BACKSTAGE PAST

by
Barry Fey

With Steve Alexander and Rich Wolfe

Forewords by Ozzy and Sharon Osbourne and by Pete Townshend

Published by Lone Wolfe Press, a division of Richcraft. Distribution, marketing, publicity, interviews, and book signings handled by Wolfegang Marketing Systems, Ltd.—But Not Very.

Photo Credits:
    P. 86, © 2011, *The Denver Post*
    Color Insert, pp. 193-197, 199-205, 208 © Dan Fong
    and pp. 198, 206, 207 © Michael Goldman

Music Credits
    P. 35 © 1968 R. Krieger/The Doors "Touch Me"
    P. 48 © 1965 Joe McDonald "I Feel Like I'm Fixin' To Die Rag"
    P. 143 © 1968 Paul Simon "Mrs. Robinson"
    P. 150 © 1973 Don Brewer "We're An American Band"
    P. 153 © 1971 Jagger/Richards "Rip This Joint"
    P. 166 © 1973 A. Bergman/M.Bergman/M. Hamlisch
    P. 223 © 1972 John Denver/Mike Taylor "Rocky Mountain High"

Layout: The Printed Page, Phoenix, AZ
Cover Design: Dan Fong, thecreativeeyellc.com

Rich Wolfe can be reached at 602-738-5889

ISBN: 978-0-9846278-3-7

CONTENTS

FOREWORD

SHARON & OZZY OSBOURNE

When we heard that Barry was writing a book, we knew two things: it would be wickedly funny and remarkable, because that's what Barry is.

Ozzy: Barry was the first promoter to book Black Sabbath in 1971. He was the first one to believe in us. He had us opening for Mountain and after the tour Barry gave each of us a gold watch.

Sharon: He felt guilty because he was paying them so little on the tour and they were a bigger draw than Mountain, so he got them the watches. But, that shows you what a good guy he is.

Ozzy: Forty years ago. I still have mine.

Sharon: I met Barry in 1977, a few years before Ozzy and I were married. I was working for the management company of the Electric Light Orchestra. What I found out immediately is that when you got to Barry's part of any American tour, you knew that you were in good hands. He's a great meet-and-greeter; he'd make you feel so comfortable and welcome. He'd go to the artist and make sure everything was okay and taken care of. Barry was always very passionate about his artists and his shows.

Ozzy: Barry was different. There were a lot of promoters who wouldn't even bother asking how I was doing and if everything was okay. With Barry, I wasn't just another artist, he booked me because he believed in me and loved my music. And, nobody knew his territory and could sell tickets like Barry.

Sharon: In 1983, Barry was promoting the US Festival. Everybody except Ozzy was being booked for this huge festival. We had an agent at the time who really didn't give a shit about Ozzy. I called Barry and I'm like, "Barry, give me a break here, what about Ozzy?"

He said, "Yeah, what about Ozzy, we've got to put him on!"

I said, "I don't care if he plays in the fucking car park, just put him on."

He said, "Sharon, I give you my word he'll be on", and he was on.

But, it was a problem for him because the show had already been fully booked. I can remember him telling me that he'd promised

Judas Priest this slot and other bands already had slots and asked, "Where am I going to put him?"

I said, "Barry, you can pay Ozzy more than any of them and then I don't care what time he goes on."

And he did! Barry was fantastic!

Ozzy: Barry threw a huge party at his house in Denver after one of our shows. It was New Year's Eve in 1996. He had all of us: Sharon and I, the band, the crew—our personal crew, all of us were invited and he opened up his house for us. There were a lot of other people there, too. It was a great time, just one laugh after another.

Sharon: Barry is just so warm. When you work for him, he gives you everything, everything. He's a great promoter, a great host. He's a very gracious man, and funny.

Ozzy: After 42 years of touring, there are maybe five promoters I have a relationship with and that says a lot. Barry is one of a dying breed, unfortunately, because he was booking acts when it meant something, when it was special, when it was really rock 'n roll, when you didn't just go to a company that booked you out worldwide. Barry knew how to promote the best of the best. He's among a handful of very special people in my life.

Sharon: We look at Barry as one of the pioneers of promoters. There are so few promoters who really do know their music and how to deal with the artists. It's a talent to deal with artists. He knows how to work them, he knows how to connect with them. He's one of the best promoters worldwide, he just is. And, combine that with a naughty personality—he's wickedly funny—it's the perfect recipe.

Ozzy: When you go through life like we all have and all of a sudden you're in your 60s and when you turn around and say, "Wow, this person has been such a huge part of my life", and that person is still respected and is still your friend, that's special. That's who Barry Fey is.

We love Barry.

FOREWORD

PETE TOWNSHEND

The Who were on tour. It was some time in the late '70s or early '80s. Barry Fey was cooking fresh hot shrimp. A big, hearty man, with a lovely family around him, wearing a floral shirt, he took his time—the butter was foaming and the chili, paprika and other hot spices fizzed in the air, stinging the eyes if you went too close to the massive fry pan warming on the outdoor barbecue burner. He gave me the simple recipe, and I still cook hot shrimp the same way, and get accolades that I dedicate to Barry.

It has been rare for me to spend family time with someone who promotes Who shows. We are usually passing through, in a rush, grabbing at days off to catch up on sleep, write letters home, deal with domestic business, laundry or small shopping. On this occasion I guess we must have been settled in Denver for a longer spell than usual. The Colorado area is not all pretty, but what is not pretty is awesome, and what is pretty is mind-numbingly awesome. I remember Barry always with great affection; he always did us proud when we played for him and the Denver audiences. Awesome is the word I was using for Colorado, Denver, Barry Fey and the people we played to there, long before the word became a High School teenage buzz-word.

Fifteen years passed, and when I met him again he was a slim man. The big heart was still there. I heard gossip that he had endured some major difficulties in his business, but he hadn't changed. He was welcoming, friendly and hospitable. Hardship hadn't changed him, but a diet had. I wonder if he still cooks those hot shrimp?

Remember that when a band like The Who came to town, we expected to get paid. We expected to get paid even if no one came to see us play. Selling tickets was not our job. In Denver, that was Barry's job and what a job he did. We have been able to build an entire West Coast leg of almost every tour we've ever done around a single Denver show. It gets us from San Francisco or L.A. all the way up to Seattle and Portland and into Western Canada. We relied on Barry, and Denver, and they never let us down.

Whatever Barry says about me in this book of his (and I haven't read it yet) will probably be nonsense. If you want to hear about me, read my book. But if you want to hear about how rock shows were evolved, elevated and turned into magnificent spectacles, read and learn. He may give away some secrets. If you're really lucky he'll include his simple, but incredible, recipe for hot shrimp. But I have a feeling that could be one rock 'n roll secret you'll have to try to get from me...

SOUND CHECK

Mick Jagger was teaching me how to snort cocaine.

It was January of 1973. He, Keith Richards and I were in Mick's hotel suite at the Hilton Hawaiian Village in Honolulu. Mick separated a line of coke from a grapefruit-sized pile on his coffee table, rolled up a dollar bill and showed me how to hold one nostril shut while I inhaled the cocaine through the makeshift tube.

The story of my journey to that hotel suite begins when I was 11 years old, the last time I was truly happy. That may seem odd coming from the man who was one of the biggest rock concert promoters in history; the man who booked Led Zeppelin's first North American appearance and the Jimi Hendrix Experience's last appearance; the man who counts, or counted, many of rock's royalty as personal friends and dozens of others, including political royalty, were more than just acquaintances; the man who was repeatedly honored in the rock 'n roll business and in the community, from "Promoter of the Year" by *Billboard Magazine* three consecutive years to a videotaped message of personal thanks from President Bill Clinton. Odd, coming from a guy who has heard countless times, "I would love to have lived your life!"

Sure, I had moments of great happiness, but anxiety was always attached to them. The last time I never wanted a moment to end was when I was playing Little League baseball in East Orange, New Jersey. It was the city championship. We were leading 8-0 and there were two outs in the top of the ninth. I was playing third base and the ball was grounded to me. I fielded it cleanly, but instead of throwing it to first for the easy out and the win, I just stood there. Everybody— my teammates, the coach, the crowd—was yelling and screaming at me to throw the ball, but I didn't want that moment to come to an end. So, I just held it, savoring the purity of the moment. No anxiety. No stress. Just perfect.

Maybe it was a premonition because the next day, my dad walked in the door after work and announced that we were moving to Pittsburgh. Less than a year of misery later, we move to Chicago, where I was even more of a misfit, choosing to join the leather-jacketed group of school bullies who beat up the Jewish kids for their lunch money instead of sticking with my own. Chicago's where my dad was swindled out of his fortune and where, one day when I was

With "Mommy", Hetty and sister Sheila

a senior in high school, I walked into our apartment to find him confined to an oxygen tent. He'd been a heavy smoker and within a week, he was dead at the age of 57.

Flat broke, my mom had to move my sister and me from a ten-room luxury apartment in a great Chicago neighborhood to a one-bedroom budget unit in a neighborhood where everyone was barely getting by. She took a job for the first time since her marriage.

We had nothing and college, which seemed a certainty for me just a few months earlier, was out of the question. I'd gotten good enough grades to be accepted at Yale and the University of Texas. I applied to Stanford, but it apparently had enough Jews. As did many schools, Stanford had a quota on Jewish students back then. But, it didn't matter. There was no way to pay for college. I had no idea what to do. I'd become pretty much a waste of skin and all I was doing in Chicago was causing trouble. So, naturally, I joined the Marines.

At 5'9" and 237 pounds, the recruiters must have looked at me the way a starving dog looks at a raw sirloin. The standard practice was that when recruits arrived, the base commander sent a form letter to the parents informing them that their sons had gotten there safely. My mother may have been the only parent in U.S. Marine Corps history who wrote back, thanking the commander for his courtesy and for taking such good care of her son! And, over my next ten weeks of hell, she continued to trade letters with drill instructor Goldsboro, who turned out to be the least abusive of the bunch.

The D.I.s made it clear immediately and repeatedly that I was there solely for their sadistic pleasures. One, Sgt. Kowalski, was an ex-boxer who ended up serving time in the brig for being a cruel, vicious bastard. Nearly every day of boot camp, he and I had this exchange as I stood at attention:

"How's the drill sergeant's left hand today, private?" and then he punched me in the stomach.

"Sir, Private Fey thinks the sergeant's left hand is very good today, sir!" Then, he'd punch me with his right and we'd repeat the question and answer routine, left-right-left-right, until I collapsed in tears. I was never so unhappy, never so miserable, never so tortured, never so beaten psychologically and physically as I was during boot camp. One of the boys in my group—and we were boys—committed suicide. Another one tried.

It was a great weight loss program, though. By the end of basic, I was down to 165, but they'd also beaten some of my soul out of me, which I guess is part of the Corps' goal; to break you down completely and then rebuild you into a killer. But, there was no one to kill at that point in our country's history. We weren't at war and I left the Marines after two years full of anger and with not just a chip on my shoulder, but a whole fucking block.

I didn't know it at that moment, but I was primed for a life in rock 'n roll.

In 1985, I was in a New York City hospital after a botched surgery. I refused to look at the row of staples around my belly and what the

Private Fey demonstrating his combat skills.

surgeon had done to me, but my visitor was curious. Bono lifted the sheet to take a peek and with a grimace asked, "BAR-ee, did you check to see if they put your legs on right?"

Nothing in my early life would have suggested that I'd become friends with Bono or any of the dozens of other rock legends to whom I grew close. I worked hard. I got lucky. I was in the right place at just the right time and was able to ride the post-Beatles wave of Janis, Jimi, Led Zeppelin, The Who and the Stones. A few people helped me, some famous, some not. A few people tried to hinder me, some famous, some not. They're all in the book.

My journey took me from misfit to myth. I vacillated between bravado and panic; between madman and saint. I was often an intolerable bastard but my goals were always the same: sell as many tickets as possible and make sure the audiences had the best possible experience.

The following pages are my memories of a special time in the lives of music lovers. All the stories are true to the best of my recollection. As I dug through the memories and memorabilia, it all seemed a bit surreal. Seeing this compilation of my 40 years promoting concerts all over the world makes me grateful for the opportunities I had and proud of the accomplishments.

I wish my mother, Hetty, had lived long enough to see this book. She was a gem, a Jewish mother who took her cues right out of the Jewish Mother Handbook. She'd say things like, "Barry, you're getting too fat". And in the next breath, "Here, have something to eat".

Her plans for me didn't include becoming a rock concert promoter. A doctor or lawyer, yes, but, "Oy vey!" not a concert promoter. When she played Mahjong with her friends and the inevitable question, "So, Hetty, what's your son Barry doing now?" came up, she'd tell them that I was lost at sea! After I'd become successful enough that she was concerned she'd be caught in a lie, Mommy told them that I'd been rescued.

She was fearless. During a Stones concert at Soldier Field, I took her back stage with me. Now, when Mick Jagger moves around back stage, people scatter, they get out of his way. Mommy just walked right up to him and asked, "So you're Mick Jagger." "Yes, I am." "I'm Barry Fey's mother and I'm from England". Mick smiled, nodded and said, "It's very nice to meet you, BAR-ee Fey's mum." He said it as if he was surprised I had one.

Hetty Fey died in February of 2001, a month shy of her 95th birthday.

Part One

OPENING ACT

Reflecting after a successful Rolling Stones concert in Honolulu

From the first concert I promoted, Baby Huey and The Babysitters, I was hooked on the business, which for me was the business of making music fans happy. The late '60s were manic years in our country and the concert business mirrored that mania, or drove it, I'm not sure which. Draft cards and bras were being burned; the Summer of Love was followed by summers of hate and fear as MLK and RFK were assassinated within two months of each other; authority was constantly challenged in ways it had never been before; police were seen as "pigs" who responded with billy clubs and teargas at the drop of a hat; streets and campuses were filled with Vietnam War protestors. And woven through it all was the soundtrack of Janis, Jimi, Jim, Jerry and others that I put on stage.

There apparently weren't many Jews in Rockford, Illinois. When I arrived in 1964, I went to the coffee shop at the Albert Pick motel. That's where I was staying, briefly, when I went to work for Robert Hall Clothing. I had finished its management training program after two years at the University of Pennsylvania and was named assistant manager of the store in Rockford.

"I'd like a bagel, please."

"What's that?"

"A bagel…you know, like a hard donut?"

The waitress had no idea what I was talking about.

At the clothing store, I was a great salesman but had no interest in the managerial work: inventory, time sheets, all that. We had a few kids working part-time for us called "will call boys" who got orders ready that customers had called or mailed in. They'd stay after their work was done and seemed to be entertained by my Marine "war" stories. But, they'd just hang around, not getting paid. I'd ask, "Why don't you get outta here…go do something?" They complained that there was nothing to do, nowhere to go; Rockford was dullsville. My roommate, Marshall Hector, and I saw an opportunity and decided we'd put on a dance.

There was a club on Chicago's north side called Thumbs Up where I used to see Baby Huey and the Babysitters play. On Easter Sunday of 1965, Marshall and I brought Baby Huey to the American Legion Hall in Rockford. We each cleared $92.50.

That was as much as I made in a week at the clothing store, so the next week, I quit and formed Thumbs Up Productions. I got a call

from a promoter in the Chicago area—I don't remember his name—
which had an offer.

"I like what you did with Baby Huey. Would you like to bring the
Beau Brummels to Rockford?"

They'd had "Laugh, Laugh" and another hit by that time.

"How much do they want?"

"$1500."

Marshall—still my partner even though he didn't quit his job—
and I rented Rockford College's gym where there was a rule that
everyone going into the gym had to take off their shoes.

There were a lot of shoes lined up outside the gym door and
after paying expenses, Marshall and I each made about $1200.

The same promoter from the Chicago area called again.

"How'd you like to do The Byrds?"

"Come on, man, are you kidding?" The Byrds were big and getting bigger. "Tambourine Man" was all over the radio.

We packed the gym for The Byrds. 6000 shoes were lined up
outside the door. I pocketed about $3500. After that, we did the
Kingsmen, but I didn't make it to the show because I was in Rockford Memorial Hospital. I had terrible headaches, couldn't keep my
balance and couldn't talk. The doctors thought I had a brain tumor.
I didn't. They thought I had leukemia. I didn't. They'd come back
nearly every day with something else they thought it was, but wasn't.
They couldn't figure it out, so they decided it was psychosomatic
and sent for a Chicago psychiatrist, Theodore Dulin. That was a
stroke of luck because he'd been in the war and had seen this before.
It was acute labrynthitis which is where a virus attacks the middle
ear. There was no medicine for it at the time, so I had to lie in bed
for three months. I had to learn how to walk again and my speech
gradually returned to normal. But, the condition never really went
away and would pop up from time to time over the years.

In May of 1966, I met Cindy Rittenberg, a Southside Chicago
girl, who was to become my wife. We were sitting in The Pickle Barrel
in Chicago's Old Town section. Man, they had the best onion rings. A
woman walked up to our table.

"Are you Barry Fey from Rockford?"

"Yes."

"My name is Pat Cole. I went to some of your shows. I'd like
to connect you to Chuck Van Duzer. He goes to the University of

Denver and his fraternity wants to put on a show. Do you think you can get him a band?"

I told her I'd see what I could do.

Because of our success in Rockford, I'd met a guy in Chicago named T.B. Skarning. He'd been booking acts like Jan and Dean and Dick and Dee Dee in the upper Midwest and really looked the part with a pinkie ring and silk shirt.

He told me, "Well, I've got a new act and they're going to be really good, but it's too expensive to just send them to Denver for one show."

"Who are they?"

"The Association."

He was right; they were going to be really good. A month later, they would hit the top of the charts with "Along Comes Mary" and "Cherish". But, I had never been to Denver and didn't know where I was going to find other places for the band to appear. So, I called Chuck Van Duzer.

"Are there any other fraternity chapters you're friendly with who'll let me put on concerts so we can make this work?"

"Sure, we've got a chapter in Boulder at the University of Colorado and in Missoula at the University of Montana."

And that's how I got to Denver.

One thing you'll know about me after reading this book—if you don't already—is how much I love food. In fact, food—and insisting on good food and plenty of it for the acts I booked and being able to find food anytime of night—became part of my success.

On my first trip to Denver for The Association concert, my hosts picked me up at Stapleton airport and drove west on 32nd Avenue, which would later be named Martin Luther King, Jr. Boulevard. The driver told me that we were driving through Denver's ghetto. Coming from Chicago and New York, I knew what a ghetto looked like and if this was the worst Denver had to offer, I couldn't wait to see how beautiful the rest of the city was. Our first stop was The Denver Drumstick, a local chain. There was an electric train running around the whole restaurant near the ceiling. A painted mural showing the Rocky Mountains was in the background and the train would run through a tunnel, into the kitchen and back out again. I liked the Drumstick because it specialized in comfort food served the old fashioned way, with lots of thick, greasy, chicken gravy. Their fried chicken smothered in gravy was amazing.

The concerts went okay. I made $2500 off the University of Denver show, broke even in Boulder and made a little in Missoula. Someone in the DU frat house, Tau Kappa Epsilon, stole about half the money from the show, so I used my "tough guy from Chicago" persona to let them know that it wasn't enough money for me to have them killed over, but there were other ways I could extract it from them. They got the message and the money showed up.

In January, 1967, I booked Eric Burdon and the Animals to play at the University of Denver in April and decided to move to Denver and try to make a go of it. I lived in the TKE house. In February, my mother, Hetty, called and really laid into me. Oh, she was pissed! "What did you do?" she yelled. "Why, Mommy? What's the matter?" She said, "Cynthia is in the hospital and she's pregnant. You get your ass home right now!" And I did, but the most I could afford was the train. Two days later, I was in Chicago. Cindy had gotten sick with something and had to go to a hospital. As they were running tests on her, they discovered she was pregnant. So, we had to come clean and tell them that we'd been married for three months. We kept it a secret because, well, I'm not sure why now, but at the time we didn't have any money or a place to stay, so we just went home. Cindy stayed in Chicago until I could get enough money together for her to join me. In March, when I had enough money saved, I sent for her.

Our first meal as a married couple in Denver was at the Denver Drumstick.

There were already concert promoters in Denver: Hugh Hooks, Andrews-Garner, which was Velma Andrews and Robert Garner and a guy named Ed Weimer.

Shortly after I arrived in Denver in 1967, I met with Ed and offered him a deal.

"Look, I'll come to work with you and give you 25 percent of what I make from my concerts. I'll work on your concerts and you give me 25 percent of what you make."

He agreed and I started working from his office in the old Petroleum Club building at 16th and Broadway in downtown Denver. After the Eric Burdon and the Animals concert, I gave him his share. But, we saw an opportunity to make more money on the ticketing. Hugh Hooks had a lock on the ticket business. He had a ticket agency and everyone went through him and he sold the tickets, whether it was his show or not. Ed wanted to break that, so when he brought Paul Revere and the Raiders to Denver, we sold our own tickets. I sat in a ticket booth at the old Auditorium Arena box office and sold Paul Revere tickets and at the end of each day, I'd take a taxi—I didn't know how to drive—to a club Ed had in west Denver on Morrison Road called The Galaxy. I'd give him the money and he'd give me cab fare home. I did that routine every day until the show, which was a big success. When I showed up at the office for my split, Ed said that he didn't have it.

"I can't give it to you this time because I'm partners with Dick Clark."

Oh my God, when he said that! I should have been prepared. That was my first really bad break in the concert business, the first time I ran into someone who didn't keep their end of a deal.

"Alright, just give me 25% of what you have left."

"I won't have enough left."

"Ed, I paid you on Burdon..."

"Yeah, well I can't pay you because of Clark."

I said, "you motherfucker", and packed up my things, grabbed a *Billboard Magazine*, which became very important, and got ready to leave.

"Barry, don't be stupid. You leave me, you'll be schlock. You'll be working out of your kitchen."

I said, "Ed, whatever I do, if I earn it, I keep it. I won't get fucked out of anything." That sure wasn't the last time somebody tried to fuck me, but it was a great learning experience.

Billboard Magazine had a story about Family Dog Promotions in San Francisco looking for groups that had original songs. During the time that I'd been living in the fraternity house, there was a group of DU students who had a band called Eighth Penny Matter. They were one of the few that played original music. Cindy and I had never had a honeymoon, so we took a tape and went to San Francisco.

I had an appointment to meet Chet Helms at Family Dog Productions. I got all dressed up with my University of Pennsylvania gear: blue blazer, blue shirt, pumpkin and blue tie, gray flannel slacks, penny loafers. I'm going to look really good. We walk into Family Dog's office on Gough Street. I introduce myself and Cindy.

The receptionist said to take a seat, that Chet would be with us in a minute. This was two weeks before the Monterey Pop Festival and Family Dog was facilitating the free food and the free stage, so there was a lot of hubbub around the office. I couldn't believe what I was seeing. Long-haired people my age were wearing beads, flowers, robes and what looked like bear skin rugs as clothing. My preppy Penn outfit couldn't have been more out of place.

Cindy and I were escorted into Chet's office. He looked like Jesus, sitting lotus style in the middle of the floor, with a desk blotter in front of him, a flower vase with a single blossom in it. So, I sat down like that and handed him the tape. He put it in the tape player and turned it on. His partner, Bob Cohen, walked in and Chet did the introductions.

The tape's still playing and Bob says, "Who are these guys?"

I said, "Eighth Penny Matter. A college group from Denver."

"Not bad, not bad. Hey, you two need to come to the Avalon Ballroom tonight." Family Dog Productions owned the Avalon, one of the happening music clubs of that time.

It was our honeymoon, after all, so we made plans to go.

Cindy and I were already wide-eyed and our eyes grew wider as we walked down to Haight Street and a shop called King Richard's (or Poor Richard's, I don't remember) where I bought a pair of Jesus sandals and tried to look more like everybody else. I so wanted to fit in, but just picture me with my blue blazer and tie and blue shirt and gray flannel slacks and my Jesus sandals. I had to be a sight. We walked into Golden Gate Park and it was unbelievable with thousands of dancing hippies everywhere. Bands were playing—I think it was either Quicksilver or The Dead—and the Diggers were giving out free food. The Diggers were community activists, although I found out later they were maybe more like community anarchists. Anyway, everybody's happy, smiling, dancing and diggin' the music...it was the most beautiful example of mass peace and harmony I'd ever seen.

After walking around all afternoon, I had Jesus blisters on my feet. Despite the pain, we went to the Avalon that night. I saw Bob Cohen across the room. I started to walk over to talk to him, but the lights went off and I had my first black light and strobe light experience. I couldn't see where I was walking. I never made it to Bob.

The next day, we went back to Denver where I'd picked up a copy of the Scott McKenzie song, "San Francisco (Be Sure To Wear

Flowers In Your Hair)" and played it over and over. (That was a pre-concert habit I picked up: whatever group I was putting on, I'd play one of their records over and over to get psyched up.) I wanted to figure out a way to bring that San Francisco vibe to Denver.

Joe Neddo, who became a good friend, was a sax player and singer in a local band, Boenzee Cryque; a really good band that got some radio play for a couple of its songs. He called and told me that a teen club, The Byrd, had gone out of business the night before and the building's owner wanted to talk to me. The owner was an attorney, Francisco Salazar, who was eventually going to use the building as his law office, but until then wanted me to open a club. I took a look at the building at 1601 West Evans. It was big enough and I thought it would work as a Denver version of the Avalon. I called Bob Cohen. He flew out the next day, liked it and called Chet Helms. He said yes and we made a deal, but Bob said, "We won't call it the Avalon. We'll call it The Family Dog."

My job was to be the Denver liaison for Family Dog Productions and book local bands that would open for the San Francisco groups Chet and Bob were sending. I'd get five percent of the net and I also had the right to do my own shows in The Family Dog.

In May of 1967, before all of the San Francisco stuff, I wanted to bring in Jefferson Airplane, so I called Bill Graham. It was my first encounter with the guy who was the biggest promoter in the business.

"Mr. Graham, my name is Barry Fey from Denver. I'd like to book Jefferson Airplane."

"Sonny, (he was older than me and in the following decades, I never let him forget it) I only handle the Airplane in California. You need to talk to Todd Schiffman at APA (Agency for the Performing Arts)." I called Todd and told him I wanted the Airplane for two nights.

"How much money do you have?"

"I've got $7500."

"That won't work. They get that much for one night. But, I've got another group that will be making twice as much as that by the time of your show in Denver, but I'll do you a favor and give them to you for two nights for $7500."

"Who?"

"The Doors."

"Who are they?"

"They're an L.A. group that's just breaking out. Go pick up a copy of their new record, 'Light My Fire' and call me back."

I said, "Yeah, yeah, sure." He could tell that I thought he was trying to screw me.

"Hey, I'm not that kind of guy, Barry. Just listen to the record."

I checked around and finally found the record and took a listen. Jesus Christ! I called Schiffman back right away and booked Jim Morrison and the Doors for the University of Denver and the University of Colorado on September 30th and October 1st of 1967. Over the summer, The Doors blew up with "Light My Fire" becoming number one on the charts and both shows were sellouts. Those were the first shows The Doors had outside of California. Todd, who discovered and promoted a lot of big acts, worked with me several more times. He was right. He wasn't "that kind" of guy.

When Chet and Bob found out I was bringing in The Doors, they wanted me to put them in the Family Dog. I'd already promised the TKE fraternity that I'd play the Doors at the DU Student Union and the second show was supposed to be in Boulder. But, I owed my San Francisco partners at least that much and I was able to move the Boulder show to the Family Dog for the second night.

The big radio station in Denver at the time was KIMN. Stations today think they're doing great if they get a six or seven share of the audience. KIMN had a twenty-four share! I called the station and spoke to Gene Winans, who was one of the greatest radio salesmen ever. I wanted to advertise the show and decided to call my company "Feline, Inc." for what I thought was an obvious reason. The Family Dog was making a big splash by bringing in the Dead and other big names, so I wanted my company to have that name association; dog, cat...Feline, Inc. But, when Gene picks up the ad copy from my apartment, I'm not there. He sees Feline and decides that I must have forgotten to put in the "y". So, he put the ads on the air and the KIMN disk jockeys said, over and over again, "Feyline presents The Doors". That's how Feyline was named and it stayed that way for 40 years.

Our first show at the Family Dog in Denver was Big Brother and the Holding Company and Blue Cheer on September 8th, 1967. I'll never forget the sound check. Blue Cheer was so loud! They had a wall of Marshall amplifiers on the stage and I started laughing because my chest started thumping and my body was vibrating so violently I had to leave.

But, that's how we opened the Dog, with Janis Joplin headlining. Denver had never seen anything like Janis. She was undoubtedly the greatest female rock singer I ever heard and, actually, the best that has ever lived.

Everybody around me had a crush on Janis. All of the stage hands, roadies, sound and lighting guys, everyone wanted to screw her. But, when I finally saw her coming out of the dressing room with her bottle of Southern Comfort—and I don't mean to be insulting—but, when I saw her, I thought, what the fuck are these guys thinking? But, man, what a great rock 'n roll singing voice! Her speaking voice had that same, gravelly, screechy quality to it.

Janis was pretty full of herself. And what a mouth! She was a bawdy, vulgar woman and scared me a little, but maybe she had to be that way.

No doubt it was tough being a woman in those days and in that business. It was a rough and tumble, testosterone fueled collection of egos and, remember, it was the '60s when women were "supposed" to be home taking care of the house and kids. Those who were working had to fend off sexual advances all the time. The women working with me were tough. Pam Moore, who started in advertising but wound up doing everything in the 20 years she was with me, remembers having to put on a tougher facade than she wanted to and would never wear a skirt to a show. She did in the office, but at the shows, she didn't want to give the bands any more excuse than they needed to treat her differently. She was so tough that managers and agents wanted to deal with me instead of her, and I was a madman.

I suppose it was difficult, maybe lonely for Janis, which sounds strange for someone who stood in front of thousands of cheering fans night after night in city after city. But, when the shows ended, then what? Guys could hook up with groupies and others in the band or crew would give their approval. Attaboy! Girls doing that would be labeled sluts. Maybe that was one of the reasons Janis seemed to always be in the company of a bottle of Southern Comfort.

The Saturday evening before the show, I took Janis and several other people to The Northwoods Inn in Littleton, a southern suburb. It was a steakhouse famous for its prime rib and peanut shells on the floor, but the crowd it attracted included a lot of cowboy types.

When we walked in, you should have seen the jaws drop. Not only were they gawking at Janis who looked every bit like the hippie rock star she was, there was Chet Helms, who was tall and with those animal skin clothes he wore and the long hair and beard, he looked like Jesus. And of course, big, fat me in my shorts and tennis shoes. The only thing that would have made it better is if Janis had started wailing the chorus from "Piece of My Heart".

The San Francisco bands we brought in to play at the Family Dog were also quite a shock to the sensibilities of the Denver establishment. Their long hair, their messages of free love and peace and urging kids to challenge authority didn't go over well. The Denver District Attorney, Mike McKevitt, and the Denver Police Department weren't going to stand for it; especially Sgt. John Gray who brought in the narcs and harassed and busted people. On our sixth weekend when Buffalo Springfield was playing, the police did a full-scale raid on the Dog. They blocked the street with their cars so no one could get in and parents wouldn't want to drop their kids off. They checked IDs, went into the bathrooms and harassed people for drugs.

It wasn't just the Denver police, though. The guys from San Francisco who came in to run the club, especially Tony Gillery, the general manager, had the attitude of, "Hey, we're from San Francisco. We'll show you how it's done." The police response was, "Oh, no you won't".

I flew to San Francisco to meet with Chet and tell him that something had to be done about the relationship with the police. I was afraid that the cops were going to plant some pot on me or in my office or car.

"Chet, what do I do if they plant me?"

"Don't worry, Barry. You won't grow."

Classic Chet.

What Chet and Bob did was hire Francis Salazar, the landlord, to sue the police for harassment. He got an injunction keeping the police from going on the property unless they were called for an emergency. That backfired, because Denver parents said, "if the cops can't go there, my kids aren't going there." Attendance started to dwindle and that was the beginning of the end. Salazar won, but we lost.

And it didn't slow the cops down, anyway. The Dead were busted in their hotel. Canned Heat was busted in their hotel. Salazar sued again and won again, but it was too late. We had a hell of a run at the Family Dog, but the San Francisco group was losing money on it, so they bailed and the doors were closed in February.

Francis Salazar asked me if I'd keep it running until he was ready to move his law offices in. Which I did, but I couldn't, in my mind, call it the Family Dog; I just called it the Dog. It didn't much matter, as it turned out. But, we put on some great shows.

One of the biggest bands I booked for the Dog, was Cream. The show was sold out. But, on Sunday night, two days before the show, Bob Fitzpatrick, Cream's U.S. manager called.

"Ginger Baker's sick. He threw up violently after the show in Phoenix. We have to postpone your show."

"Oh my God, I'm sold out! What am I supposed to do?"

"Don't worry about it", said Fitzpatrick. "We'll call you tomorrow." That's the first time I made lemonade out of lemons. When he called back, I was able to convince him to add a second show. So, the following week, Cream put on two sold-out shows at the Dog.

Then there was this guy named Matthew Katz, an attorney from San Francisco who I booked Moby Grape through. So, get this: they go on stage and never face the audience! They kept their backs to the audience the whole time. I said, "What the fuck?" They were phonies. Katz and the real band split up, but he owned the name, so he hired some other musicians to masquerade as Moby Grape. He also owned the names Jefferson Airplane and It's A Beautiful Day.

The Dog managed to stay open through the spring, but barely. It was a struggle. The Byrds had been long booked for two shows, June 7th and 8th, 1968, but two nights earlier, Robert F. Kennedy was assassinated. I didn't know what to do, but the band was on its way, so we held the shows, though definitely under a cloud. Also, Public Service Company turned off our power the morning of the first show because we hadn't paid our bill. One of the Byrds' roadies used to work for a power company, so he shimmied up the pole and threw the switch and the shows went on.

We closed the Dog the next week with Janis. That was the second Friday in June after only 9 months. The show still goes on there, though. For several years now, the building has housed a strip club. But, the Family Dog really got me on the map with The Doors and a bunch of other big name acts. Look at the lineup:

1967

9/8 and 9	Janis Joplin, Big Brother and the Holding Company/ Blue Cheer/Eighth Penny Matter
9/15 and 16	Quicksilver Messenger Service/The Charlatans/ Superband
9/22 and 23	The Grateful Dead/ Mother Earth
9/29	Captain Beefheart/Lothar and The Hand People
9/30	The Doors/Captain Beefheart
10/6 and 7	Buffalo Springfield/Eighth Penny Matter
10/13 and 14	Van Morrison/The Daily Flash
10/20	Canned Heat/Allmen Joy
10/21	American Standard and other local bands
10/27 and 28	Lothar and the Hand People/Allmen Joy
11/3 and 4	Blue Cheer/Superfine Dandelion
11/7 and 8	The Jefferson Airplane/The Other Half
11/10 and 11	The Sons of Champlin/The Other Half
11/17 and 18	Chuck Berry/The Sons of Champlin/New World Blues Dictionary
12/1 and 2	The Jim Kweskin Jug Band/Solid Muldoon
12/8 and 9	Canned Heat/The Siegal Schwall Band
12/15 and 16	The Box Tops/Soul Survivors/Jimmerfield Legend
*12/21	Allmen American Standard/Leopold Fuchs/Eighth Penny Matter/Joy
12/29-31	The Doors/Allmen Joy/Jimmerfield Legend/ Allmen Joy

1968

1/12 and 13	Beggars Opera Company/American Standard/ Eighth Penny Matter
1/19 and 20	Eighth Penny Matter/October Country
1/26 and 27	New World Blues Dictionary/Last Friday's Fire
2/2 and 3	The Fugs/Leopold Fuchs
2/9 and 10	Leopold Fuchs H. Bomb/American Standard- Tommy Bolin
**2/14	Jimi Hendrix/American Standard -Tommy Bolin
3/5 and 6	Blue Cheer
3/8 and 9	Siegal Schwall Blues Band
3/15 and 16	Climax

3/19 and 20	Cream
4/6	The Fugs
5/3	Frank Zappa and the Mothers of Invention
6/7 and 6/8	The Byrds
6/14	Fever Tree
6/19	Janis Joplin and Big Brother

*Otis Redding was scheduled on this date, but he died in a plane crash on December 10, 1967.

** Hendrix had played a show at Regis College in Denver and afterward jammed at The Dog.

"Summer of Love" or not, 1967 was such a fucked up time politically, racially and with the Vietnam War. I wanted Denver to see and feel that peace, love and freedom and hear the great music that I'd experienced in San Francisco. What better way than with a Love-In?

The time for a Love-In seemed right after the Family Dog opened on September 8, 1967 and great bands like Janis Joplin and Big Brother and the Holding Company and Blue Cheer and Quicksilver and The Grateful Dead started coming to Denver. The Dead played Friday and Saturday nights, the 22nd and 23rd and on Sunday, the 24th of September, was the Love-In at City Park.

About 30,000 jammed the park, and what a collection of characters! Everybody from the San Francisco scene showed up: the most dangerous man in America—as proclaimed by Richard Nixon—Dr. Timothy Leary; Ken Kesey and his Merry Pranksters arrived in their Furthur Bus (Furthur was a mash up of future and further); Janis Joplin; Jerry Garcia; Owsley—Owsley Stanley, the guy who mass produced over a million hits of LSD. (The DEA was looking for him in Denver, but he was posing as a roadie for the Dead—not much of a stretch because he was their first sound man—and they didn't get him in Denver, but he was nailed a year later at his home in Orinda, California. Owsley's partner in the LSD making business was Tim Scully. When California made LSD illegal in 1967, Owsley and Scully decided to move their lab to Denver. Scully set it up in the basement of a house across the street from the Denver Zoo. He made the LSD there and shipped it to Owsley, who put it in tablets for distribution.)

Of course, I didn't know any of that at the time, but there I was, the least likely person to be thrust into the middle of Hippiedom's royalty. I was among the All-Stars of the '60s Counterculture and I was the only one who wasn't dropping acid. It was a crazy, exciting time and the Love-In worked pretty much the way I'd hoped. If nothing else, it gave music fans of Denver a firsthand look at the Psychedelic Era. I was thrilled.

After that, there were all sorts of rumors that the Dead and others from the San Francisco Haight-Asbury scene would be setting up shop in Denver. Some of that happened, but the Dead didn't move here. They did become regular visitors though, because they really enjoyed hanging in Colorado. And where the Dead went, so did the Deadheads. Their cross country pilgrimages were legendary. Rickety old school buses and rundown Volkswagen buses with a freaky, fun bunch of people who wanted nothing more than to be able to enjoy the Dead and each other. They were a community of thousands wearing tie-dyed everything who had nothing better to do with their lives than to travel from city to city, hear their favorite jam band jam and share the communal experience of getting high.

I lost track of how many Dead shows we did at Red Rocks. It became Mecca for the Deadheads. It was their temple for the worship of Jerry and Bob and the others. I loved them for several reasons, including that they were generally peaceful hippies who didn't cause problems and they bought a LOT of tickets. They guaranteed that every show was a sell out and we did dozens of shows over the years. The Dead shows were a trip and I mean that in every way that you want to define it.

Backstage was crazier than normal because the shows would last for hours. The Dead traveled with their own gourmet chefs who created some recipes that you probably wouldn't want to try at home. They dropped acid into random dishes. Pam Moore, my longtime colleague at Feyline, remembers getting dosed at Dead concerts simply by eating. When we got wise to that, they found other ways to share, or force, their acid with us/on us. We all learned real early in our experience with the Dead that you couldn't drink anything backstage out of a cup because someone would dose the drinks. So, we'd bring in cans and bottles that were sealed, but that didn't stop the merry pranksters. We'd put our drinks in a big trash can full of ice. As the ice melted, someone would drop acid into the water and a little bit of it would wind up on the lip of the can or bottle and away you went. In Albuquerque, my national tour guy Joel Brandes rented some vintage luxury cars and hired some University of New Mexico students to drive the band to and from the show. When it ended and the college boys were supposed to drive the band back, they couldn't. They'd been drinking the Kool-Aid or whatever the Dead had backstage and were too trippy to drive.

As much as I loved Jerry, I have to admit that I never saw a complete Dead show. I couldn't stand the hours and hours of jamming. It was boring. I wasn't the only one who didn't see the whole shows. Jerry would vanish for 15 or 20 minutes at a time. Because of the long jams, it was easy for him to leave and go backstage and eat or whatever. When he'd go back and start playing, Bob Weir would take off and have dinner.

The Dead were good to their fans. Make that great to their fans. They'd have a Tapers' Section fairly close to the speakers where they'd let fans set up tape recorders. There was a huge industry of people exchanging Dead tapes. There still is.

The Grateful Dead were the band of the people. They didn't want to charge too much for tickets. They loved their fans and their fans loved them.

We did have a problem at Red Rocks one time when too many people showed up for a concert. A DJ at a Boulder radio station didn't help. He was announcing that everyone should go to the concert if they had a ticket or not.

He said, "Hey man, I'm going and I don't have a ticket." Asshole.

It was another one of those moments when the fans demanded that they be able to see THEIR music. The police used teargas and it got a little ugly.

In 1995, I'd blown the speakers out, again, on my custom made 1980 450 SLC Mercedes Benz. It came from the factory as a two door hardtop, but I wanted a convertible. So, I sent it to Camera Ready Cars in California. It took almost a year, because the conversion had never been done before and we had to engineer it from the wheels up. Once, someone told me, "Barry, I thought your Mercedes was a one of a kind." I assured them that it was. They said, "I saw it on Belleview the other day and it wasn't you driving." That was my first clue that my son Geoffrey was sneaking out and driving at the age of 13.

There were a few other times that he went joy riding while I was out of town; probably more than I know about, and then there are the parties at our house when I was gone which I suspect Geoffrey had something to do with. But, I digress.

Anyway, I'd blown the speakers out again because of my love of loud rock 'n roll and while I was waiting in the car stereo shop, I heard the tail end of a radio news report saying something about Jerry Garcia. I'd heard enough that a sense of dread came over me. Someone at my office must have told KOA Radio, a Denver news station, where to find me because they were on the phone in minutes, confirming the worst and asking me for a statement about Jerry. I said a few words, but I can't remember what. I was in shock.

As I drove home, I had to pull over to the side of the road because I was crying so hard. I didn't know why it was affecting me so, but I was bawling. When I finally made it to the office, the TV news crews started showing up. Over the next couple of hours, every station came to interview me and I'd talked to every radio station on the phone. I broke down in nearly every one of them. My son Jeremy called me and said he saw me crying on TV.

In the early days, the late '60s, Jerry and I had some fun together and were fairly close. What struck me most about him is how kind he was. A very gentle man. And very clever. Not in a sarcastic way; just a really quick wit, a very funny guy. But in the last several years, Jerry got deeper into his nearly constant state of being loaded and we didn't speak as much. Not much more than a simple "Hi, how ya doin'?" So, I couldn't figure out, at first, why his death was hitting me so hard; much harder, it seemed than when Tommy Bolin, Ronnie Van Zant and Jimi Hendrix, whom I knew much better, died tragic deaths at young ages.

At Jerry's candlelight vigil, I realized the tears weren't just for Jerry, but for me and for our generation. When he went, a piece of us did, too. For all of us who'd grown up in the '60s, Jerry was part of the musical and social fabric that we were wrapped up in.

Jerry meant so much to so many. He and the Dead were always faithful to their music and fans. They always sold out for me, but never sold out.

I took out a full page ad in the Denver newspapers in honor of Jerry.

◇◇◇

Dear Jerry,

"The Sixties" died today,

August 9, 1995

Rest in Peace

By December of 1967, I'd heard about Jimi Hendrix. I called up a guy named Chuck Barnett, who worked for G.A.C., Hendrix' agency. Now, this guy didn't know me from Adam, but he knew of The Family Dog— everybody in the business did. It was famous, or maybe infamous.

"Chuck, I want to book Hendrix. Three shows: Tucson, Phoenix and Denver."

"You got enough money?"

"No."

"Well, send me $10,000 for one show and I'll sell you all three shows."

So, in February of 1968, we set up shows at the University of Arizona in Tucson, A.S.U. in Tempe and Regis College in Denver. That was kind of an interesting time because there were no computers, no Ticketmaster. I put up a card table outside the A.S.U. field house and sold tickets. But, in Tucson, the president of the University saw a poster we'd put up of Hendrix with his big Afro and colorful clothing. He said, "I don't care if these people have a contract or not, they aren't coming on our campus."

He wouldn't listen to our protests, so at the last minute, we had to scramble and find a place for a concert, which turned out to be a converted bowling alley. We easily sold out because the space was so much smaller than what we'd been planning on, but I barely made any money. Maybe 50 bucks. But, that's important because, as we'll find out later, I didn't have a losing concert until July of 1971, which, in 2011, is an amazing string...nearly impossible.

A guy named Kent Lewis was helping me with the Regis College show in Denver. On the tickets, he spelled Jimi Hendrix, "Jim Hendricks". Thank God the tickets sold out so Jimi never got to see that.

The Regis show is a day away and I go to Stapleton to pick up Jimi. That was back in the day when you could walk right to the gate. I've got my shower shoes on, shorts and a t-shirt, even though it was February. I'm quite a sight. But, Jimi gets off the plane with his giant Afro with his plumed hat, animal skin coat and multi-colored this and that and people in the terminal, my God, they parted like the Red Sea. No one wanted anything to do with us. They just stared as we walked down the concourse.

Somebody drove us to the Cosmopolitan Hotel, which wound up being Jimi's favorite place to stay. We were sitting around getting acquainted and Jimi said, "I'd like to buy some Indian jewelry."

I found a store on 16th Street, within walking distance of the hotel, called Kohlberg's. You have to remember what a strange sight he was, that we both were. We stood around in the store and the clerks ignored us, giving us the stink eye now and then just to let us know that they knew we were there, but they had no intention of waiting on us. That kept up until Jimi pulled out a roll of hundreds and they descended like locusts. Long after that day, I'd get letters from Mr. Kohlberg saying, "Dear Mr. Fey, When is that nice Mr. Hendrix coming back?"

At Regis, they allowed us to sell 4700 tickets. We could have filled a space twice as large. People were sitting on the steps outside the field house, trying to hear the music. It was a great show and afterwards, Jimi was still amped up, so he went to the Family Dog and jammed with Tommy Bolin. That's where they got their relationship going. Tommy was just 16, maybe 17 and he was already a great guitar player. Not as great at Hendrix, but the audience that night was blown away.

One time when Jimi was in Denver, we sent our runner, a young woman, to pick him up at the Cosmopolitan and take him to the show. They didn't show up, didn't show up. Where were they? They got there about 25 minutes before he was due to go on. I found out later what happened: Jimi had seduced her on the way to the concert. So much for that.

For some reason, I don't remember why, we had to get Jimi to an appearance or performance in the morning. Rock stars generally don't see the morning light, unless it's because they've been up all night. My assistant, Leslie Haseman went to the hotel to get him and he was still in bed. He told her to stay while he got ready. She said watching Jimi get up was unbelievable. He was washing down some kind of pills with Mateus Rose and smoking pot. This was at nine in the morning!

After the Family Dog in Denver closed, I heard about this great place for a concert called Red Rocks. It was only a few miles outside Denver, but since I didn't drive, I'd never been there. But, I booked a show for September 2, 1968 with Jimi Hendrix, Vanilla Fudge, The Soft Machine and Heir Apparent. I remember talking to Ken Palmer at KIMN, the AM radio powerhouse. Ken didn't care for me much because we competed in the concert promotion business. I usually won. On the same night he booked Donovan, I booked The Doors. He had to cancel.

"You're bringing Hendrix to Red Rocks? What are you going to charge?"

"Five dollars."

"You'll never get that much."

"Well, I think we will." We sold out in a week. 9000 tickets times five.

A few days later, Hendrix' people called and said, "We have to move the date."

"What are you talking about?"

"We have to play September 1st. We can't play September 2nd."

We had three months, so I figured we'd have plenty of time to let people know that the date was changing. No problem.

The night of the concert—remember, I'd never seen Red Rocks and neither had Jimi. We arrived at the same time and both of us were awestruck. The seats were full, it was an amazing sight. All these other venues were made by men, but Red Rocks was made by God.

I got the full exposure to the grandness of Red Rocks when I walked on stage, stepped up to the microphone, looked up at the seemingly endless rows of fans going up the mountainside and said:

"Ladies and gentlemen, please welcome to Denver, the Jimi Hendrix Experience!" That was my first stage announcement at Red Rocks. The first of many.

Some of Jimi's equipment didn't make it, so he had to use some of Vanilla Fudge's gear. It wasn't his finest show because he was using borrowed gear, but combined with the majesty of Red Rocks, it was good enough. The fans went wild and went home happy.

We had a police escort to the Cosmopolitan. Jimi and I went to his room where he talked for a while. Just the opposite of how he was on stage, Jimi was a pretty quiet, introspective guy who'd had a tough childhood that he seemed to carry with him. He was soft-spoken, but articulate to the point that he spoke almost with an aristocratic sound to his voice. We had become pretty close by then—and while I was sitting on his bed, he wrote the album liner notes for "Electric Lady-land" which eventually went double platinum. I'm sure my presence during the writing of the album notes was a major inspiration for him.

After Jimi died in London on September 18, 1970, his stepmother June called and said, "Barry, it would mean a lot to me if you came to Jimi's service."

What could I say? "Ma'am, it'll be an honor. Thank you. I'll be there." It was scheduled for October 1, 1970.

My ears were bothering me and I needed to see my Ear, Nose and Throat guy, Dr. Paul Dragul, to get some sprays and whatever to make sure I did okay on the airplane.

"Where are you going?"

"Seattle."

"Seattle?" He thought for a while as he was peering into my ears. "Could you do me, and yourself, a favor on the way and stop in San Francisco?"

"I guess so, but why?"

"I own part of a horse that we've been cheating with. He's much better than we've let on and he's running a big race at Bay Meadows that I know he's going to win. He'll be a longshot and I want to put a bunch of money on him to win but I don't know anybody who'll do it for me."

That was before Off Track Betting.

So, I take his money, fly to San Francisco, take a cab to San Mateo and at the Bay Meadows betting window, I put all the money on his horse to win. I'll be a son of a bitch, he did!

I go to the window and collect between $20,000 and $30,000 cash. That was a lot of money in 1970. I get a cab back to the airport, get on a plane for Seattle and head for Jimi's funeral.

I don't know what to do with the money. I can't let it out of my sight, so I take it with me to the funeral. There I am, sitting between the remaining two members of what had been The Jimi Hendrix Experience, Noel Redding and Mitch Mitchell, with every pocket I had bulging with cash. It was a big funeral at a Baptist church in south Seattle. The pews were jammed with Jimi's family, friends and all kinds of people from the music business. His managers, record label execs, etc. Several well known musicians were there; the most famous of them was Miles Davis. Next to the coffin at the front of the church was a six-foot tall floral arrangement that was made to look like a guitar. Before the procession to the cemetery, the coffin was opened for those of us who wanted to pay our final respects. Nobody looks good dead, and that included Jimi. Outside the church, there was a line of limos, probably a couple of dozen, waiting to take us to the cemetery. The Seattle police had the streets roped off and there were reporters, camera crews and a couple of hundred fans, many of them holding or waving some sort of Hendrix memorabilia or makeshift tribute. I remember it was a clear day, not a cloud in the sky, unusual for Seattle. His casket was lowered into the ground at a cemetery on a hill in the Seattle suburb of Renton. Afterwards, there was a party, for lack of a better word, at an airport hotel, the Hilton, where a lot of the out-of-towners were staying. There was some jamming with the hotel's bar band going on and the typical post-funeral chit chat, but all I could think about was that cash in my pockets. I couldn't wait to get to the airport.

Back in Denver, I dropped off half the cash to Doc Dragul who thumbed through it and one of us, I think it was him—I hope it was him, because I'm ashamed if it was me—said, "Jimi Hendrix should die everyday."

Jim Morrison was probably the most intelligent, cerebral rock star I ever booked. Not only was his IQ supposedly way up there, the way he thought about things was on a much different plane than most of the rest of us. He also brought a new type of sexiness to the stage. Elvis was probably the first sex symbol, at least for young white audiences, but ten years later Jim ratcheted it up a few notches and took it to a different place. He had a bad boy edginess that Elvis didn't have. Where Elvis gyrated on stage, Jim glided and jumped and pranced and slithered and uncoiled.

When he wrapped both hands around the microphone and sang,

> *"I'm gonna love you 'til the Heaven stops the rain,*
> *I'm gonna love you 'til the stars fall from the sky for you*
> *and I"*

every woman in the hall felt as if he was singing to her and only her.

With all that Morrison had going for him, he was a complex guy. Introspective genius, okay, but he had his moments on and off stage where his behavior matched or exceeded what we had come to expect from a rock star of that era. An example of that was at the Family Dog on September 30, 1967. The 25,000 square foot floor was the shiniest I'd ever seen. The logo was in the center with the signs of the Zodiac in a circle around it. And when the black lights and strobes were turned on, there was an illusion of the floor rising. But, the floor had to be waxed a lot. We had 55 gallon drums of floor wax lined up on the balcony between the dressing room and the stage. As Jim walked out to go on, he popped the lid off one of the vats, stuck his head in, took a deep breath and with a smile of satisfaction said, "Oh my God! Now I'm ready." I remember saying to myself, "What the fuck kind of business did I get myself into?"

No one knew Jim Morrison better than my former head of security, Tony Funches. Before he came to work for me, Tony worked for and toured with the Doors, and specifically with Jim, as his personal security guard. Here are some of Tony's memories:

"Being a rock star was just a means to an end for Jim. At least that's the way it was supposed to work out. He told me he wanted to be a poet, and he would have made a great one, I'm sure.

"Jim, the Doors and I came to Denver in 1967. That was my first time there. After their shows, the rest of the band went back to L.A., but Jim wanted to cruise around Denver for a bit, relax and meet 'the poetry lady.'

"At the Doors L.A. office, there was this 12 year old kid always hanging around. He idolized Jim. I threw him out several times, told him to go to school, go home, go anywhere; but, he always came back and begged to be allowed to do something for the Doors, so we gave him a desk and put him in charge of sorting and answering fan mail. His name was Danny Sugerman, who several years later, after Jim died, became the Doors' manager. Anyway, one fan letter was different than the others and Danny put it on Jim's desk for him to look at. It was poetry, written by a Denver woman.

"Some of Barry's people guided us around town and we had some killer pizza at a straight-ahead hippie pizza palace called "Straight Johnson's." We also visited The Denver Folklore Center on 17th Avenue where we shopped and Jim visited with everybody that walked in the door as well as the really great folks that worked there. A guy named Harry Tufts owned the place. I bought so many blues albums that I ran out of cash. Jim put them on his credit card for me until we got back to L.A.

"After the Folklore Center, we headed over to the home of the lady in question. It was in the Park Hill section of Denver, which at that time was one of the wealthier sections with large, two-story brick homes and immaculate yards with white picket fences. When we got to her house, and I don't recall her name, I checked it out to make sure it was cool and then I went and sat in the car while she and Jim discussed poetry.

"They spent hours in there and I could see them in the living room through the open drapes. It was so peaceful and serene compared to the glare he usually endured with the media circus that followed him. This was who the man really was. This was the Jim Morrison I knew. When they had finished their conversation she thanked me for being so patient. Actually, I was stoned on some killer herb one of Barry's folks had laid on me: What is time, anyway? We headed to the airport and back to California.

"Jim enjoyed the encounter with her. I didn't get an inkling of there being romantic interest by either of them in the other, they were just a couple of intellects that traded observations on common topics. Almost scholarly is how I'd put it."

Part Two

THE BIG SHOWS

O **The Denver Pop Festival
June 27-29, 1969**

O **The Woodstock Music Festival
August 15-18, 1969**

"Denver's 'first annual' Pop Festival blasted off into a three-day orbit of screaming and wildly vibrating animal sounds Friday night before more than 8,000 outlandishly clad and thoroughly delighted young fans."
—*Alan Cunningham, "The Rocky Mountain News"*

"A flying bottle hit a cop's helmet. A chase resulted in the arrest of a zonked-out black dressed in an orange jump suit. Sirens blared while the P.A. system played 'Street Fighting Man' on stage."
—*Jim Fouratt in "Rolling Stone"*

"Let's make up in our minds that we make our own world here tonight, starting tonight. We've seen some teargas, that's the start of a Third World War. Just pick your side now."
—*Jimi Hendrix, while tuning up on stage at the Denver Pop Festival*

THE DENVER POP FESTIVAL

In February of 1969, I did a show with Iron Butterfly. I wasn't a fan. Compared to Cream and Janis and Zeppelin and Creedence, come on, Butterfly didn't have much talent. They got lucky, like Grand Funk Railroad was later; they sold a lot of records and a lot of tickets, but they really didn't have much talent compared to the big acts. Their hit was "In-A-Gadda-Da-Vida" which was supposed to be "In the Garden of Eden". But, they were so stoned when they went into the studio, they slurred through it and it came out "innagadda-davida". It was a HUGE, HUGE hit. That night, after their show at the Auditorium Arena, some kids broke windows and vandalized stores in downtown Denver. That's when Denver politicians stuck their noses into my business.

After Mayor Tom Currigan, who'd been friendly and support-ive of me, resigned to become head of Continental Airlines, Bill McNichols became mayor. After the vandalism, he put out a decree that there would no longer be rock concerts in downtown Denver and no more rock concerts at Red Rocks. The only place we could put on rock concerts was at the Coliseum. There was no way I'd be able to sell the 11,000 plus seats, plus the acoustics were awful. It was all concrete and sound bounced all over the place.

After that Iron Butterfly show, I didn't put on another concert in Denver for about four months. I decided to put on something called The Denver Pop Festival, outdoors, at Mile High Stadium, where the NFL Denver Broncos played. Now, I didn't really know quite what a pop festival was, but I picked out three dates: June 28, 29 and 30, 1969 and started calling groups.

My budget was about $120,000 hoping that I'd do $150,000 to $200,000 and make a shitload of money. So, I started booking.

David Geffen had been working in the mail room at William Morris Agency in New York and had just become an agent when I met him. We became friendly and I called to see if he knew of any acts. He tried to sell me on a new group as one of my headliners.

"Barry, I've got a super group for you. Crosby, Stills, Nash and Young."

Now, I knew Stephen Stills and Neil Young from Buffalo Springfield. I knew David Crosby from The Byrds and Graham Nash was in The Hollies.

"They've got an album coming out in a few weeks, Barry. Your concert will be the worldwide debut of CSNY. It'll be great timing."

So, I signed them for $10,000! That was a lot of money, especially for a band with no album, which meant they weren't being heard on the radio.

April comes and goes, no album. May, no album. Early June, no album. I called up David.

"David, I like ya, but I'm not going to pay $10,000 for a group with no album!"

"Barry, you can't do that. It'll break Stephen's heart!"

Stephen was living up in Gold Hill (in the foothills west of Boulder) at the time and was apparently looking forward to doing a local concert.

"I don't care, David. I can't do it." That was the end of that.

David wasn't happy with me, but he was a classy guy. "Okay, Barry. We'll work together again on something." We would, and it would cost me a hell of a lot more than $10,000.

That was one of two brilliant moves I made when booking bands for the Pop Festival. The other was when I had a choice between Santana and Aum. Of course, I chose Aum. Fuck.

For the headliner of the first night, Friday, I booked Iron Butterfly. The second night headliner was Creedence Clearwater Revival.

But, I didn't have a headliner for the third night, because that's where I had planned to put CSNY.

So, I go shopping and everybody in the world got wind of this festival and some people decided to try to muscle me into bad deals. There was a group in Seattle called Concerts West that was booking The Jimi Hendrix Experience. Ron Terry told me I could have Jimi for $100,000.

"Fuck you."

"Then you can forget Hendrix".

What he didn't know was how close Jimi and I were. I called his manager in London, Mike Jefferies, and got Jimi for $50,000. But, it wasn't easy, thanks to his business manager, one of the worst people who ever lived. His name was Stevens Weiss. He was also the business manager for Led Zeppelin.

"Alright, Barry, we'll need $25,000 by cashier's check immediately."

We sent it and everything was fine.

The week before the festival I sent another check for $25,000 because Weiss wanted all the money up front. The Friday morning of the festival, he calls me.

"Barry, where's the money?"

"Stevens, I sent it to you a week ago. You should have it."

"Barry"—and he had this piercing, whiny, nasally voice— "Barry, I'm not putting Jimi on the plane if I don't have the money."

Fuck. I didn't have $25,000 sitting around, so my assistant Leslie sent runners to all the ticket outlets and collected enough cash. We wired him the money and Jimi got on the plane.

About five or six weeks later, I get the cashier's check back in the mail. Stamped on the outside of the envelope was "Received" on such and such a date. Right on time. The envelope had been opened. The check was still in it. Weiss had gotten it a week before the show and just did that to fuck with me.

It turned out to be the final performance of the Jimi Hendrix Experience. Jimi's bass player, Noel Redding and his drummer Mitch Mitchell, warned me before the show that Jimi had changed.

Noel said, "You won't even recognize him" because he'd become so hooked on heroin. "We're not going to play with him anymore" because he'd become impossible to work with.

I had him in September of 1968 and we'd become really fast friends; ate together, shopped together, spent a lot of time together. But when he showed up for the Pop Festival, he barely recognized me. He went through the motions, but he was so far gone. It broke my heart to see him that way. After the Pop Festival, Jimi kept performing, in fact was at Woodstock the next month with his hastily formed Band of Gypsies, but we had the last appearance of The Jimi Hendrix Experience at the Denver Pop Festival.

The money was going fast and I needed help. $25,000 for Butterfly, $25,000 or $30,000 for Creedence, $50,000 for Jimi and it kept going up and up. And, I didn't know how much sound and lights were going to cost. Some promoters from Philly tried to muscle me on the sound and lights. The Spivak Brothers, Herb, Alan and Jerry were going to charge me $25,000 or $30,000 for stage, lights and sound at Mile High Stadium. And, they were going to bring in Chip Monck, the finest production guy ever who, a couple of months later would be one of the announcers at Woodstock. Remember the guy who said, "Stay away from the brown acid"? (He joked with me later about that announcement and said he did it, "Because I was making the blue acid.")

Chip calls me one day.

"I understand that you want me for your show."

"Yeah, well so and so is providing you."

"He ain't providing me. I don't work for him."

"But, he's doing my sound and lights."

"I'll do your sound and lights and I'll be your emcee, too."

And he was cheaper than the guy from Philly. So, I called the guy from Philly.

"Guess what? You ain't coming to Denver."

"You can't do that."

"Watch me."

So, one of the Spivak brothers flies out to Denver. We sit down at the Cherry Creek Inn for coffee and he starts trying to muscle me.

"Let me tell you something", I interrupted. "You're west of Chicago. That shit doesn't go on here, so go back home 'cause you ain't doing it."

So that's how I got Chip Monck.

As we got closer and booked more bands, it was clear that we were going to be way over budget. I wanted to keep it around

$120,000. We were at $300,000. I called in Nate Feld, a local beer dealer, who took out some loans. I mortgaged my car and whatever I could and we scraped up enough.

Feyline came very close to being out of business. Not because of the money. Because of the rain. Starting in May of 1969, it rained just about everyday. It was a monsoon that kept pouring in June. The week of the festival, it poured on Monday and I thought it was going to rain the rest of the week and that would be the end of Feyline. I'd be out of business, out of everything.

But on Thursday, the day before opening day, I was listening to the radio and the forecast said, "zero percent chance of rain Friday, zero percent chance of rain Saturday, 5 percent chance of rain Sunday." The forecast was right. It was dry all weekend. Monday, it poured.

The Festival was right in the middle of anti-establishmentarianism and, because I was a businessman, I was viewed by the young people as part of the establishment. That was ironic because the real establishment, many parents who thought I was ruining their kids, the City of Denver politicians and the police were anti-me. So, from the first night of the festival, hundreds gathered outside the gates and protested against having to pay to hear the music. They said it was their music and they weren't going to pay for it. What bullshit. I paid over $300,000 so they could hear their music! They tried to crash the gates and crawled over security fences. The Denver police got out their riot gear and kept most of them from getting in.

On the second night, when Zephyr was on stage, the cops used teargas against the 300 or so gatecrashers. But, they apparently didn't check which way the wind was blowing first and a cloud of gas settled over the stands where the fans who paid were sitting. Plus, some of the canisters were lobbed back into the stadium by the protestors. It was awful. People were choking and crying and running into the concourses and onto the field to get away from the gas. Most of them didn't know what it was. The only reason I knew was because of my time in the Marine Corps, where they'd make you go inside a quonset hut with a gas mask. They'd fire the teargas and before they'd let you out, you had to take off your mask and sing the Marine Corps Hymn.

Chip and I took turns going up on stage, trying to calm people down.

THRONG TEAR-GASSED

Festival Flap: 33 Arrested, 6 Hurt

"Don't rub your eyes, that'll only make it worse. Get something wet, a cloth or something and put it over your eyes."

Eventually, as the gas dissipated, we talked everyone back off the field. Zephyr got back on stage and finished their set, but outside the gates, the battle continued the rest of the night.

After the show, we had a meeting with the cops. The police chief, George Seaton, who was the uncle of Bill Thompson, the manager of the Jefferson Airplane, used to enjoy cocktails when he was off duty and his officers found him at the Harem Lounge in Cherry Creek. They brought him out to the stadium around midnight where we all agreed that we didn't want another night of violence. I had a big mouth and a reputation for being a tough guy, but I hated the violence. Just hated it. So, we agreed that as soon as the show started, at 6 o'clock, we were going to let everyone in. Just open the gates very quietly and let anyone in. Good. Great plan.

Sunday afternoon comes and Captain Stan Cayou, the head of the police detail, walks up.

"We've changed our mind. We're not going to let these fuckin' punks push us around. We're not opening the gates. If they want a war, we'll give them a war."

I felt like telling him it was my show and I'd do what I want, but it was their police department and their city and their stadium. Instead, Leslie and I took a couple of thousand tickets and went outside to hand them out to people. We planned to hand them out to the gate crashers and that would take care of that. I went up to one guy, and Leslie had the same experience, I handed him a ticket. He brushed it away and said, "I don't want any fuckin' ticket. We don't care about the show, we came to fight the pigs." A bunch of people from California had come just to fight the police and cause trouble. And they did. They threw bottles and rocks at the cops. They were throwing teargas that they'd stolen out of the police cars into the stadium. It got worse when some of the kids already in the stands started throwing bottles and stuff at the cops. Really ugly.

When it was Joe Cocker's time to go on, I found him hiding in a restroom in the north stands. He was terrified.

"So, this is America?" he asked.

He told me he wasn't just concerned about his safety, he was insecure about his music. But, he had an incredible set. I'd never seen anyone on stage like him, with that kind of spastic, jerky movement. He did a hell of a show.

Hendrix? God! The cops fired more teargas and the crowd reacted as you'd guess people would after getting gassed—jumping onto the field and running toward the stage. Jimi was playing "Voodoo Child" and instead of there being a 20-yard buffer of grass between the stage and the stands, people were jammed up tight against the stage. And, he didn't help things by telling the crowd between songs:

> *"Let's make up in our minds that we make our own world here tonight, starting tonight. We've seen some teargas, that's the start of a Third World War. Just pick your side now."*

I couldn't wait for him to finish his set so we could end the Festival. Thank God it was over. What a mess. But, I wound up netting about $50,000.

The Denver Pop Festival Lineup

June 27, 1969

- Big Mama Thornton
- The Flock
- Three Dog Night
- Frank Zappa and the Mothers of Invention
- Iron Butterfly

June 28

- Aorta
- Zephyr (with Tommy Bolin on guitar)
- Poco
- Johnny Winter
- Tim Buckley
- Creedence Clearwater Revival

June 29

- Aum
- Rev. Cleophus Robinson
- Sweetwater
- Joe Cocker
- Three Dog Night
- The Jimi Hendrix Experience

Attendance: 62,000

And how about these ticket prices? $6 per day or $15 for all three days. Can you believe that? $15 for all that music?

Announcements I Heard at Woodstock

"Alan Fey, please come to the information booth. Alan Fey, please come to the information booth." *

"There's a rumor that there is some bad acid going around. If you are worried about the acid you are taking not being good, just take half a tab."

"It's a free concert from now on. That doesn't mean that anything goes. What it means is that we are going to put the music on for free. We've had thousands of people come here. We're going to need each other. We'll be bringing food in. Remember, the man next to you is your brother and you damn well better treat each other that way. If you don't, we're going to blow this whole thing."

*Alan, my son, wasn't there, but I knew they were making an album of the concert and I wanted to get his name in it.

BY THE TIME I GOT TO WOODSTOCK

There are probably millions of Baby Boomers who will tell you they were at Woodstock. It's one of those phenomena like Vietnam—way more guys claim to have served there than actually did. The people who say they were at Woodstock and tell you how great it was, those are the ones who weren't there. I was at Woodstock and it was undoubtedly a significant event—and turned out being far more significant than any of us knew at the time—but great? Not so much.

I was invited to attend Woodstock as a V.I.P., but I had a Diana Ross and The Supremes concert at Red Rocks on August 14, 1969, the night before the Woodstock Festival was to begin. So, I made sure the concert got started and then headed for the airport. I took a red-eye to New York and then another plane to the Sullivan County Airport, which was about nine miles from the site. My invitation included helicopter transportation to the festival. When I showed up with my big suitcase—which I took because I had to be in Houston after that for a Blind Faith concert— the people loading the chopper had other plans.

"Hi Barry, we knew you were coming. We'll take your bag, but we can't take you. We don't have enough room. We're transporting medicine and food."

So, I walked. Nine-point-three miles from the airport to Max Yasgur's cow pasture. This was when I was at my heaviest, around 325, but I kept up. There were thousands and thousands of us walking. Hundreds of cars were abandoned. Locals stood along the road and looked at the parade of weird-looking crazy people. But, they were nice and the kids were nice. I met a couple from Georgia and we talked while we walked. They said they had no tickets and no money—the word had gotten out about Woodstock and they just had to be there. Well, I was supposed to be a V.I.P., so I told them that I knew some people and could probably get them in. When we got to the backstage gate, I asked the guard if they could come in with me. He pointed up the hill and said, "Look up there." The fence was down. The concert was free.

I got there about three minutes before Richie Havens went on stage. I was standing on the side of the stage and was absolutely stunned at what I saw. I'd never seen so many people in one place. About a half million were jammed into a space equipped for 150,000.

When Richie started playing "Here Comes The Sun", I thought, "Where?" Of course, he was phenomena. Woodstock made his career. But, he hadn't played Denver yet, so I booked him at the Auditorium Arena in November of 1971 and, thanks to the name recognition he got from Woodstock and its album and movie, it was sold out and was a great show.

But, oh, what a mess Woodstock was. It was raining off and on and the pasture was muddy. There wasn't enough food or water. There weren't enough toilets. Forget about getting much sleep. My V.I.P. status meant that I got a blanket to wrap myself in when I could find a dry spot to lie down on. I stayed a couple of days and couldn't take it any longer. I was wet, tired and hungry and couldn't wait to get out of there. Even in the V.I.P. area, food was hard to come by. I had a shot at getting a sandwich when a tray was being passed around, but Grace Slick grabbed it just as I was reaching for it.

Thankfully, I didn't have to walk the nine miles back to Sullivan County Airport. They had three colors of t-shirts: red for medical, blue for crew and black for VIPs. Well, I was so big that my black shirt wouldn't fit, so I wrapped it around my arm, making sure they could see it and I could get on the chopper. It flew me back to the airport and I spent the night in a motel room with five people I didn't know, then caught a flight the next day to New York. I was so hungry, I went to a place called Tin Lizzie's where I had the biggest steak I could get and some onion rings. Then, I flew to Houston for Blind Faith.

On top of all of the logistical problems at Woodstock, some of the bands didn't get paid. But, the exposure they got was priceless. Woodstock made the careers of a lot of groups.

What was amazing about Woodstock was how well everyone got along; that there was no violence among all those people. It was really pretty remarkable. Everyone was pretty mellow, most of them, I suppose, because of something they ingested. I was very proud of them. But, the conditions were ridiculous.

Another Woodstock act I booked, was "Country Joe and The Fish". Wherever they played after Woodstock, fans demanded the "Fish Cheer".

> *"Give me an F!"*
> *"Give me a U"!*
> *"Give me a C"!*
> *"Give me a K"!*
> *"What's that spell?"*
> *"What's that spell?"*
> *"What's that spell?"*

And then he went into the "I Feel Like I'm Fixin' To Die Rag"

> *Yeah, come on all of you, big strong men,*
> *Uncle Sam needs your help again.*
> *He's got himself in a terrible jam*
> *Way down yonder in Vietnam*
> *So put down your books and pick up a gun,*
> *We're gonna have a whole lotta fun.*
> *And it's one, two, three,*
> *What are we fighting for?*
> *Don't ask me, I don't give a damn,*
> *Next stop is Vietnam;*
> *And it's five, six, seven,*
> *Open up the pearly gates,*
> *Well there ain't no time to wonder why,*
> *Whoopee! we're all gonna die.*

A year later, on September 19th, 1970, what Country Joe's F-U-C-K spelled for me was a $5000 fine for indecency by the hall manager at the Arizona Coliseum in Phoenix. I'm sure he stuck it in his pocket.

Part Three

THE GODS OF ROCK

- ○ **The Beatles**

- ○ **The Rolling Stones**

- ○ **The Who**

- ○ **Led Zeppelin**

THE BEATLES

The Beatles were the only major group I didn't book and that was because they stopped touring by the time I really got going with Feyline. If I had been here, Denver wouldn't have been the only place on the Beatles' first U.S. tour that didn't sell out. The promoter was Vern Byers who had a teen club and the only place you could buy tickets was at the teen club. So, they came up short of selling out. But, the thing about the Beatles at that time was that it wasn't as much of a concert tour as a social revolution. They never got a chance to be heard. There was so much screaming at their concerts that you could barely, if at all, hear their music. But, they were incomparable.

Paul McCartney

In January of 1973, a guy named Vinny Romeo called me. I had only known him as an assistant—not even that—an assistant assistant, a glorified gofer, to famed New York talent agent Frank Barsalona.

"Barry, I'm now managing Paul McCartney."

"Really? Congratulations."

"I'm going to London to meet with Paul. Why don't you come with me?"

"Hell yeah, I'll go." At that point in my life, I'd fly anywhere for anything. I was one of United's favorite customers. It's really what kept me married to Cindy as long as I was. I was neither a good parent nor a good husband and my traveling took pressure off the relationship.

We get to London and go to meet with McCartney. We hang out for a couple of days. Paul was nice enough, but something seemed off. He was very nervous, very agitated. I asked Vinny what was wrong. He said that Paul was going to debut his new single and there was no rock 'n roll radio then in England. Bands had to go on TV, on "Top of the Pops", a BBC show and perform live.

When I heard that, I told Paul, in my smart-ass condescending way, "Well, Paul, come on, you are Paul McCartney! Don't worry about it. Everything'll be fine."

So, we all go to the TV studio and McCartney goes on the show and does his new single that he was so worried about: "My Love". He walks down from the stage after the show and asks, "Well, what'd you think, guys?"

"Fuck you!" I said, which was my way of saying he'd been sand-bagging us.

"I beg your pardon!?"

"You were worried about that song? That will be number one in two days in the United States. That's a beautiful song!"

He seemed to like hearing that.

That night, he invited us to go with him to Rod Stewart's 28th birthday party. It was at a place called The Champion, a restaurant/bar which they closed for the party. It had absolutely great hamburgers. I don't normally like thick hamburgers but these things were four or five inches high and the meat was so tasty, seasoned just right, they were just perfect. Listen to me: I'm at Rod Stewart's private birthday party and there were naked women and everything else connected with the rock star life all over the place and all I cared about was how great the burgers were. But, a good time was had by all. I said goodbye to McCartney and that was that.

The next significant interaction with McCartney came twelve years later, July of 1985. I was with U2 in Dublin before we went to London where they played at Live Aid. I'm backstage at Wembley Stadium and I flew my oldest son, Alan, in to be with me.

My God, what a line up: Queen, U2, Elton, The Who, David Bowie and many others with McCartney as the last performer before the grand finale. During the show, McCartney and Bowie had an impromptu news conference backstage and as it broke up, Paul was walking our way. When he was close enough, I held out my hand and said, "Hello, Paul. Remember Vinny Romeo, 1973?"

He clasped my hand, looked at me, smiled and said, "You're BAR-ee Fey!"

"Yes sir, I am, thank you very much. Nice to see you again. How are you?"

Alan was nearly in shock. After Paul had moved on, he said: "Dad, that was one of the Beatles and he said 'hi' to you. That's so cool!" This is the same son who Mick Jagger put to bed during a party at our house in 1972. Earlier in the day in 1985 at Wembley, Alan was with me when Bowie and U2 and the rest came by to say hi. He didn't seem much impressed by them. But one of the Beatles, that was cool!

The next real McCartney moment—and it's tainted my opinion of him, unfortunately—was when he was playing Folsom Field in Boulder and it was at the time that his wife Linda was really heavy into her anti-meat, anti-leather campaign.

Make-A-Wish contacted me and said they had a dying child whose biggest wish was to meet Paul. I contacted McCartney's people and they agreed to it, no problem, he'd be happy to make the boy's wish come true.

On the day of the concert I pulled up to Folsom and noticed a fairly steady stream of roadies and other backstage people walking the couple of blocks to a business district. They were going to buy food, food with meat in it, because Linda had banned meat backstage. Talk about a groupie, that's basically what Linda was. A photographer-groupie. But, Paul fell in love with her, even though he was engaged at the time.

The Make A-Wish child arrived in his wheelchair. We took him backstage and told Paul's security guy that we're ready. We waited about ten minutes and the security guy came out with two signed CDs and a signed photo and an apology. "I'm sorry, but Mr. McCartney isn't able to meet with you."

Now, I know he's adored by millions but, I have never been able to forgive that. All he had to do was stop what he was doing for two fuckin' minutes and come and say hello to this kid and make his life a little bit better. And he wouldn't come out.

And that's the memory of Paul McCartney that still stands out for me. With all the good times before that, including making my son prouder, I think, than he'd ever been of me backstage at Live Aid. But, I felt so ashamed and hurt and felt for this kid so badly. Look, God blessed McCartney—and all of these stars—with such talent and such an ability to make people feel better just by playing or singing. They're so lucky. All Paul had to do was say 'hi'. No excuse for that. What possible excuse could there be? He came out awhile later to play for two hours.

That's the last time I saw Paul.

George Harrison

George was just a nice, decent man. Undemanding, never a problem. A great guy. I booked him and Ravi Shankar at the Denver Coliseum in 1974.

John Lennon

I never booked John, but had the pleasure of meeting him at an art gallery. One of the great human beings of our business. He was obviously very much in love with Yoko, which I couldn't figure out. I'm sure I wasn't alone in that.

Ringo Starr and his All Star Money Losing Band

Ringo would show up with an amazing band, great players, heavy hitters like Joe Walsh, Nils Lofgren, Dr. John, Billy Preston, Levon Helm, Clarence Clemons, Todd Rundgren, Randy Bachman, John Entwistle, Jack Bruce, Eric Carmen—but they would never draw the big crowds. And every time I played him, I was reminded of what Elvis' manager Colonel Tom Parker told me in Hawaii in 1973: "Don't ever let 'em come one at a time."

But, every time I got a call from Ringo's people, I could never turn him down. I'd just ask, "How much are we going to lose this time?" Ringo was a good guy, I just couldn't fill the seats and I lost money every fucking time.

I wanted to petition the IRS to allow me to add Ringo as a dependent.

THE ROLLING STONES

Jethro Tull was playing in Phoenix in early June, 1971. I had them at the Del Webb Townhouse, a hotel in Phoenix that also had a theater in the round that held about 2500. It's about a quarter of five in the morning. I'm sound asleep when the phone rings.

"This is the overseas operator. Is this Barry Fey?"

"Yeah, this is Barry."

"I have a Mr. Thor Knudsen calling you from Sweden."

"Oh, okay." I'd never heard of him, but I figure if he's calling from Sweden I should probably talk to him.

"Barry?"

"Yes."

"I'm calling on behalf of the Rolling Stones. Would you be interested in doing their 1972 tour of the United States?"

Now, if the call hadn't been introduced by an operator, I probably would have hung up. But, I talked to him and he said the Stones gave him my name, told him to get a hold of me and to tell me to be prepared to fly to France—they were staying in Nice—to meet with them about the '72 tour.

"Well, I don't have a passport, but I'd love to."

What I couldn't figure out is why the Stones were having him call me. I'd spent maybe a total of 20 or 30 minutes with them at my 1969 show in Fort Collins and their impression of me couldn't have been that great because when they asked for food backstage, I told them to go back to the hotel. What an idiot.

So, I got a passport, but then I waited days, then weeks and I didn't hear anything from Thor. Finally, in early July, I got a call on a Tuesday and he asked me if I could be there on Saturday. I left Denver Thursday and after a stop or two landed in Paris. I changed to a smaller plane for the trip to Nice. A driver picked me up and took me to Hotel le Negresco, a famous, old hotel.

The driver said, "You'll be having dinner tonight with the boys."

The boys. Sure, I eat with the Stones all the time. No problem.

So, we go to dinner. There's Keith Richards, Bill Wyman, Charlie Watts and Mick Taylor. They told me that Jagger couldn't make it because he'd had a rather large fight with Bianca, his wife at the time. They'd only been married a couple of months, so I guess the honeymoon didn't last long. Later, after they divorced in '78, she was quoted as saying, "My marriage ended on my wedding day."

Domestic dust up or not, I'm not so star struck that I didn't know it was rude for him not to come. I flew all the way from Denver and he couldn't walk 200 yards?

We didn't need Jagger to make a deal, or so I thought. They wanted me to do all of their shows on their 1972 U.S. tour—over 50 shows starting in Vancouver and ending in New York. Why me? Because the Fort Collins show, which happened only because I had pestered their manager, Ron Schneider, every day for weeks and he wouldn't give me Denver, but finally agreed that Moby Gym would be a good place for the boys to open their 1969 tour, was the only one of the tour that went well. Their next show in Los Angeles at The Forum was a disaster because they had to wait until after a hockey game and didn't get started until about 2 am and they said it didn't get much better after that. They hated Bill Graham, who did most of the tour and Bill hated them. So, we made plans and the boys all agreed with me that the top ticket price should be $6.50 and Barry Fey would do the whole damn thing!

But, what a stupid ass I was because I talked my way out of doing the whole tour. "Look, I don't think I can do the whole country. I'm just a small company." It didn't occur to me that I could hire people to help me do the whole tour. Idiot. I picked out the cities that I knew I could do and we agreed on 17 of the dates. They loved the plans, all of the arrangements, everything was great and they would talk to Mick. We had a deal.

On my way home, I stopped in London to visit John Morris. John was the other guy on the microphone at Woodstock besides Chip Monck. *("It looks like we're going to get a little bit of rain, so you'd better cover up...everybody just sit down, wrap yourself up... hold on to your neighbor, man. Hey! If we think really hard, maybe we can stop this rain! ...please move away from the towers...please move away from the towers.")*

John was the one who did me a favor by announcing my son Alan's name at Woodstock. He wasn't there. He was only two years old. I just wanted his name on the recording. We'd become real friendly, so I dropped by his house. We're getting caught up on Saturday when the phone rings.

"It's for you", John says. "It's Mick Jagger."

I picked up the phone.

"Barry (he and the other Brits always pronounced it BAR-ee), this is Mick Jagger. I'd like to apologize for not being at the meeting. Will you come back to Nice?"

Now, I'm a person who's really set in his ways and had a drawer full of noses I cut off to spite my face and I wanted to tell him no, but, it was Mick Jagger, man! So, the first thing in the morning, I fly from London to Paris and then to Nice. He and Bianca met me for lunch in their villa—each of the Stones had their own villa, huge, gorgeous homes. When I was in Keith's during the first trip, I was marveling at how big and beautiful it was.

"God, this place is amazing. What's the upstairs like?"

Keith looked at me and with that famous grin said, "I don't know man...never been up there."

Anyway, I'm at Mick and Bianca's villa for lunch and I'm suitably impressed. They're very nice to me, but, oh my God, the tension between them. Even had I not known they'd argued the day before, I would have thought that there was trouble in paradise.

You need to understand that there were few things more important to me than eating. I weighed about 300 pounds. When I was hungry, forget it. That ruled everything for me. There was one more piece of chicken on the platter and as a pregnant (by about 6 months) Bianca reached for it, I beat her to it. That lightened the mood a little.

Everything's fine and Mick agrees with all of the tour plans the boys and I had made two nights earlier and he says, "Let's do it. BARee, it'll be a pleasure working for you."

That was a very important trip for me, a career maker.

The next year, the Stones asked me to come with them for the opening of their '72 tour in Vancouver. It was called the S.T.P. tour, for "Stones Touring Party". They picked me up with their private plane that had the famous lips and tongue logo on the tail. This was a few weeks after "Exile On Main Street" came out and, really, when you think about all of the fantastic, unbelievable years the Stones have had, 1972 may have been their peak. The Beatles had dissolved a couple of years earlier and people started calling the Stones "The World's Greatest Rock and Roll Band". I've written elsewhere that I think The Who deserved that title, especially since the Stones had become less a band of equals and more like "Mick Jagger and the Stones". His popularity as the front man had separated him from the rest of the guys. Mick was flying high, but what made the Stones so interesting to me, was Keith. Just by his looks and reputation, he represented danger and, obviously, a lot of people were drawn to that. And between the two of them, they had a wide range of fans covered. But, there was nothing dangerous about Keith. Well, he did carry a .38 during the tour because the Hell's Angels supposedly had a contract out on Mick, but that was just self-defense. Keith's the coolest guy ever in rock 'n roll.

That tour was far more than just a tour. It's hard to explain what it was like to be around the Stones then. I mean, that's where that strange little dude Truman Capote and I became good friends. It was such a heady time and while, when it came to concerts, I was always more into counting the ticket money and going home, there was something very addictive about being immersed in that craziness and being treated by them as a fully accepted participant. It was like I was half a Stone. It was just fucking awesome and, thankfully, I realized that as it was happening.

The night of the show at the Pacific Coliseum, there's a lot of excitement. I have nothing to do with it, no financial interest. When I walked outside the arena, I spotted trouble. The kids were starting to line up and the Mounties or whatever they called themselves, were lining up opposite them, a few yards away. There were a couple of thousand kids. Far fewer cops. I tracked down the head of the police force.

"Sir, I'm not from here and I don't want to interfere, but I'm a concert promoter from Denver and I've had quite a lot of experience with crowd control. You're going to have trouble. But, what you should do, instead of lining up like this is go and immerse yourselves among them, so that wherever they turn, they see a police officer. Don't make it your line against their line."

Clearly he was impressed by my vast experience and willing-ness to share it.

"Sir, mind your own fucking business and get out of here."

Which I did. I went back inside and it wasn't long before there was a riot out there. The kids were burning cop cars, throwing rocks at the cops and the cops were beating and tear gassing the kids. It was a mess. 30 or so cops were treated for injuries. I have no idea how many fans went home bloody.

I flew home after that concert, but caught up with the tour a couple of weeks later, when they played for me in Tucson. The cops there did a marginally better job than the ones in Vancouver. A few hundred fans trying to crash the gates were tear gassed. Violence seemed to follow the Stones on that tour. In San Diego, 15 fans were injured and several dozen arrested; more violence and dozens of arrests at RFK Stadium, Detroit and Montreal. Montreal is where somebody blew up an equipment van and then fans rioted because they'd been sold counterfeited tickets. Jagger and Richards wound up in jail after a fight which almost made them miss a show in Bos-ton. The mayor was so worried there'd be a riot if there wasn't a show; he got the boys out of jail in time.

After the Tucson show, I had three more in a row: Albuquerque and then two in Denver. And this is unbelievable in 2011, but the Stones played TWO shows on the same day; June 16. A 3 pm show and a 7 pm show at the Denver Coliseum. That was on a Friday.

The next day, we had a luau for the Stones in my backyard. Dan Fong, in addition to being the great photographer whose work is seen throughout this book, was my chef/caterer. He was a fabulous cook and the boys—and other bands—loved his food. Mick always requested Dan for the backstage food.

Dan went all out. He flew in pineapples from Hawaii, buried and roasted a couple of pigs. There were ribs, chickens, ducks, oysters on the half shell, lo mein, egg rolls, fried rice—it was a 13 course meal. He had a three and a half foot high "lips and tongue" logo made out of papier-mâché with a bubble machine, but the machine wasn't working right and instead of bubbles, foam kind of oozed out of it all night. There were big, papier-mâché mushrooms all over the place and tiki torches lighting long, low linen covered tables where everybody sat on the ground. He hired a bunch of good looking babes to help serve. At the end of the party, they disappeared with the boys. It was supposed to be a dinner for 40, but about 80 showed up. It was chaos, but my God, what a great fuckin' party. One of the best ever.

When Mick arrived—remember, this was an off day for them—rather than having something on more ordinary than his stage costumes, he had on something even more flamboyant. He was wearing a sequined jacket-vest with feathers along the edges of the sleeves, toreador pants with slippers and glitter and makeup on his face. Well into the evening, the bartender yelled to someone who was closer to Mick, "Tell the faggot in the fairy costume that his drink's ready!" Mick didn't seem to hear it, but Charlie Watts, who'd been sitting on a couch, fell on the ground laughing.

Like I said, it was a great party which all of us enjoyed, and my neighbors, who until then probably thought I was the gardener, liked it too. There were kids perched in trees trying to catch a peek of the Stones.

In 2011, I was at a Starbucks getting a drink when a guy came up to me. "I used to be your neighbor. My parents lived next door and I remember the Stones party you had in 1972. I was 22 and had my girlfriend with me. We were sitting on a little grass knoll separating our properties, trying to see the band. A guy started walking toward us and all we could really see was the glowing ember of his cigarette until he got within a few feet. It was Keith Richards."

"Well, that must have been pretty cool for you and your girl", I said.

"Oh yeah, but that wasn't all. Keith made small talk with us for a couple of minutes and then hit on my girlfriend. He tried to pick her up!"

She declined his offer. Keith wasn't lonely for long. I saw him with two gorgeous blondes hanging all over him.

Before the party broke up, we played basketball. I had a court in my backyard and Mick fashioned himself as quite the player. So, we had a Feyline vs. The Rolling Stones game and we kicked their asses! Of course, I had a couple of security guys who were 6'7", 6'8". The Stones' team didn't stand a chance.

My son Alan was five years old and when he was too tired to stay awake any longer, Mick carried him to bed, tucked him in and said, "Now, you go to sleep."

The party broke up about four in the morning. That was some party.

We set the all time attendance record for the Tarrant County Convention Center in Fort Worth with two shows on June 24th. The next day, in Houston, the boys did two more shows, at "The Hof"; the Hofheinz Pavilion at the University of Houston. Judge Roy Hofheinz, was a wealthy businessman who had been the mayor of Houston, was part of the group that built the Astrodome and brought Major League Baseball to Houston. He was close with LBJ and John Connally. He was a big, big deal in Houston.

A week or so before the show, Judge Hofheinz called me in my Denver office.

"Mr. Fey", he drawled, "my daughter would really like to get some tickets to the Rolling Stones concert."

"Yes, sir, I bet she would. It's going to be a great show."

"She'll gladly pay, but she doesn't want to have to go out and stand in line."

Now, before the tour, I made up my mind that nobody got comp tickets. You want to see the Stones, you pay. Comp tickets took money out of my pocket.

"Judge Hofheinz, I tell you what. Tell your daughter to get a sleeping bag and go wait in line like everyone else has to do."

"But, Mr. Fey, the hall the Stones are playing in has my name on it."

"Yes sir, but I rented it."

I had the feeling that Mr. Hofheinz wasn't used to hearing "no", especially over something as seemingly insignificant as Stones' tickets that cost $6.50. But, he was a businessman.

"All right, all right, Mr. Fey. I understand."

In those days, the ticket sales lines were almost as much fun as the shows. There were no computers, just first come, first served. And people would line up for days, some even more than a week, camping out in front of the box offices or record stores or wherever the tickets were being sold. Waiting on line was a great scene. At the St. Louis shows, ten days before tickets went on sale, these two guys rolled out their sleeping bags and set up camp. They were easily the first ones in line. And nearly everyday, the television stations would do a story about the growing line of people waiting for Stones tickets and nearly everyday, those two guys at the front would be interviewed on TV. The moment the box office opened and tickets went on sale, they just got up and left. Didn't buy tickets. They were just there for the party and maybe so that all their friends could see them on TV.

That's another thing that Ticketmaster took away: the ticket line parties. People brought lawnchairs, blankets, sleeping bags, food, guitars and transistor radios. I'm sure there was a good bit of mood altering material being passed around. Some people would bring their dogs. The lines were a good time, but I always had my security guys around to make sure that the ticket line experience was a safe one for the fans.

I was staying in the Rice Hotel in Houston. Before the show, I got a call from a guy named Jones.

"Mr. Fey, my name is John Jones. I'm not one of these big Texas landowners you read about. I only own 15 acres. But, they're all in downtown Houston, including the hotel you're staying at."

I thought about that for a moment.

"Mr. Jones, how would you like tickets to the Rolling Stones?"

"Well, I would appreciate that, sir."

So, I violated my no-comping policy, but not really. He comped my hotel room.

Before the Kansas City shows, an executive with Nabisco called and tried to get free tickets from me.

"I'm sorry, sir, I can't give you tickets, but I sure like your Oreo cookies." What a smartass. I acted like a little king.

Stevie Wonder was the opening act on the '72 tour. He was killing audiences. Stevie was so good. He'd already had huge hits with "Signed, Sealed, Delivered", "My Cherie Amour", "Yester-Me, Yester-You", "If You Really Love Me" and others. I think "Superstition" had come out by then, but I'm not sure. Crowds were just going crazy for him. City after city, he got standing ovations and several times, the boys would bring him back on stage to play with them in the finale.

Well, you didn't need to be Barry Fey to know that there were a lot of tickets waiting to be sold in a lot of cities with Stevie as the headliner. I went to his manager.

"Listen, Stevie is doing so well, we should bring him back in six or eight months, and headline him. He'll make a lot of money."

His manager, and I'm sorry I can't remember his name, said, "Barry, that's a good idea. But, I gotta tell you—and I don't like telling you this."

"What is it?"

"Stevie only plays for black promoters.

I said to him, "I won't tell him if you won't".

He laughed his ass off, but I never got to take Stevie on tour.

The Stones' New York dates coincided with Mick's 29th birthday. July 26th, the final concert of the tour. I was invited to his birthday party. Now, what do you buy for Mick Jagger? He's going to get all of these expensive gifts. I know I'm not going to out-present any of his rich friends.

Somehow, I got the idea to buy him a bed. A hospital bed. At National Jewish Hospital in Denver, they sold me a bed and put up a plaque stating that the bed was donated by Mick Jagger. They gave me a photo of a kid lying in the bed with the plaque in the foreground. I had it framed, packed it and took it to New York.

A day or two before his birthday, I went to see Mick at his hotel suite. He was staying at the Pierre. I gave him the present and he seemed to love it. He took down one of the hotel's pictures and put that one up. I did my job. How do you compete with a photo of a sick child in a bed with Mick's name on it?

Peter Rudge, the Stones' manager, called me a day before Mick's party and said it was being moved to a secret, secure location: The Starlight Room on the roof of the St. Regis Hotel. Hell's Angels was still trying to kill him. Mick had said some things about them after the Altamont disaster where the Angels were supposedly in charge of security and fucked it up badly. A guy got stabbed right in front of the stage while the Stones were doing "Under My Thumb". The Angels wanted Mick dead and word got out that they were in New York and were going to get him.

Everyone who'd been invited was under orders not to tell anyone where it was. Security was ridiculous, but I finally made it up the elevators. It was packed; a great party. Mick survived.

My only disappointment was that I couldn't get my picture taken. All the fuckin' paparazzi in Manhattan and not one god damn one of them would take my picture! That's how important I was. Either that or none of them had a wide-angle lens.

Eliot Janeway. There's a name you wouldn't have expected to find in my book, right? The noted economist and writer had interviewed me about the Stones tour. He'd never written about rock music and needed my help to figure out the economics of the tour, I guess. A few months later, he was in Denver and asked me to meet him for dinner at the Brown Palace Hotel.

"You know, Barry, I'm a very good friend of Wilbur Mills and he's looking for new members of Congress to be on his team. Do you know anybody?"

I thought for a moment. "Well, there is this lady here named Pat Schroeder who's going to be in the election. But, she's really a longshot. She doesn't seem to have much of an organization behind her.

"I'd like you to visit her Barry."

"I don't know her, how am I going to visit her?"

"Just go see her and tell her that she'll have the support of Wilbur Mills and we'll get her some Milk Fund money."

I had no idea what the fuck that was, but I remember going to Pat Schroeder's house and knocking on her door. She'd kind of heard of me and found my message from Janeway to be very interesting.

As the November election approached, it was clear that Pat was going to be crushed by Mike McKevitt, the Denver District Attorney who had all of the GOP power and money and name recognition behind him. And, he was monopolizing the radio stations with his appearances and commercials. There was no Fairness Doctrine, so Pat couldn't get on the air.

A week before the election, I gave all of my commercial time— and I was running a bunch of spots for different concerts—to Pat Schroeder. And through Eliot Janeway, Wilbur Mills had Ted Kennedy cut a commercial for Pat.

"I look forward to serving in Congress with Representative Pat Schroeder." Ted had no fucking idea who she was, but the commercials worked.

Pat has often credited me with getting her elected.

That story hooks up to the Stones via Bill Carter, who I'd met through the Eliot Janeway-Wilbur Mills connection.

Bill was a lawyer from Arkansas and had been a Secret Service agent during the JFK and LBJ years. He'd done some legal work for me and is a great guy who I think the world of. One of his best qualities is that he's just fearless. He asked me to keep him in mind if any of my rock 'n roll clients needed some legal help.

"Absolutely Bill, I'll see what I can do."

After the riotous 1972 tour, the State Department, I'm sure on orders from Nixon, decided the Stones should not be allowed back in the country. That made touring, and my job, a little difficult. I was talking to Peter Rudge about it and told him I knew this attorney who had some connections with Wilbur Mills and Eliot Janeway. I spoke to Janeway, who mentioned it to Mills, who, full circle, recommended Carter.

I set up a meeting with Bill, Peter, Mick and myself at a hotel in New York. With all of us watching, Bill picks up the phone and calls Wilbur Mills in Washington. Well, Congress is in session and Mills is on the House floor, but when he's told that Carter's on the phone, he leaves the floor and gets on the phone. Wilbur briefly says hello to Mick, but spends several minutes on the phone with Rudge and gets the ball rolling to straighten out the problems.

That was good enough for Mick and before long, Bill became the Stones' new attorney in the U.S. He did an incredible job for the Stones in a bunch of different ways, most notably challenging all of the cops in every city they toured who wanted to make their name by arresting the Stones for something.

Bill went on to become especially close to Keith and helped him out of a number of jams, the kind that only a superstar heroin addict can get into, many of them detailed in his memoir, *"Get Carter— Backstage In History From JFK's Assassination To The Rolling Stones"*.

In my opinion, which is shared by Keith, Bill deserves as much credit as anybody for keeping the Stones, Keith especially, out of prison, together and on tour. Keith writes about the story in much more detail in *"Life"*. (What you failed to point out, Keith, is that I also deserve credit because if there's no Barry Fey, there's no Bill Carter.)

A few years after I introduced Bill to the Stones, he gives me a call. Things were going great with the boys and they're keeping him real busy. But, he explained that he'd also been doing some work for several years with a Little Rock businessman who had a company that was going public in April of 1978.

He asked me if I wanted to get in on the ground floor.

"What's the name of the company?"

"Federal Express."

"What does it do?"

He explained.

I replied, "Bill, I love ya, man, but who the fuck is going to pay $10 to mail a letter?"

I passed.

That was another great Barry Fey decision. Can you imagine how much...?

Fuck.

Thanks in large part to Bill and Congressman Mills, the Stones were able to get back into the United States for a Nicaraguan Earthquake Benefit Concert, which was essentially a scam to get the Japanese government to allow them in. Just before Christmas, 1972, Peter Rudge called.

"Barry, we've got a problem and need your help."

He wanted to take the boys to Japan and then on to Australia and New Zealand. The Stones had never played in Japan and it had been six years since they were in the other countries. But, the S.T.P. Tour, which I consider one of the most successful tours in history, had gotten so much media coverage around the world for the violence and drug related decadence that getting visas and work permits was becoming a nightmare. In fact, it didn't appear likely that the U.S. was going to let the Stones tour again after all of the '72 bullshit until Carter and Mills got involved. Sounds weird now, but remember the mentality of the crowd in the White House that year. The Japanese government said Jagger wouldn't be allowed in because of his drug convictions. It didn't even bother mentioning Keith's problems—Jagger's were enough.

Peter went on to tell me that they had just gotten a big break. On December 23rd, a huge earthquake had devastated Nicaragua and killed about 5,000 people. Bianca was from there and started a Nicaraguan relief effort. Peter's thinking was, if we can get the U.S. government to allow the Stones to do a Nicaraguan Earthquake Benefit—how could it say no?—then the Japanese government would see what great humanitarians the boys are and, if the U.S. would let them back in after the turmoil in '72, the Japanese would remove the ban. The U.S. government, with the pushing of Carter and Mills, said yes. And because it let the Stones do Los Angeles, it gave permission for us do Hawaii, too. Rudge said the boys really liked the way I ran their shows and asked me to do three more in Hawaii, which I booked at the Blaisdell Center on January 21 and 22, 1973. He also asked me to help with the charity shows in Los Angeles, which were booked at the Forum on January 18th and 19th.

Perfect!

A few days later, Rudge called again.

"Barry, just to preserve the peace since we promised him the dates, would you mind co-promoting Hawaii with Bill Graham?"

"Why the fuck does he have to be in it?" Graham had badly botched the '69 tour, which is why I got my chance with the Stones, but he'd apparently redeemed himself during the '72 tour.

"Barry, please." Okay.

I flew to Hawaii in late December to set up the ticket sales for the shows. One on the 21st and two on the 22nd. They sold out quickly. While I was there, Cindy was close to delivering Jeremy. I took a red eye from Honolulu to Los Angeles and called the doctor when I got in. He told me that there was no need to rush, that he wasn't going to be born for a couple of days. He was born that night. I missed the birth of my child for a second time and both times, I was at LAX. Geoffrey was born in 1970 as I was waiting for a flight back to Denver: "Barry Fey, pick up the white courtesy telephone. Barry Fey."

Someone, I don't recall who, told me that I was the proud father of a healthy baby boy. And in 1972, the same thing for Jeremy, who wasn't healthy when he was born prematurely. He was pretty sick for a while with jaundice, but after a few days he was in the clear.

The two shows at the Forum went okay, except the security guys were being assholes. Anytime kids would stand up while the Stones were playing, the guards, who were strolling up and down the aisles, would shine flashlights on them until they sat down. I went up to the head of security and asked, "If these kids were at the Rose Bowl watching a football game, would you keep them from standing up?" He got the message, but I think they were so worried about having another Stones riot that they overreacted. But, the concerts, despite the ulterior motives, actually raised a bunch of money. With Mick kicking in another $150,000, the total was around $350,000.

The Japanese government was unimpressed. It still refused to let them into the country. After the Hawaii dates, the band went on to Australia and New Zealand.

In May, 1973, Mick, Bianca, Bill Graham and I went to Washington, D.C. to present the earthquake benefit check to Senator Ted Kennedy, who was connected to the Pan American Development Foundation. We got there on a Friday and a car takes us to the Capitol. The senator comes out to greet us and there's a ceremony where the check is presented. It's the typical check presentation, except that a lot more media showed up to see Mick and Bianca. When it was over, it was about 12:30 pm, time for lunch. Ted said, "Why don't you come with me and we'll eat in the Senate Dining Room?"

What a privilege! And just as the rest of us are about to follow him to lunch, Bianca, the bitch, said, "No thank you, we have plans to eat at San Souci." San Souci was a very exclusive French restaurant on M Street, near several of the foreign embassies. That was the first the rest of us had heard about the "plans". How embarrassing...good God!

We shook hands and thanked Senator Kennedy for his gracious offer and took a taxi to San Souci. When we're inside, I'm standing next to Bianca; Mick and Bill are right behind us, but in plain sight. The maître' d looks up from his podium and says, in his probably phony French accent, "May I help you?"

"Yes, sir", I said. "Four for lunch, please."

"Oui, monsieur, I'll be right with you." He looks down at his reservation book, starts running his finger down a page, flips a page, runs his finger up and down, then another page, then another, then another and finally stops and looks up. "Oui, I can take you on Wednesday."

I was stunned! I'm standing there with Mick Jagger. Forget Bianca; I mean she's strikingly beautiful and was a quasi-celebrity in her own right, but it's Mick Jagger. "Wednesday! We're hungry now."

"Oh, I'm sorry sir, it would be impossible to accommodate you until Wednesday."

Just to make sure he could see Mick, I took a step to the side. "Do you see who I have with me?"

"Oui monsieur, I believe I know who that is."

He didn't care. Napoleon Bonaparte could have been sitting on Mick's shoulders, we weren't getting in.

So, I said to the others, "Let's go back to see if we can still get into the Senate Dining Room." We took a cab back to the Capitol and the pages or whoever they were called for Senator Kennedy to come out. While we're waiting, Congresswoman Pat Schroeder walks by.

"Barry! What are you doing here?"

"We're going to eat with Teddy in the Senate Dining Room. Come with us!" Ted had arrived by then.

She said, "Oh, I can't, Barry. That's for senators only."

Ted, who'd blindly done radio commercials for Pat's campaign a year earlier, but now knew who she was, overheard the conversation as he walked up and said, "Come on, Pat; have lunch with us."

So, Mick, Bianca, Pat, Bill and I follow Ted into the dining room, stopping conversations and turning heads at every table, and we have lunch.

Backtracking to the Hawaiian shows in January of 1973, I had the Stones there at the same time that Elvis was working on his television special, "Aloha From Hawaii". We had the 29th and 30th floors of the Rainbow Tower in the Hilton Hawaiian Village and Elvis had the top floor. Here's how different the Stones and Elvis were. Keith, Mick and the boys were just acting like normal guys—as normal as the world's biggest rock stars could act. They'd walk around on the beach and sit by the pool without worrying too much about who was around them. Elvis would take the service elevator down the back and go directly into a limo in the hotel garage that would drive him to the arena for his rehearsals.

One day, several of us went to the arena where Elvis was rehearsing, just to see what was going on. I met Colonel Tom Parker, Elvis' "50-50" manager. He supposedly got 50% of everything Elvis made. I was teasing him a little about the Beatles surpassing Elvis in popularity. "Elvis is still awfully big", I said, "but look at the Beatles, they're the biggest thing ever."

Parker said, "Yeah, you're probably right about that. They sold more records, but don't ever let them try to come one at a time."

He was right. None of them, Lennon, McCartney, Harrison or Starr, could match Elvis one-on-one.

There were several suites per floor and I did the room assignments. Strategically—I thought—I put Charlie Watts right across from me. Mick and Keith were down at the other end of the hall, or maybe on another floor. I didn't want to be anywhere near the circuses that would surely occur in their suites. I figured with quiet Charlie next to me, I'd be able to get some sleep. What I didn't know was that he was an insomniac. The first night, there's a knock on the door at three a.m.

"BAR-ee, it's Charlie. Let's rap." I let him in and we sat and talked for over two hours. He knew that I loved horses, as did he, and we talked a lot about horses. Another night, I woke up for some reason at about four a.m. and looked out the window. There was Charlie, walking by himself along the beach.

I did spend some time in Keith's and Mick's suites. Most notably, one night I was walking down the hall. The door to Mick's suite was open. Keith's in there with him and they wave me in.

"BAR-ee, come on in!"

"What's up?"

"Come on and do some of this with us."

There was a big pile of white powder on a table. It had brown flakes in it.

I figured it was cocaine, but I'd never done any before and told them I wasn't interested. When they found out they had a virgin on their hands, they wouldn't let up. They wouldn't take no for an answer.

"Okay, okay. What do I do?"

Mick rolled up a dollar bill (you'd have expected Jagger to use a C-note, right?) and said, "You put your thumb over one nostril and then you snort it up through this with the other nostril."

So, I snorted one line. Then another. And it was having no effect on me. I was a big boy then, probably 250 pounds. They're laughing their asses off as I keep snorting. I probably did $10,000 worth, but it had absolutely no effect on me. That seemed like a huge waste of money, but at least it was Mick's or Keith's money. There was no shortage of people trying to get me to try this drug or another. I did try someone else's cocaine again in 1973. I had Leon Russell and Little Feat at Folsom Field in Boulder. I was really tired and Leon and I were backstage talking. "Barry, I've got something here that'll wake you up." He laid out a line and I did it, but again, it did nothing for me. One other time, when I had Flo and Eddie playing at McNichols in Denver, their manager, Skip Taylor, gave me something—I guess it was coke, who knows—but, it burned my throat so badly that I told him, "Skip, if I wanted to feel this crappy, I'd stand out in the rain all day." That was the extent of my drug experimentation until I was with Keith again in 1980. Oh wait, there was one other time. A woman I was dating rubbed cocaine on the tip of my penis.

"That'll keep you harder longer, Barry."

"Yeah, but I can't feel anything."

"That's okay. I do."

The Hawaiian shows were great. I'd brought ZZ Top over to open for the Stones and introduced them before each show: "Ladies and gentlemen, please welcome that little 'ol band from Texas, ZZ Top!" Nobody knew who these guys were, but they found out in a hurry.

In 1978, the Stones played Folsom Stadium in Boulder on my birthday, July 18th. Peter Tosh opened for them. After the show, they wanted to take me out for my birthday, so we headed for Denver. Traffic on the Boulder Turnpike, the main highway between Boulder and Denver, was jammed up with Stones fans, so the driver of the car the boys were in drove on the median. We were right behind them. I can imagine what the people stuck in traffic were thinking about these assholes driving down the median.

There was a restaurant on south Broadway in Denver called The Little Shanghai that stayed open for us. They served up platters full of Mongolian beef, Chinese chicken salad and stuff like that. Mick loved Asian food. And somehow, at one in the morning, they were able to satisfy Tosh's request for fish heads and rice. The boys signed a menu that the owners framed and put on the wall. We stayed there several hours. It was a very nice birthday.

The Stone's business manager, Prince Rupert Loewenstein—real name, Prince Rupert Ludwig Ferdinand zu Loewenstein-Wertheim-Freudenberg, a descendant of the dynasty that ruled Bavaria from 1180 to 1918 —flew into town for the show. Rupie looked every bit the aristocratic banker that he had been; the unremarkable, expensive suits and ties; the gray, thinning hair; a round, pale face. But, he had a great sense of humor and was very likable. When he started working with Jagger in 1968, he had no idea who Mick was. He rescued the boys from financial chaos, if not ruin. That was shortly after Jagger was seen by guests at the London Savoy Hotel, chasing his business manager, Allen Klein, shouting, "Where's my money?" Klein had practically given away the rights to their '60s music library and they owed millions in taxes. Prince Rupert ran their income through a company he set up in tax-friendly Holland and the boys became consistently ranked among the top earners of rock 'n roll.

Around the first week of December, 1980 when I was in London, my phone rang in the middle of the night. It was Keith Richards, calling from Paris.

"You've got to come over here and talk some business. I need you."

Keith was used to being surrounded by people who said "Yes" to anything he wanted. I needed a little more information. He went on to say that he didn't trust Mick with the business end of their next tour. They weren't the Glimmer Twins who grew up together anymore. It had become "Mick Jagger and the Rolling Stones" and Keith wanted me to help him run their US tour and help him take back a bigger role in running the Stones. Look, to me Keith was the heart and soul of the band. He wasn't trying to replace Mick, he just wanted to have a say in how the band was run.

The weather was terrible when I got to Paris. Cold, sleet, rain… just miserable. They had a room for me in a beautiful hotel, great neighborhood. The Plaza Athenee. I was so cold and when I found out the bathroom floor was heated, I just turned it on high and sat down. A few hours later, I called Keith. Somebody else answered.

"Oh, Barry...Keith left for New York this morning."

I said, "What the fuck! Didn't he know I was coming?"

"Yeah, but he had to leave and we couldn't get hold of you."

I was pissed. So, I flew to New York on a Sunday morning and checked in to The Navarro on Central Park South which is where I often stayed with The Who. (It was rebuilt in '82 as the Ritz-Carlton.) The next night, I was watching the Patriots and Dolphins on *Monday Night Football* and got Keith on the phone. We chit chat, small talk, you know, even though I was still privately annoyed at the Paris thing. It was senseless for me to even ask what happened. Getting a reason from Keith Richards...yeah, that's a worthwhile pursuit.

Keith said, "Hold on, Barry. The other phone's ringing." He came right back. "I gotta go, Barry. John's been shot."

I went back to the television and Howard Cosell was announcing that John had been shot and was dead. I didn't know what to do. John Lennon! Who the fuck would want to kill him?

The next morning, as I approached The Dakota, John and Yoko's apartment building, the streets and sidewalks were filled with mourners. People were crying, leaving Teddy Bears, notes, photos, candles, flowers and all that. I cried. We were all in shock. The world was in shock. God, it was sad.

That was on Tuesday. On Thursday, Keith asked me to go over to Patti Hansen's apartment around midnight. Patti was gorgeous; one of the top models in the world, but a really nice, solid girl with her head on straight—so unlike many of the previous women in Keith's life. She and Keith got married a few years later. When I walked in, Keith, Patti and Jane Rose (the head of Rolling Stone Records who later became Keith's personal manager) were sitting on the floor playing jacks.

"Oh, hi ya BAR-ee. Come on, sit down and we'll play a little bit."

I was tired and had no interest in playing fucking jacks. I wanted to talk business, but I knew that would have to wait. "No, that's alright, you go ahead. I'll just sit and watch."

They finished their game and of course, after a strenuous game of jacks, they gotta have something to eat. Patti made Shepherd's Pie. I don't know what all she put in it, but it wasn't very appealing to me and I didn't eat much, which for me was a rare occurrence.

We talked for a long time about John and other things, no Stones' business, before finally—at about 2:30 a.m.—Keith says, "Alright, BAR-ee, let's go talk business."

"Keith, I'm sorry man. We'll have to do it some other time. I can't keep my eyes open."

He pulled this red, cylinder shaped thing out of a drawer. It was a few inches long and had a pointed top; a grinder. "Do some of this. It'll wake you up."

Now, my short history with cocaine pretty much started and ended with Keith and Mick in 1973.

I reminded Keith of the '73 failure to launch.

He said, "Shut the fuck up, just do what I say."

I did. And, man... instantaneous BOOM! We talked for several hours and worked it out so that I was getting 11 dates on the next tour. About 7:30 a.m., I went back to my hotel and was still so wired from the coke that I started calling all of my employees back in Denver, where it was five a.m. I woke up everybody I could. Even the receptionist.

"We gotta get ready for the Stones! We're going to do this city and that city." I was so fucking high. At noon, I got on a plane at Newark and I was still high. I felt like I could have flown home without the plane. That was some strong shit. I found out later that it was some of the pharmaceutical grade pure cocaine that Freddie Sessler helped Keith find.

The tour happened and of the 50 shows between September 25th and December 19th, 1981, I did 11.

Toward the end of the '81 tour, we did two shows at Folsom, Saturday and Sunday, October 3rd and 4th. That was the tour where Mick got in a cherry picker and moved around above the audience. It was also when they wanted to play small places as well as the stadiums. So, we were going to play them at the Rainbow Music Hall on Monday. We couldn't tell anybody, but we printed up a bunch of tickets and we were going to announce the show at noon on Monday. At the Rainbow, we had a big board with the logo on it that all of the groups signed. For some reason, we took it to Boulder on Sunday for the boys to sign. Keith signed his with a dot-dot-dot going over the logo. He said, "See? Over the rainbow." Historians looking at that sign will conclude that the Stones played the Rainbow. And, I'm sure there are fans who say, "Oh yeah, I was there when the Stones played the Rainbow". They didn't. After Sunday's show, Keith, or maybe it was Mick, said, "Aw, let's just get on the plane. Sorry, Barry." And they left. It's probably just as well. Right before the tour began, they tried to put on a secret show, a public rehearsal, at a small club in Boston under the name "Little Boy Blue and the Cockroaches", but word got out and about 10,000 fans showed up to storm the place.

Ian Stewart died in 1985. He was one of the original Stones. What a good, good guy he was. He was their piano player, although the rest of the band kind of demoted him to part time piano player/ road manager in the '70s. He was into golf, not groupies, and in his role as road manager, he'd often book hotels that were on golf courses, not in city centers where the rest of the guys would have easier access to groupies. When they came to Colorado, I got Ian on the Cherry Hills Country Club and he was in heaven. Just a nice, sweet guy who died way too young. 47. Heart attack.

In 1990, they invited me to Japan when they played ten shows in the Tokyo Dome, which is where, just a few days earlier, Buster Douglas took the championship from Mike Tyson. Michael Cohl was managing the tour at that point. I'd never seen anything like it; 50,000 fans had jammed the stadium and when the show was over, they were so polite and orderly. They left the stadium by section. One section would stand up and leave. Then the next. And the next. There was no rush, no pushing and shoving.

The summer of 1994 was the biggest grossing summer Feyline ever had with the Stones' "Voo Doo Lounge" tour, the Eagles "Hell Freezes Over" tour and Pink Floyd's "The Division Bell" tour. All of them were stadium shows and ticket prices were around $70.

I also had the Stones for two nights at the MGM Grand, the first time the band played Las Vegas. It was great, such an exciting atmosphere with all of the glitz and glamour that goes with everything else on the Strip. It was the "Bridges Over Babylon" tour in the fall of 1997, after I'd retired, so they didn't play Denver for me. But, part of my retirement deal was that I could still play groups in Vegas. Jay Marciano, the head of Universal, which bought me out, said, "I can't imagine the rock 'n roll business without Barry Fey in it somewhere. Since he started Vegas, let him do Vegas. It doesn't interfere with us." The Stones played the MGM Grand on November 22nd, which sticks out in my mind also because that's where Freddie Sessler was arrested in the hotel lobby, scalping tickets to the show.

In 2005, way, way after I retired, I was having Thanksgiving dinner at my son Geoffrey's house in Denver, and it's about four o'clock. We'd already eaten and I was stuffed, parked on the couch in front of the TV where the Broncos were playing the Cowboys. I was getting very comfortable in the tryptophan zone. It was cold outside, warm inside. It was perfect.

The Stones were playing that night at the Pepsi Center in Denver, part of their "Bigger Bang" tour. Somebody called from backstage, I don't remember who.

"Barry, the boys would really like you to come down."

I said, "Nah, come on, it's Thanksgiving. I'm with my family. Football's on. It's cold outside. Tell them I appreciate the offer very much, but 'no, thanks.'"

My family looked at me like I was crazy and made me go. Geoffrey, his wife Erin and I went. We had another turkey dinner—which was fine with me. There's nothing better than crisp, brown, roasted turkey skin. We ate, joked around and talked about old times. It turned out to be a lot of fun and I'm glad I went. We stayed around for a little bit of the concert, but I was so full, I left early. Part of why I left was that Keith just seemed to be going through the motions. Maybe the turkey and the trimmings were getting to him, or maybe it was because they were in the last few dates before taking a break from the tour, but he didn't seem into it at all. Mick had the crowd going, though, congratulating the Broncos on their overtime victory earlier in the day against the Cowboys. He had an inflatable turkey wheeled onto the stage and said something about if the Pilgrims had killed a cat instead of a turkey, we'd all be eating pussy.

THE WHO

I walked into a record store in downtown Denver and the owner held up an album.

"Have you seen this? It's a rock opera. Tommy."

"A rock opera? What the fuck is that and who do they think they are?"

Just one of the best performing groups ever, that's who. Four men, two or three of them arguably—not arguably for me, but just to prove I'm open minded—the best ever at their positions: John Entwistle and Keith Moon. Moon was the Jimi Hendrix of drums. I think he's the only one to play lead with both feet and he's widely acknowledged as the best rock drummer ever. Entwistle was a phenomenal bass player; the best ever, bar none. The only proof you need is his riff in "My Generation". On top of that you have Roger, one of the best rock singers ever and Pete, easily among the top rock guitarists ever, up there wind-milling his guitar. And what a fuckin' song writer! The best show I've ever seen was June 9, 1970. The Who played Mammoth Gardens in Denver.

But, before I tell you about that, I need to go back a few years to when my relationship began with Frank Barsalona. He was a very big agent in New York; there's never been an agent like him. He was so hot, and had so many groups, that record companies would give him a half a point or point on the albums if he would take on the groups to book. His agency was Premier Talent and all of the big groups were with Premier. In 1969, I worked with Frank to book Joe Cocker at the Denver Pop Festival.

When I'd go to New York, I'd hang out with him at his office at 57th and 7th. We were a couple of fatties and there was a Chinese restaurant on the first floor of his building. We'd go there, eat, and eat some more.

Frank and I booked the show with The Who at Mammoth where the capacity was 5000. We sold out quickly. Peter Rudge was managing The Who then. That day, June 9th, was so hot. It was over 100 degrees. Mammoth Gardens didn't have air conditioning, but had huge windows that opened up. After we let 3500 people in, I stopped it. It was just too hot. It was inhumane. So, there were 1500 people who had tickets, but I wasn't going to let them in for their own good. I got together with Frank, Peter and the band and they agreed to add a show the next night. So, we sold another 2000 tickets and there was a second show on the 10th.

But that show on the 9th was one I'll never forget. With those windows open, The Who were so loud, you could hear the music ten blocks away at Denver's Civic Center Park.

One of the greatest things about The Who is that they're loud as a jet plane, but you can still hear everything. Nothing's distorted or muddled.

That night, Pete stepped to the microphone.

"I'm sure you've all heard or read that we'll never do 'Tommy' again live. Bullshit."

And with that, the band played about two and a half hours of "Tommy". And I witnessed something at the end of that show that I'd never seen. The crowd didn't yell, "More, more, more." They just turned around and quietly walked out. The heat may have had something to do with it, but I believe it was because they knew what they had just seen, the greatness they had just heard. The Who had left it all on stage. And there was no sense in yelling for anything more. The fans just walked away, The Who walked off and that was it. Without a doubt, the best show I'd ever seen.

A couple of years later, I had them at the Denver Coliseum. They'd done a few numbers and Daltrey was complaining that Entwistle's monitor was too loud. Entwistle refused to turn it down. They sniped at each other through another few numbers before Daltrey kicked the monitor over. Entwistle said, "Fuck this" and walked off the stage. This was late enough in the show that the crowd thought it was their cue to call for an encore. But, The Who didn't do encores. I went back stage and the boys had calmed down a bit and were deciding whether to go back on and finish their set. The crowd was screaming for more. Townshend said, "Listen to that, they really want us back". I, the smart ass, trying to lighten things up and get Entwistle and Daltrey to go back on, said, "Yeah, they really want me back." Pete kicked me in the ass, and, fuck, it hurt! Hurt for days. Anyway, they went back on and finished their set. The crowd thought they were getting the first ever Who encore and went wild.

As crazy as it was with them, no band created energy on stage like The Who. Maybe the Stones or the Beach Boys could follow them and maintain the energy, but they're about the only ones.

And loud? Oh, my God! How people sat in the front section for two and a half hours and withstood that volume, I don't understand. I'd go out front, as I did during every show to make sure things were going okay and the audience was getting a good show. But, for the Who, I could make it from the back only to the first aisle, maybe a third of the way up, before I had to go back, it was so loud. But, like I said, the thing with The Who, as opposed to many other loud bands, like Ted Nugent—Nugent was just noise—with the Who you could hear all the music, all the words.

After Keith died and Kenny Jones took over on drums, I flew to New York for the 1979 shows at Madison Square Garden, their first tour without Moon.

They did many stadium shows for me. We had the Cotton Bowl in Dallas and a couple of days before that was a show in Houston. I had gone on to Dallas when I got a call from them in Houston; I think it was Bill Curbishley who called.

"Barry, the boys and I want to bring you something from Houston. What would you like?

I said, "How about a steak? Yeah, I'd like a steak. There's a great steak place called Brenner's."

About an hour before the show in Dallas, some of the Who crew came to me and said, "Curbishley wants to see you. It's important." So, I start walking and another couple of guys, two security guys, picked me up and carried me around a corner and put me on the back of a steer, a Longhorn steer! And the steer starts walking down a ramp backstage and I'm a little freaked out until its handler runs up and stops it. That was the steak I'd asked for. The boys figured I could have it butchered and fill my freezer, but I couldn't do that. I don't have any problem eating meat; I love steak. I just couldn't have an animal killed so that I could eat it. I gave it to a petting zoo or kids' 4-H farm or something.

I also loved shrimp, and loved to cook it. I make great Louisiana style barbecued shrimp. The Who loved it and I'd often take some backstage before their concerts. Sometimes I make it extra spicy and during one concert, Daltrey couldn't hit some high notes, so he apologized to the crowd.

"It's not my fault. It's Barry Fey's shrimp!"

Townshend, on one of the guitars he gave me, wrote: "To Barry, for shrimp and risk." Two of the things he remembers me for.

The Who had some great people working with them. Not only Curbishley, but their security guy, James Callahan; J.C. And, their sound guy who's been with them forever, Bobby Pridden. We had a party at my house after one of the Who shows where Lynyrd Skynyrd opened for them. I've got a photo of Bobby playfully holding a gun to Ronnie Van Zant's head.

Not long after Entwistle passed away in 2002 from a cocaine overdose—he had no business using that shit, he had a bad heart—I introduced the band at Fiddler's Green in Denver. It was Roger, Pete, the drummer was Jason Bonham, John's kid and I think Simon Town-shend, Pete's little brother, was on bass.

I stood at the microphone and said, "Ladies and gentlemen, please welcome the greatest rock and roll band that ever lived."

I saw them all. Nobody could match the energy those guys, all together as one unit, put out. Hendrix was Jimi and Springsteen was Bruce, the Stones turned into Mick and the boys. There's never been a band like The Who.

My admiration for The Who aside, what a bunch of crazy fuck-ers. I mean, Keith Moon was legitimately bat shit crazy. Moon the Loon is the nickname he picked up. I booked a private room in a fancy restaurant for all of them and as the meal went on, course after course and bottle after bottle, I noticed that Keith was ignoring most of the restaurant food. That's because he was eating the floral center-piece. Flower by flower, stem by stem, until it was nearly gone.

The others, Townshend, Daltrey and Entwistle were relatively normal by rock star standards, except I think Moon's craziness rubbed off on Pete. He may have had his own "moments", but I think being around Moon made him do a few things he might not have ordinarily done. I'm not sure which of them started destroying their instruments first, but Pete's smashing of guitars and Moon's destruc-tion of his drum sets became iconic moments in rock 'n roll history. Pete's guitar smashing has been emulated hundreds of times over the years by wannabes. In 1967, a few years before I booked them for the first time in Denver, they were on the Smothers Brothers televi-sion show. Moon put some kind of explosive in his bass drum, which was supposed to go off at the end of "My Generation". But, he put too much in and shrapnel from the drum kit flew everywhere.

In the early '70s, we were in Los Angeles for some shows and their record company had just delivered their first gold albums. There was a party in the penthouse of the Continental Hyatt House Hotel, better known in rock circles as the Riot House. It was the same hotel where legend has it Moon threw a TV set out of a window—ditto for Keith Richards, from the 10th floor; Led Zeppelin used to rent several floors at a time for all of its entourage. Someone from Zep-pelin—some say it was John Bonham—drove a motorcycle through the hallways; it's where Little Richard lived for years; where Jim Mor-rison lived until he was evicted for dangling out a window, hanging on by his fingertips; THAT hotel. Anyway, their record company had given them the gold record party and the boys decided to distribute the wealth: 12 floors below the penthouse is the hotel pool. They took turns trying to hit the water with the records. Some splashed. Some smashed.

No surprise that my main problem with The Who when I took them on tour, was finding hotels that would take them. They'd been banned for life from all Holiday Inns, mostly because of Moon. He had this thing for blowing up toilets by dropping Cherry Bombs, M-80s, dynamite and other explosives into them. Entwistle was a pretty quiet guy, although I'd heard that he had some part in Moon's toilet bombings. As a group, they were known for doing some crazy things—most of it instigated by Moon. He was interesting, to say the least. A tragic life, in many ways and certainly a tragic end. I was attending a *Billboard Magazine* convention in 1978 where I was being honored as "Promoter of the Year" when I got a call from Rudge—or it might have been Barsalona.

"Barry, Keith died. Would you please be the one to announce it to everybody at the convention?"

I interrupted the speaker and made the announcement.

What a waste. One of many. Janis, Jim, Jimi, Tommy Bolin...

WHAT'S A LEAD ZEPPELIN?

In 1968, two momentous occasions occurred in rock 'n roll history. The first was the debut of the singing radio commercial. I was the first concert promoter to sing his own commercial.

"You'd better not shout, You'd better not cry,
You'd better not pout, I'm telling you why;
Vanilla Fudge is coming to town!"

We sold out. 7500 seats for Vanilla Fudge and Spirit.

About 10 days before the show, Ron Terry, the agent for Vanilla Fudge calls. I'll never forget this.

"Barry, I need you to add another group to the show."

"No."

"What do you mean 'no'?"

"Ron, we're sold out. There's no more advertising. We're sold out. No."

"Barry, this is going to be a very big group soon. You've got to put them on."

"Ron, I printed 7500 tickets. They're all gone. I'm not spending another fucking dime on this."

"Barry, this group is called Led Zeppelin. They're going to be huge."

"Oh, I get it. Lead Zeppelin, like a lead balloon. It's a joke. Very funny."

"No, no, no, Barry, I'm not teasing. I'll call you back."

"Don't bother; I'm not putting them on."

Ten minutes later, Ron calls back.

"Vanilla Fudge has agreed to take $750 of the money you were going to pay them and they'll give it to Led Zeppelin if you'll pay them $750, too."

I was about to start screaming at him, but then I started thinking; wait a minute, Barry. Here's the headliner that's willing to give some of its money to a group that no one's ever heard of, that's never played in North America.

"Ron, you've got a deal."

So, I got Led Zeppelin for $750.

The night of the concert, I get on stage to make the announcement to open the show.

"Ladies and gentleman, please welcome, direct from England for their North America debut, Led Zeppelin!" There was a smattering of polite applause. Then, Robert Plant let it rip and everybody in the audience was stunned. Frankly, I don't know how Spirit went on after that. You didn't have to be a genius to know Zeppelin was going to be a smash. Oh, my God. People were going crazy!

The next morning, I get a call from Max Floyd, the program director at the Denver FM rock station, KLZ.

"Who did you have on last night? Our phone lines are jammed!"

The band had given me a white copy of their album, one that hadn't been released yet. I took the album to the radio station and they played it continuously, all day.

Over the years, Led Zeppelin was a trip and not always in a good way. Except for Robert Plant and John Paul Jones, they were among the worst bunch of individuals I've ever dealt with. First of all, you've got the manager, this 350-pound giant Peter Grant, who was good to me at first—I even introduced him to my mother—but it didn't take long for him to show his true colors. You couldn't pay him in anything but cash. He had a red flight bag in which he used to carry all the concert money, often hundreds of thousands at a time. John Bonham might have been a great drummer, but he was a mean son of a bitch. And he died a mean death, choking on his vomit after drinking 40 shots of vodka and passing out at Jimmy Page's house. When I was in New York with Tommy Bolin in the early '70s, we ran into Bonham. He wanted to go for drinks, so we found a bar and after a few minutes, Bonham pulled out a gun and started waving it around. We tried to get him to stop, but he said not to worry, it wasn't loaded. I said, "Are you crazy? There are probably ten guns in here that ARE loaded! You can't do that in New York City. Maybe Omaha, but not here."

John Paul Jones was a quiet guy, kind of a loner, but a hell of a bass player. Plant was the best guy of the bunch, the only one you could really talk to. In early 1970, Zeppelin went on a U.S. and Canadian tour. I had four dates: the Denver Coliseum on March 25th, the Salt Palace in Salt Lake City on the 26th, the Arizona Coliseum on April 18th and Las Vegas on the 19th, but Plant's voice gave out and the Vegas show was cancelled. But, the whole band, their agent Frank Barsalona and I went there anyway. Who knows what disgusting things Bonham did in Sin City; Frank was the only one I spent time with. Of course, Zeppelin went on to become one of the biggest bands in the world, but in their wake, was a lot of carnage. In 1977, the band's thuggery was in full bloom. Bill Graham, who I'd had my own issues with over Led Zeppelin, told me about this one: one of his employees spotted a kid backstage, about ten, who was pulling signs off the band's trailer doors. He told him to stop and took the signs away. The kid went crying to his dad: Peter Grant. Graham said Grant, Bonham and John Bindon, the head of Zeppelin's security got the guy alone in a trailer and beat him to a bloody pulp. They kicked him repeatedly in the balls, knocked out a tooth and tried to gouge his eyes out. Graham says he tried to jump in, but Grant—who, again, was 6'3" and nearly 400 pounds—flicked him aside to one of the others who threw him out of the trailer. Graham said he wanted Grant, Bonham and Bindon arrested that night, but there was still a sold out show the next night and Oakland authorities were worried that cancelling it would have led to a riot. So, the morning after the second show, the Oakland police arrested them. I wish I could have been there to see the perp walk, captured on all the local TV news-casts with Grant, Bonham, Bindon and tour manager Richard Cole in handcuffs. But, the most serious charges Bill could get the DA to file were misdemeanor assault and battery charges and they were turned loose right away. The four wound up settling a civil suit with Graham and the others.

Just after the Oakland shows, when Zeppelin had moved on to New Orleans and I was negotiating to play them later in the tour at Mile High Stadium, the tragic news broke that Bobby's five-year old son, Karac, had died of an infection. That ended their touring for over a year and, coupled with Bonham's death two years later, led to the end of Zeppelin.

In early 2011, Robert Plant was at the Fillmore, which is the renovated and renamed Mammoth Gardens in Denver. I walked in during the sound check. Robert was on stage, saw me and started singing to me. He came down and we got caught up and he men-tioned again just how big that moment was for them on December 26, 1968. The first appearance of Led Zeppelin in North America. And as bad as most of the rest of the band was, they never forgot that I was the first one to play them and helped get their songs on the radio.

One more thing about Frank Barsalona. Years later, I was with him in his New York apartment when he got a phone call. It was Peter Grant, Zeppelin's manager and Stevens Weiss, their business man-ager. They told Frank he was fired. After all the money he made for that group. He'd done such an excellent job, but they just fired him. Frank was brokenhearted. It's the first time I'd ever seen him cry.

Frank and I became even closer friends over the years. He's the godfather to my youngest son, Tyler, who was born in 1991.

Here's how good Frank Barsalona was. He's the only agent inducted into the Rock and Roll Hall of Fame. He was the greatest agent, the biggest agent. By the way, the only promoter inducted was Bill Graham, and that was done posthumously.

I have a jacket in the Hall. It's a black Rolling Stones jacket I designed and had made for one of their tours.

Part Four

THE ROCKS OF GOD

- O **Red Rocks Amphitheater**

- O **The Jethro Tull Riot**

- O **The Feyline Summer of Stars**

RED ROCKS SUMMER SERIES 1975

July 17 Stephen Stills Sold Out 9000	July 27 James Taylor Emmy Lou Harris Sold Out 9000	August 6 Linda Ronstadt Nitty Gritty Dirt Band Sold Out 9000
August 7 America J. D. Souther Sold Out 9000	August 18 & 19 Eagles Dan Fogelberg Sold Out 18000	August 26 Seals & Crofts Sold Out 9000

Thank you for a wonderful summer.
See you again next year.

Barry Fey

RED ROCKS AMPHITHEATER

There is no concert venue on Earth, indoors or outdoors, that compares with Red Rocks. The grandeur, the majesty...there aren't enough superlatives to describe the experience of not only seeing a concert there, but performing there. Let's simply say that Red Rocks is perfect.

Located about fifteen miles west of downtown Denver, and about a thousand feet higher at 6300 feet above sea level, Red Rocks is thought to have been first used as an amphitheater by the Ute Indians. The first documented "white man" concert was in 1906. (The first documented riot was in 1971, because of me. More about that later; let's get back to the majesty.) There's a large, tilted disc-shaped rock at the bottom of the mountain behind the stage; a huge, probably eighty-foot tall rock angled up hill from stage right, the north side; and several smaller, but still large outcroppings angled up and away from the stage on the south side, or stage left. In between, is where nearly 10,000 fans are treated to unforgettable concert experiences.

The acoustics are flawless. You can stand on stage, nestled at the bottom of the amphitheater, clap your hands, and it'll be heard perfectly in the top row.

The night air is crisp, cool and refreshing after hot, summer days. There's the scent of pine trees that line the seating area. It is intimate, yet, as I said, holds nearly 10,000. As you look down at the stage from your seat, you can simultaneously see for fifty miles with a panoramic view of the Denver metropolitan area. It's the only concert venue in the country that is also a tourist attraction.

After the concert film "U2 Live At Red Rocks: Under A Blood Red Sky" was released in 1983, every act wanted to play there. And we played just about all of them. The only three major bands that didn't play Red Rocks were the Stones, the Who and Zeppelin.

Pollstar, which is a concert industry magazine, annually ranked the concert venues and Red Rocks consistently won in the "Best Small Outdoor" category. After it won for the 11th time, the magazine decided to name the award "The Red Rocks Award" and remove Red Rocks from the running.

Now, about the riot.

Roberta "Bobbie" Niles worked in the Denver Theaters and Arenas office for the director, Sam Feiner. I liked trying to do business with her because she was very nice to deal with, but whenever I said "fuck", she'd hang up on me. I said "fuck" a lot and still do. I'd call her back and, again, she was very pleasant, but when I inevitably said "fuck" again, she'd hang up. So, I stopped saying it. But, I was so persistent and it got to be—especially after the previous mayor Tom Currigan had intervened on my behalf—they weren't going to fight me and the music anymore. She told me that Feiner told her, "Give him whatever he wants, but don't let that schlub come down here. No meetings."

After the Denver mayor banned rock concerts everywhere but the Coliseum, I booked Diana Ross and The Supremes at Red Rocks, convincing Bobbie and Feiner that it wasn't a rock concert. Which it wasn't, and it went well. We also played John Denver, Sonny and Cher, The Carpenters (I was downstairs in a hospitality room with The Carpenters' manager when a huge roar went up from the audience. He looked at me in surprise, because Karen and Richard didn't normally elicit that kind of response. He said, "Jesus, Karen must have taken off her clothes!"), Seals and Crofts and other soft rockers whose audiences were well behaved and helped me slowly get back into the city's good graces.

The city policy bent a little when KIMN Radio general manager Ken Palmer got permission to stage Three Dog Night at Red Rocks. Palmer came to me to produce the show, which was really strange because he didn't seem to like me or the music I put on. When I wanted to run ads promoting Vanilla Fudge, I asked if he would play one of their records so the kids could get familiar with the band and I'd sell more tickets. He refused. He was more of a Dave Clark Five guy at that time and didn't like the psychedelic rock. So, on my 60-second commercials, I played 50 seconds of "You Keep Me Hanging On" followed by a quick tag telling where and when the show was. The kids loved hearing that song and were jamming the KIMN request lines asking for the commercial to be played. We sold out Three Dog Night and it was peaceful, no problems. So, with that as a precedent, I called my gal pal Bobbie at Theaters and Arenas and asked for permission to book Jethro Tull at Red Rocks in July of 1971. My pitch was, "Well, it is rock, but the lead guy plays a flute." They let me.

This is where I really screwed up. Jethro Tull sold out and sold out so quickly, I should have booked two or three shows. Huge mistake. There was still this feeling among some young people that it was "their" music and that if they wanted to see it, they should be allowed to. I'd heard rumors about people saying they were going to get in, no matter what. The night of the show, way more people showed up than the amphitheater could hold. Probably a couple of thousand. Most of them were kids, good kids, and when I walked among them, they'd say, "Here, take my money, I want to get in." But, there was no room. The cops tried to keep them in an area at the top of the amphitheater where they could hear the music, but not see the stage. That wasn't good enough for some of them. When they tried to crash their way in, the cops reacted with riot gear and teargas being fired from the police helicopter. But, once again (see The Denver Pop Festival chapter), the police miscalculated and the gas drifted down over the crowd and onto the stage where Livingston Taylor was the opening act. He started choking and crying and stumbled off the stage and the audience scattered, looking for shelter and help. Many of them wound up backstage; there were kids and babies and it looked like a M*A*S*H unit. Performers, stage hands and fans were sprawled out everywhere getting treated by doctors and paramedics.

Outside the amphitheater, it was worse. A cop car was on fire and police had the road leading to the backstage area blocked off. My assistant, Leslie Haseman, sent one of the cops down to the barricade and told him that if he didn't let the band get through, there were going to be 10,000 more pissed off people who'd join the riot. The cop didn't get there in time and the band drove through the police blockade. Here's Ian Anderson's memory, as told to Ricardo Baca of *The Denver Post* in June, 2011 when Tull played Red Rocks again:

> *Anderson called it a "Top 10 strange/weird moment." "It was an overreaction by the police. We charged through police roadblocks, and I ran straight onto the stage and talked to the audience. (The police) knew there would be a full-scale riot if they arrested me."*
>
> *Anderson remembers charging through the police barricade and knowing that he was the only person who could calm the capacity crowd—which was swimming in tear gas at the moment.*

"(*The police) tried to turn us back and say, 'You're not allowed to go up there,' so we just charged the gate,*" Anderson said. "*We jumped out of the cars and ran straight on stage to talk to the audience.*

"*It was like the Russians putting a flag on the ocean bed under the Arctic ice. Once you've done it, staked the claim, it's tough to dislodge you.*

Once I was on stage in front of a microphone, they cops realized that they had to stand back."

Anderson soothed the crowd and told them they were going to get a full set of music. He told them to put clothing over their mouths, and he encouraged parents with babies and small children to come to the apron so they could access the makeshift hospital set up backstage.

"*People were passing babies down through the audience,*" Anderson said.

It was a mess of an evening. But like Woodstock and Altamont before it, the concert was also a snapshot of America as it formed its relationship with rock 'n' roll.

"*Back in the early '70s, they didn't know how to cope with rock concerts and rock people,*" Anderson said. "*The big production and how the audience behaved.... People now have more understanding, and civil and social savvy. They have an awareness about what it all is.*"

Anderson also said that getting out of Red Rocks was nearly as tough as getting in. The Denver cops weren't going to let these long-haired hippies get the best of them, so they were waiting for them to leave. Some of my security guys put them in the back of station wagons and put blankets and crap over the top of them. It worked.

But, I've got to give Ian Anderson credit. He played his entire set, jumping all around the stage playing the flute like he did in every show, maybe even with more abandon to get the crowd settled down. Now, he could have refused. There was a clause in Tull's contract that said that if anything crazy happens beyond the control of the band, they have the right not to play. But they did play, and I don't even want to think about how bad it would have been if they hadn't. Ian's still my hero to this day.

Obviously, after that night, the city banned rock concerts again at Red Rocks. I didn't bother asking for a while, but when it refused to allow me to book America—good God, soft rock America! —there on July 4th, 1975, I sued. A Denver District Court judge ruled in my favor, that the city had acted in an arbitrary and capricious manner. I recall Judge Kingsley lecturing the city's attorney. "Who do you think you are? Czars? You're going to decide what people should listen to?" That cleared the way for me to start booking rock bands again, and led to some of the most memorable concerts in history from iconic rockers like The Grateful Dead and U2 to The Moody Blues with the Colorado Symphony.

You gotta love this irony: The band with the most sellouts at Red Rocks has a name that reflects what was going on the night of the Tull concert. Widespread Panic has sold out the Rocks more than 35 times.

The increasing success we were having at Red Rocks each summer, illustrated in the accompanying newspaper ad showing the sellouts we had in 1975, gave me the idea that we should turn Red Rocks' summer concerts into a major, yearly event: "The Red Rocks Summer of Stars". It was an instant hit in 1976 and continued every summer through my retirement in 1997.

We generated such publicity and excitement about the series that even the announcement of the concert line-ups each spring became a huge, eagerly awaited event. In the second week of April, people would wait in line for the morning newspapers to go on sale because we'd place double-truck (full pages facing each other) ads. I had a strict embargo on the information. No leaks to anybody about what shows we'd booked. That secrecy, plus the proper amount of hype and teasing through the media, created a huge amount of excitement in those pre-Internet when you actually had to get your news from newspapers, radio or television and pre-Twitter and Facebook where "viral" meant sharing something verbally with another human. Fans would hang the ads on their refrigerators or walls and circle the concerts they wanted to see and then stand in line at the ticket outlets to buy the shows.

We had everybody who was anybody in rock and pop at the Summer of Stars, except for the Stones, Who and Zeppelin. Our best year was 1985 when we did 55 Red Rocks shows with 92% capacity and put a nice exclamation mark on the season with two sold-out Springsteen shows at Mile High Stadium: 137,000 tickets on September 23-24, the largest two-day concert crowd in Mile High stadium history.

Part Five

U2 AND US

- ⭕ **U2**

- ⭕ **The 1983 US Festival**

To our tried and true friend
BARRY FEY
With gratitude and affection,
U2 and Principle Management

Dublin, July 1996

Barry

A voice louder than any rock 'n' roll band,
a belly (used to be) wider than any stadium,
a willy smaller than any singer's ego,
hairier than any fuzz box,
a heart bigger than a bass drum,
a brain bigger than his 'phone book,
lips on loan from Engelbert Humperdinck,
chest on loan from Tom Jones,
moustache on loan from Freddie Mercury,
legs on loan from me (a bad deal),
diet on loan from Pavarotti,
styling and investment advice courtesy of Caesar's Palace.

Happy Birthday... may you face a chocolate cake the size of Red Rock Mountain
and may you decide to climb it,

Love to a generous life,

U2

I love this group. No band was as close to me as U2. I had great, close relationships with The Who, the Stones and others, but what U2 did for me went far beyond the promoter-artist relationship. I'll get to that a little later.

In 1980, I was in New York hanging out in Frank Barsalona's office as I often did. Barbara Skydel, who worked for Frank, called me into her office.

"I want you to meet someone, Barry. This is Paul McGuinness. He manages an Irish group called U2 and they're going to be great."

I said, "How ya doin' Paul? It'll be great to play you. Give me a call." I didn't know U2 from the Irish Rovers, but if Frank was behind them, so was I.

Not long after that, Paul calls and wants to play the boys in Denver, so I booked them into the Rainbow Music Hall on March 28, 1981. This was part of their "Boy" tour, which was in support of their album of the same name. Four mop-topped kids showed up: a lead singer, two guitars and a drummer. They were so young: 18, 19. They started off with "The Ocean", which was a slow, soft, haunting kind of song and I wasn't quite sure what I had booked. But, after they turned it loose with "Tick Tock" and "I Will Follow", I called Frank at his home.

"This fuckin' group is going to be the biggest group in the world, Frank. They're unbelievable."

They just knocked me out.

Their set list at The Rainbow:

1. *The Ocean*
2. *11 O'Clock Tick Tock*
3. *I Will Follow*
4. *I Fall Down*
5. *An Cat Dubh (The Black Cat)*
6. *Into The Heart*
7. *Touch*
8. *Another Time, Another Place*
9. *The Cry*
10. *The Electric Company / Yankee Doodle*
11. *Things To Make And Do*
12. *Stories For Boys*
13. *Boy-Girl/Let's Twist Again*
14. *Out of Control*
15. *Encore*
16. *A Day Without Me*
17. *Twilight*
18. *I Will Follow*

After the show, I went into the box office and grabbed four, $50 bills and went into their trailer.

"Listen", I said, "You guys are amazing. I know how tough this is." I handed Bono, The Edge, Adam Clayton and Larry Mullen the money and said, "Please, go have a good meal on me. You deserve it." They never forgot that. And Bono never forgot seeing me, as I stepped outside the door and bought a U2 button off a guy for $3.

He'd never seen a promoter act that way, and I'd rarely acted that way about a band.

Jonathan King had a hit in 1965 called "Everyone's Gone To The Moon". He was doing a BBC music show from London called "Entertainment, U.S.A." and would check in with me now and then for my opinions on what was going on musically in the States. A few days after the U2 show he called and put me on the air.

"Hello Barry, have you seen anything new? Anything good?"

"I'll tell you, Jonathan, I saw a group from Dublin, Ireland that is going to be the biggest band in the world. They remind me of a young Who."

Well, U2 saw or heard what I said, so our love affair got off to a good start. I brought them back to the Rainbow a few months later, in May, 1981 and, the following year in Denver and Fort Collins.

We talked a lot in those early years. McGuinness and I and Bono and I. When I was booking them for the US Festival in 1983, Bono called and asked me to change their days.

"Barry, you've got us playing on the day headlined by The Clash. We'd rather play on the second day, with Van Halen, because we don't want to be labeled as a punk act; we want to be known as a rock 'n roll act."

"No problem." I switched them. In fact, you can still see or hear on YouTube a clip of me introducing them to the US Festival. U2 was getting bigger and bigger and we got closer and closer.

During one of their 1981 stops, I had my associate Chuck Morris take the boys for some sightseeing and he took them to Red Rocks. Clayton remembers that they were blown away by its beauty and that they were all thinking that someday, they'd play there.

"Someday" came in 1983. McGuinness was in my Denver office and we're talking about playing Red Rocks.

"Barry, we want to film the show, but I don't know if we'll have the money to do it."

I asked, "Do you want a partner?"

Paul said, "Well, we might. What would the deal be?"

"Here's the deal, Paul: you tell me how much you need and you tell me how much I get. That's the deal." And that's how it worked. U2 and I were 50-50 partners. Later, Chris Blackwell from Island Records wanted in, so we made it three equal partners: "U2 At Red Rocks Associates". But, it wasn't as simple as that. It never was in this business.

Barry ta Baja
the last time I saw yar
ye use 'Roasting' an the spit '
of yee mates...... I would like
far to know that I / we hae
equally great 'associations and
resonances... whenever we hear
far on the radio.....??
Fey live at the Roast" has
just edged into the all time
top ten along with 'Fey "shants
at the punters in the red rock rain "
my particular favourite.
love to you and yours
a far
Bdo

PS hope they put the legs an the
right way round nest time. thanks for
the thoughts.

On June 4th, 1983, I'm flying back to Denver from the US Festival's country music day—I had to leave early to get back for U2's "Under A Blood Red Sky" concert and filming. As the plane approaches Denver, the weather's terrible! Thunderstorms, sleet, snow, hail, flooding, famine, pestilence, locusts—all kinds of shit. I'm thinking that there's no way U2's going to play in this weather. But, we always had a backup in case of weather.

When I got off the plane at the Denver airport, I ran to a payphone and called backstage at Red Rocks.

"What's going on? Where's the show been moved to?"

One of my employees hemmed and hawed and wouldn't tell me what was going on. So, Paul McGuinness gets on the phone.

"Barry, they aren't talking to you because I ordered them not to. We're having the show here. We've got too much invested in the filming to not go on."

I may have said something about me not allowing them to rain on my audience, blah, blah, blah. So, then Bono gets on the phone.

"Barry, I love you, but I just went on the radio and made these unauthorized announcements saying that the Red Rocks show is going on tonight, whether one person comes or ten people come, the show's still happening tonight. I said that I know it's raining now, but, I'm sure it won't be by the time the show starts, so please come. And, I said that tomorrow we'll play indoors at Boulder for nothing and people can use their ticket tonight and come again tomorrow, they can do that. Or if they want to just use their ticket tomorrow night, they can do that. But, the show will go on."

I know I wasn't happy about it, and that's probably a huge understatement of my reaction. The Edge said later he was sure that I thought they'd lost their minds. It was crazy, but they insisted and I finally agreed. I ran home from the airport, put on my Israeli army jacket and heavy clothes and hurried up to Red Rocks. When I got there, the amphitheater is in a cloud. Literally, in a fucking cloud. It's raining. It was barely above freezing. Stagehands are using squeegees to get the water off of the stage and away from the wires. They were throwing ice melter onto the stage so Bono wouldn't slip. I'm just not believing that one of my audiences is going to have to sit in these conditions! There were supposed to be a couple of opening acts, the Divinyls and somebody else but they refused to go on because they didn't want their equipment to get ruined. Only about

4400 fans showed up (which means 5600 didn't) and they were all scrunched down as close as they could get to the stage. But, it was an incredible sight with the bonfires above the stage flaring into the clouds. The boys asked me to introduce them and by that time, I was fully into it. I made some reference to Dylan's "Hard Rain" show several years earlier and then screeched, "From Dublin, Ireland, please welcome U2!"

I'm sure that each of the fans who was there (and the thousands of others who claim they were) will go to their grave saying it was the most phenomenal night of their musical lives. Twenty songs and several different endings for the video's editing purposes. But, talk about dramatic! At the beginning of "The Electric Company", Bono walked to the microphone and held up a white towel. "There is but one flag, the white flag." And a few minutes into the song, he climbed onto a roof next to the stage and held up a ten foot pole with a big white flag on it. That may have been one of the stupider things he's done because of the conditions, but it worked out and added an extra layer of emotion to an already amazing night.

That same night, I had Neil Diamond in concert in Denver. I was supposed to drive down and say hello, but I never made it. From the minute U2 began playing, I couldn't move. I stood off stage right and didn't budge until it was over.

It was so cold that you could see Bono's breath. How The Edge was able to play, I don't know because his fingers had to be freezing. But, I think all of us agree that it wouldn't have been nearly as great a video if it had been clear and 70 degrees.

If you haven't seen the DVD and you don't see any other video from it watch "Sunday, Bloody Sunday". *Rolling Stone Magazine* called the performance one of "the 50 Moments that Changed the History of Rock and Roll". That moment when Bono marches like a soldier to the edge of center stage holding a white flag and then leads the crowd in a "No more! No more! No more!" shout-back was magic. Magic is a much overused word, but that moment, that whole night, was pure, fuckin' magic.

"Sunday, Bloody Sunday" was part of another dramatic moment during the "Rattle and Hum" documentary, which was shot during the 1987 tour. Their plan was to film in Chicago and Buenos Aires. Chicago didn't work for some reason, so the band asked me to find another venue. I booked them for two nights at McNichols Arena in

Denver, which The Edge liked; he was hoping lightning might strike twice after the band's Denver success with "Under A Blood Red Sky". Did it ever!

On the day of the second night, an I.R.A. bomb killed eleven people at a Remembrance Day ceremony in Enniskillen, Northern Ireland. During "Sunday, Bloody Sunday", just before he would have normally gone into the "No more!" shout-back, he went into a rant about the bombing and the so-called revolution that the I.R.A. and many Irish-Americans glorified, but most of his countrymen didn't support.

"Let me tell ya somethin'. I've had enough of Irish Americans who haven't been back to their country in 20 or 30 years come up to me and talk about the resistance, the revolution back home…and the glory of the revolution, and the glory of dying for the revolution. Fuck the revolution!

"They don't talk about the glory of killing for the revolution. What's the glory in taking a man from his bed and gunning him down in front of his wife and children? Where's the glory in that? Where's the glory in bombing a Remembrance Day parade of old-age pensioners, their medals taken out and polished up for the day? Where's the glory in that? To leave them dying, or crippled for life, or dead under the rubble of the revolution that the majority of the people in my country don't want?

"No more!" Powerful shit.

"Rattle and Hum" could have been called Bono's "Cuts and Bruises Tour". I had them booked to begin the tour in Tempe, Arizona where Bono fell during rehearsal and cut his chin on a light and had to have it stitched up. Later in the tour, Bono's arm was in a sling for several shows after he fell during a show at RFK Stadium.

But, the three Arizona shows were sold out. Bono's chin was sore, but it was a sore throat that caused us to cancel one of the shows. Everything was ready to go, but we nearly cancelled shows on April 2nd and 4th and another in Tucson because Arizona's jag-off governor, Evan Mecham, had cancelled Martin Luther King, Jr. Day. Now, U2 had written two songs in memory of King; "Pride (In The Name of Love)" and "MLK", and probably, more than any other white group, had consistently tried to honor his legacy.

Mecham was inaugurated in January of 1987 and not only did he immediately cancel Martin Luther King Jr. Day, he also defended the use of the word "pickaninny" to describe African-American children. What an asshole.

Of course, the April dates had been locked in long before Mecham came on the scene. But, Stevie Wonder started a performers' boycott of Arizona. That left us in a philosophical and financial jam. What we came up with was this: let the mood of the community dictate whether the shows went on. We talked with fans and members of a Mecham recall campaign and the band decided the best way to highlight their opposition to Mecham was to go ahead with the concerts and use them to state their disgust with him.

Ten minutes before the first show, I was called into the dressing room. Bono said:

"Barry, we've written a statement about the governor..."

"Good. Great!"

"...and we want you to go on stage and read it."

"I beg your pardon?"

"Yeah, we think it would be better coming from you."

He handed me a piece of paper. On it were the boys' thoughts about what a shame it was what the governor did and how wrong it was, that the band was outraged by it and called Mecham an embarrassment to the people of Arizona. Later in the show, during "Pride", Bono got a huge cheer when he said, "I think the people of Arizona know what they need to do". The band also gave a donation to the Mecham recall effort.

But, what a shit storm that got me into. Even though they were U2's words, they came out of my mouth. The TV show "Entertainment Tonight" started this running battle between Mecham and me. One night they'd interview him and the next night they'd interview me. Mecham ridiculed me by saying, "What does this guy know? He's from Denver. What does he know about what we do here?" The next night I replied: "You don't have to be from Phoenix to recognize ignorance."

Mecham didn't last long. He was impeached the following year.

The band's idea for the "Rattle and Hum" documentary was for some of it to be shot in black and white. As I've said, they shot most of the black and white portion in Denver and were planning to shoot the color part in Rio.

After one show, Bono called me into the dressing room.

"BAR-ee, we were going to do Rio for the color portion, but the costs are getting out of control and the politics down there are crazy, so we've got to figure out some other place to play."

"Well, why don't we do Phoenix?"

"Phoenix? Why?"

"That'll add a certain symmetry to it. You began Joshua Tree there, you end it there. Mecham is gone. I can try to get the big football stadium, the Sun Devil's stadium in Tempe. It'll be great."

Bono said, "Why don't you get in the limo with us and come back to the hotel. We'll talk about it."

I could be such an asshole, just as I was in 1971, when Mick asked me to return to Nice. I just wanted to go home; I didn't want to go to their hotel suite.

I put up a lame excuse: "But Bono, my car's here."

He said, "We'll take care of your car. You come with me."

I agreed and when I walked out of the dressing room, I slammed the door so hard that people all around backstage stopped and looked to see what had happened. One of my people asked, "Barry, what happened? Is everything okay?"

"I've gotta go back to the fuckin' suite with Bono!" I grumped. I don't think I even realized at the time how ridiculous that sounded.

They looked at me like I was nuts and pointed out that there had just been over 17,000 people in the arena who would have loved to have been invited to Bono's suite. And I'm bitching about it.

So, at the suite we're talking about ending the tour in Tempe. Bono and McGuinness said they wanted to give it some more thought and set up another meeting when they got to San Francisco. They asked me to fly out and when I get there—it was at the Clift Hotel—there's a room full of people discussing what they should do. Everybody had an idea of where the final shows of the tour should go. But, I prevailed. The band agreed that the tour would end in Tempe.

But, McGuinness was concerned. He didn't think the boys could sell out a football stadium on back to back nights.

"I'll take care of that, Paul."

"How?"

"We'll sell tickets for $5."

"$5?"

"Yeah, it'll fill the place up and it'll stop scalpers." Little did I know that the scalpers would have a field day with the cheap tickets. Anyway, I told him not to worry, the place would be sold out.

Getting the stadium was a little tougher.

The university told me that the field could not be touched within ten days of the Fiesta Bowl. That was part of their contract. Well, it turns out that I knew the president of A.S.U., J. Russell Nelson. In the 1970s, when I was trying to put Fleetwood Mac at Folsom Field at the University of Colorado, Nelson was the chancellor. Nelson refused for a variety of reasons; none of them good enough for me. I called my friend, Dick Lamm, the Governor of Colorado, who called Nelson and explained that the state could probably use the $250,000 that the concert would deliver. I got my concert.

When I showed up at A.S.U., Nelson joked (I think), "Why are you following me? I left Boulder to get away from you!" We worked it out. I got my concerts.

The concerts sold out in a day.

The band wanted me to do some of their introductions, but the director of the film didn't like my white tennis shoes. Look, I dress how I dress. I wore shorts and tennis shoes to the White House. When the director asked me to wear black shoes, I said, "Fuck you, I'm wearing what I have on." I was very stupid like that. Before I was supposed go on stage and do the intros, Dennis Sheehan, the tour manager walked up to me, knelt down and with a can of spray paint, made my shoes black.

The boys got on a plane for Dublin the next morning so they could be home for the holidays. But, I was nearly crying when they left, I'll tell ya. That was a wonderful experience, that '87 tour.

Jumping back to April of 1987, I took the band to Las Vegas for a show at the Thomas and Mack Arena. A few days before the show, the boys wanted to go to see the Sugar Ray Leonard and Marvin Hagler fight. Hagler was the champion, Leonard was coming out of retirement. I got tickets for Bono, The Edge, Adam Clayton, Larry Mullen, Frank Barsalona and Chris Blackwell. Frank bet on Hagler. I put my money on Sugar Ray. After about one round, Clayton, who doesn't like violence, left and waited in the limousine. It was a great fight. Sugar Ray won, as did I. After the fight, the night was still young and the boys wanted to go somewhere. Playing at the Golden Nugget was

Frank Sinatra and Don Rickles. Sinatra had always been a hero to the band, so they asked me to get them into the show. No problem.

Rickles opens the show and does his routine and then he brings out Sinatra.

"Hey, Frank. Before you start, there are some people in the audience you really should meet. It's a band called U2. They're going to be very, very big."

The spotlight shines on the band as they stand up.

Sinatra looks at them and tells Rickles, "Well, they may be getting big, but they sure as hell aren't spending their money on clothes!"

Backstage after the show, Frank Sinatra was sweet as sugar and so gracious. He could not have been nicer. He sat and talked with U2 for over an hour, telling them about his days on the road with Buddy Rich and all about his career. It was a great night.

It was a Labor Day weekend one year and Bono called me in Denver.

"BAR-ee, I've got a friend who's meeting me in Las Vegas, but I really don't want to go there by myself and neither one of us knows anything about it. Will you go with us and show us around?"

That's the kind of relationship we had. He'd call me to do things like that and I'd do it in a second.

Bono remembered it this way at my roast in 1992:

"I was in Las Vegas as an innocent and following behind Barry like a puppy dog through the Golden Nugget. I was asking Barry to explain the whole phenomenon which, coming from Europe, was a bit strange. Barry was just walking through the tables going, 'No.' 'No.' 'No.' 'No.' 'No.' I thought, wow, this man really doesn't approve of gambling. I was asking, 'Barry, what's all the "no" thing?' He said he would just get a feeling. He said gambling is sort of a spiritual pastime and you follow your instinct. In that case, his instinct was telling him no."

In the late '80s, U2 had gotten so big that Chris Blackwell of Island Records couldn't afford to give them what it would take to re-sign them. That's saying something, because Chris was one of the most influential men in the record business, with all sorts of great acts from Jethro Tull to Bob Marley and the Wailers. He and I were sitting in Frank Barsalona's apartment in New York and Chris is explaining his dilemma.

Frank said, "Why don't you give them no money and 20% of the label?"

Chris agreed. U2 agreed. Not long after that, Island Records was sold to Polygram Records for $150 million. Frank was a genius.

Here's something about Chris that has nothing to do with anything, but I think is interesting: His mother, Blanche, whose family owned banana plantations in Jamaica, divorced Chris' dad and had a long-term relationship with Ian Fleming of James Bond fame. She was his muse for several of his stories including "Quantum of Solace" and, as the story goes, was the inspiration for Pussy Galore. She also gave Fleming a boat named "Octopussy".

U2 and I spent a lot of time together over the years; in the U.S., in Ireland, in London and in Paris in 1984, where I felt the urge to give them a career assessment and advice. It was about three in the morning and Bono and I were relaxing in the hotel lobby.

I said, "You might be the biggest group in the world, but you still don't have your 'Hey Jude'."

Bob Hilburn, a legendary music critic for The Los Angeles Times from 1970 through 2005, was interviewing Bono a short time after that and when the conversation came to U2's status in the industry, Bono told him that he wasn't sure because Barry Fey told him they still don't have a "Hey Jude".

That was the same trip to Paris where we went to a wonderful restaurant and for dessert, when the waiter brought the trolley around, there was a luscious looking piece of chocolate cake, which, of course, I devoured.

I said, "Oh, my god! That was delicious."

McGuinness said, "Well, have another piece."

"No, no, no, I can't. That's Nazi cake."

"What do you mean, Barry? We're in France."

"Paul, take my word for it. That cake has killed more Jews than Hitler."

It wasn't the cake that nearly killed me. It was a doctor on Long Island who talked me into surgery. I had lost a lot of weight, from 320 to 180 and I had a tremendous amount of loose skin. In March of 1985, a doctor convinced me it was going to be easy to take off the skin. So easy, in fact, he told me to bring some money and while I was recuperating at his house, I could use his Rolls Royce and go to the track. He made it sound like a spa weekend. The surgery went horribly wrong. I had to have transfusions of five pints of blood. I'm at this dog and cat hospital on Long Island and just feel like shit.

But, the doctor says he wants to discharge me and take me to his house. Luckily, a nurse wouldn't let him, because I had phlebitis in my left leg, the only thing I ever had in common with Richard Nixon. Another doctor transferred me to Columbia Presbyterian Hospital in New York (where I was just across the hall from Sunny Von Bulow, not that she would have cared had she not been in a coma). Anyway, after a couple of days at Columbia I was feeling better and was strong enough to call my best friend in New York, Frank Barsalona. Another couple of days go by and the bleeding has stopped, the infection's gone and the doctors say I'm going to be fine. I was scheduled to go home on a Monday. On the Saturday night before, there's a knock on my door and it's Bono and Paul McGuinness. They'd heard, probably from Frank, that I was in the hospital and they were checking up on me. Now, the way Bono tells the story, he pulled back the sheet to see what they'd done to me and there were about 160 staples around my waist, holding me together. He said, "Well, they got your legs on right." He also said later that he saw my dick and that, "it's great to see a man with an ego in proportion."

Bono and Paul brought me a piece of Nazi cake.

When I told them I was going home on Monday, they couldn't believe it and neither—after seeing my staples—thought it was a good idea. Dr. Bono and Dr. Paul were convinced that I should stay a few more days. What I didn't find out until later, is that after they said goodbye to me, they spoke with my doctor and, despite their second opinions, were told by my doctor that yes, I would be going home on Monday. My 12-year-old son, Jeremy, was coming from Israel and the plan was for us to meet at the Newark airport and fly home together.

It was Monday morning, April 1, 1980. A little after six o'clock, there was a knock on the door.

"Excuse me, Mr. Fey?"

"Yes," I said as I was struggling to get dressed.

"My name is Detective Sergeant so and so (I wish I could remember his name) and my instructions are to make sure you get to the airport okay."

"Instructions? Who gave you instructions?"

"The band, sir. U2. Bono and Mr. McGuinness."

Well, I'd already ordered a limo and didn't think I'd have any trouble, and told him that was very nice, but I wouldn't be needing him.

"No, sir, your limo was cancelled and Bono and Mr. McGuinness sent one of theirs. And, they insist that you allow me to escort you to the airport."

Okay. Fine. He helped me get dressed, which was really difficult because I was so swollen from the surgery.

When we got to the airport, he wheeled me to the gate and walked me onto the plane. As I was about to thank him for his help, he sat down next to me and buckled his seat belt.

"What are you doing?"

"Sir, Bono and Mr. McGuinness insisted that I travel with you to Denver."

"That's really not necessary. My son's here. I'll be fine."

"Sir, my instructions are to stay with you and make sure you make it safely to Denver."

So, he did, and when we got to Denver, he made sure there was a wheelchair at the gate for me and that someone was there to meet Jeremy and me and drive us home. I thanked him and as soon as he left us to catch a flight back to Newark, I got up from the wheelchair and walked to our car.

I'll never forget Bono, U2 and Paul for doing that for me.

After I retired, whenever U2 played in Denver, they'd invite me to the shows. We'd have something to eat backstage and get caught up. Then I'd go out and sit in the crowd. After about three songs, Bono would say, "Where are we tonight?" The crowd would scream, "Denver!" He'd say, "Well, if we're in Denver we need to talk about Barry Fey." And he'd say something about me and Red Rocks or whatever. Then, they'd dedicate a song to me, always the same one: "Running To Stand Still", which is about a heroin addict. I could never figure out why they chose that one.

THE US FESTIVAL

The biggest single show I did was the US Festival near San Bernardino, California for Steve Wozniak, the co-founder of Apple. He had a vision for a festival for "us", uniting music, computers and new technologies, television and people. There were large, air-conditioned tents with the latest in computers and electronic music players.

It was a three-day New Wave, Heavy Metal and Rock show over Memorial Day weekend in 1983, plus a fourth day a week later for a Country show.

The numbers were huge; the conditions were miserable. 670,000 people over four days. It was disgustingly hot and dusty. The daytime temperatures were well over 110 degrees and Woz had installed sprayers, or misters, to try to cool people off. The wind had sucked all of the smog from the Valley up into the hills. My throat was so raw from breathing that crap I barely was able to introduce Ozzy and U2 on Sunday night.

You can see the complete line-up below, but the first day was New Wave headlined by The Clash.

The second day was Metal/Rock with Van Halen headlining. That was a huge day, setting a single-day attendance record for a concert in the United States of approximately 375,000.

The third day was more rock 'n roll and didn't start out that way, but it turned out to be David Bowie day.

We're all booked and I get a call from Wozniak.

"Barry, you know I love David Bowie."

"Okay", I said.

"Is there any way we can get him on our show?"

"Steve, we're already booked, there's no room."

"Barry, please, it *is* my money."

"You've already got the most expensive back stage pass in history, but I'll call."

I called and found out that David was in the middle of a European tour and the only way he could make it is if we put his whole crew on a 747. Bowie was getting $750,000 a night, so that would cost Wozniak $1,500,000, including the cost of the plane.

But, Van Halen had a Favored Nation clause in its contract, which meant no other band could be paid more. I called Steve back and explained that with the added $500,000 for Van Halen, Bowie would cost him $2,000,000.

"Book it." No hesitation. Book it. Woz lost about $10,000,000 on that show. We asked him how it felt to do the biggest rock show in history and lose that much money?

Woz said, "At the rate I'm going, I can only do 44 more of them."

Wozniak was great. He was a practical joker. We'd been warned that The Clash, the headliner of New Wave night, was going to blast

Wozniak when they got on stage for being a capitalist pig, blah, blah, blah. When he heard that, he was furious. He wanted to kick them off the show, but we convinced him he couldn't do that. He was pissed, rightfully so, at how hypocritical the band was. The Clash was getting paid 500,000 capitalist dollars, so Woz had us photocopy a transparency of the check and when The Clash started dissing him, we flashed it on the big screens next to the stage. "Pay to the order of The Clash. $500,000.00." They got laughed at for that one. What punks.

Bill Graham had done the show in 1982. Woz said that while he personally got along fine with Graham, his staff who dealt directly with Bill had a very negative personal experience. He said, "There had been too much ego conflict and control conflict between the two entities. I tried to talk my staff into seeing it differently but they had been trod upon and wouldn't give in." But, Graham didn't give in. Right up until the day that the lineup was announced, he was trying to interfere, sabotage us and steal the show. Chuck and I were at a hotel in Los Angeles where a news conference was scheduled to announce the 1983 US Festival lineup. David Lee Roth was there for it. Woz was there. It was going to be a big deal. Graham called and he begged, yelled and threatened me about the bands we booked for "Metal Night". He told me I'd have blood on my hands if I went ahead with the groups we'd booked because of the violence they'd surely cause with a crowd that big. That seemed like an odd warning since Bill had booked the same groups together before, without any problems. What he was really concerned about was that someone other than him was promoting one of the biggest festivals in rock history. When he didn't get anywhere with me, he called Woz.

Woz remembers, "Bill Graham, and [his assistant] Nick Clainos (whom I had a good relationship with going back to college days) did call me shortly before the '83 US Festival with warnings about violence from our strong heavy metal lineup. In my head, [I knew that] they'd put on shows with these same groups, however. They pleaded with me to drop the show. The groups were being way overpaid. I frankly wish I had taken their advice. The overpayment was based on some bad advice I got from a top notch "Big-8" accounting firm that we had basically lost money on the first US Festival due to gate crashers. I felt that we could secure that. One problem was that press reports as to attendance of the '82 event were much higher than our sold ticket numbers. For the '83 show we had controls on ticket stubs, turnstile entrance devices with counters and aerial photography to back up our ticket sales numbers. It turns out that we didn't have massive gate crashing for the first show after all. But using the info from our accounting firm, which we trusted at the time, we knew that we'd make money even paying the groups so much. But, Barry did his job and he brought a good feeling along with it and I consider him a good friend always."

The lineup was pretty amazing, even though I had to kick one band off the bill. John Cougar Mellencamp wouldn't agree—as every other band had to and did—to allow three of his songs to be used on an album and in a film. Mellencamp wouldn't budge, so I uninvited him. We did okay without him:

Saturday, May 28 – New Wave Day

- Divinyls   INXS
- Wall of Voodoo   Oingo Boingo
- The English Beat   Missing Persons
- A Flock of Seagulls   Stray Cats
- Men at Work   The Clash*

*Mick Jones' last appearance with The Clash

Sunday, May 29 – Heavy Metal Day

- Quiet Riot   Mötley Crüe
- Ozzy Osbourne   Judas Priest
- Triumph   Scorpions
- U2   Van Halen

Monday, May 30 – Rock Day

- Los Lobos   Little Steven & The Disciples of Soul
- Berlin   Quarterflash
- Missing Persons   The Pretenders
- Joe Walsh   Stevie Nicks
- David Bowie

Saturday, June 4 – Country Day

- Thrasher Brothers   Ricky Skaggs
- Hank Williams, Jr.   Emmylou Harris & The Hot Band
- Alabama   Waylon Jennings
- Riders in the Sky   Willie Nelson

Part Six

OFF STAGE
AND OFF KEY

In a business rife with odd characters whose egos, insecurities and mental defects created some of the oddest stories, there were many who stood out from the rest. Several stories resist categorization, but they reside in this section which is devoted, not always lovingly, to the oddest of the odd.

BILL GRAHAM

My phone rang .

"Barry, it's Bill." I hadn't spoken to Bill for about a year.

"Yeah, Bill. What's up?"

"Barry, I want you to know that I just did crack for the first time. I had the greatest 15 minutes of my life. But I know if I do it again, I'll be dead."

"Yeah, okay" and I hung up. Bill was weird like that. He'd treat me like a confidant one minute and the next he'd be trying to take my living away and destroy me and my family.

That was my last conversation with Bill Graham, long after I cared anymore whether he was dead or alive.

He died a few weeks later, but it was a helicopter crash that killed him, not crack.

Our relationship started well. In 1967, I wanted to bring the Jefferson Airplane to Denver. Someone told me to call Bill. Everybody knew Bill Graham. His Fillmore Auditorium shows were legendary. He told me, "Sonny, I only handle the Airplane in California. If you want to book them outside, you call this guy: Todd Schiffman". Which I did, and that's how I got started with The Doors, but that's another story in another chapter.

In 1973, Graham and I and Concerts West were the only three promoters handling Led Zeppelin. I got to the place where I had seven shows, which required a 50 percent deposit, $12,500, for each show. Those were wired to the management office. But, we had to pay the other half in the settlement room immediately after each show. Zeppelin's manager at the time, Peter Grant and the tour manager, Richard Cole, wouldn't take anything but cash. We didn't receive the ticket money until a couple of days later and I was a little short, so I called Bill to explain my problem.

"Can you possibly loan me $25,000 for Zeppelin?"

"Sure, come on out and I'll give it to you." Just like that.

So, I flew to San Francisco and he takes me to his safe deposit box and it's full of cash. He takes out $25,000 and gives it to me and tells me to bring it back after the show. Which, I did.

With Bill Graham at a 1981 Rolling Stones concert in Boulder.

After one of the Zeppelin concerts, I'm at the airport with my mother, who's 70 or so at the time. I hear this booming voice yelling my name and it's Peter Grant. He comes up and I introduce him. He gives her a hug and is charming as can be. He brags to my mother about how wonderful a job I'm doing with Zeppelin's shows. It was a nice moment.

The next time I see Peter, a few months later, I reached out to shake his hand. He said, "Are you kidding? Why the fuck would I shake hands with you?"

I said, "Peter, what's the matter!?" This was a guy you didn't want mad at you, because he was huge in the industry and, he was huge.

"What kind of human being are you? You introduce me to your mother and all the time, you're trying to fuck me!"

"Peter, I'm sorry, but what are you talking about?"

"Graham told me that he found out you had no intention of paying us, so he made sure he gave you the money so you'd pay. And you have the nerve to introduce me to your mother knowing all the time that you're planning to screw me."

I protested, "Peter, that's not true!" and tried to tell him what had really happened.

"Don't bother. I think I'll believe Bill Graham before I'll believe you."

I was stunned. Why would Bill—and you have to understand that he was a big deal at the time, he was the one who set the table for the rest of us and I was just getting started, I wasn't even a pimple on his ass—why would he do that? He and I had been close, I thought, and I just didn't understand why he'd treat me like that. Here's a guy who had stayed at my house a couple of times, playing with my kids and dogs. I stayed at his house. He picked me up at the airport one time in his convertible. It was cold, but he had the top down. Miles away, we were crossing some big bridge and I couldn't take it anymore. I yelled, "Bill, can you put the fucking top up? I'm freezing." He yelled back, "I don't know how!" We were buddies, or so I thought. That's why I took all of the shit he was pulling very personally. So what if he had a messed up childhood—and it was horrific—but that was no excuse to try to ruin me.

In 1976, I was riding a bike, flipped off the front and broke both of my thumbs. When I showed up in Oakland for the George Clinton, P-Funk national stadium tour, I had both hands in casts. Most of the dates, we did by ourselves, but in Oakland—because he was my buddy and, despite everything, he was still Bill Graham—I let him be my co-promoter. Stories started getting back to me that Bill had spread, one saying that he'd had my thumbs broken to make sure I knew who was the boss and the other that they were broken because I hadn't paid my gambling debts. What is the matter with this guy? It was almost like he was obsessed with me, and had no reason in the world to be. It was like he was the equivalent of the Beatles and I, on my best days, my BEST days, might have been the Rolling Stones. Night and day. He was Bill. Fucking. Graham. I knew my place and never left my place. He had absolutely no reason to feel threatened by me. But, he sure acted like he was.

I wasn't the only one he was screwing. He sold black market t-shirts at his own shows. Bill was also screwing bands out of hundreds of seats every time they played. Jane Geraghty, the controller at the Fillmore East who later went to work for Frank Barsalona at Premier Talent, told me how she'd sell the tickets and sell them again, because Bill had instructed his ticket takers at the door to not tear the tickets and then they'd take them back down to the box office.

And, to avoid paying taxes, Bill took thousands of dollars in cash from each show, $5,000 to $10,000 a week from the Fillmore East and Fillmore West and sent it overseas. I was with him a couple of times when, each time, he took a suitcase full of cash to JFK. Once was in March of 1974. I remember the date because it was when the first edition of *People* magazine hit the newsstands. Bill picked up a copy and flipped through it. I could see in his eyes that he wanted *in* there. I mean, I've got a big ego, but with Graham, it was a combination of a huge ego with the craving to be noticed. He wanted recognition. He wanted to be a star. After he put down the magazine, we walked to a gate where he traded the suitcase of cash for an empty one. The courier was his brother-in-law, who owned a trucking company with Bill's sister in Geneva, Switzerland. I went there once to visit them. It was during the time when Nixon and his men were trying to make my life miserable and I toyed with the idea of sheltering myself in Switzerland. It was quiet and peaceful there. Bill's sister, whom I liked, took me to a restaurant and Burt Lancaster was at one of the tables. That was a sign for me; that the highest level of excitement I could expect in quiet, neutral Switzerland would be an occasional sighting of Burt Lancaster. I needed more than that, so I went home.

There was a time that I got crossways with Frank Barsalona, who was only the most powerful agent in the business and with whom I had a great relationship. I was doing a ton of business with him. He liked me and would give me every act that he could. Two of his people, Barbara Skydel and Bill Elson, were trying to pull some shady shit on me behind Frank's back and I wouldn't put up with it. I was so angry at Elson; I called him and said, "I'm going to be on the next plane to New York. You'd better get a cop, because when I get there, I'm going to throw you out the fucking window". I confided in Graham and he told me he hated Skydel and Elson, too. He kept egging me along, saying, "Barry, you've got to stand up to those pricks. Don't you dare give in." Every time I had second thoughts about going against Frank, Bill would give me a pep talk. "Don't let them get away with it, Barry." I listened. After all, Bill was the most powerful promoter in the world. The way he talked to me, I thought he was really in my corner and backing me up on this. We were fighting the good fight together. What I didn't know until Frank told me later was that after Bill would get me all pumped up, the motherfucker would go to Frank and say, "I don't understand what Barry's doing. He's crazy."

So, following Graham's advice, I told Frank he had to choose between his employees and me. What a fucking idiot I was. Of course, he chose them, but Frank asked me repeatedly to reconsider because he really liked me.

So, I made a deal with Graham. I said, "Bill, why don't you do Frank's shows in Denver?" He agreed. "Okay, and I'll give you half the money." "Bill, I don't want any of the money. You just do the shows and keep the money. I don't want anything to do the shows or with Frank."

Bill sent Dave Furano out to do shows in my area, but he didn't know his way around and my people and I still wound up doing most of the work. We did the advertising and the tickets and I was getting more and more annoyed that we were doing Graham's work. That was before computer ticketing. We'd have a printer make the tickets and then we'd take them to the ticket outlets. For one show, we'd already had the tickets printed and Bill was on the phone screaming at Dave, demanding a second show. When Furano told me that, I said, "You want two shows? Here ya go". I started ripping the tickets in half. Dave gave up. He said, "I can't be between you two madmen", and went back to San Francisco.

After that, I knew letting Bill do shows in my territory wouldn't work, so I called Frank and patched things up. Frank said, "Barry, I just don't understand why you were so stubborn about this. We could have worked this out long ago." That fucking Graham.

Shortly after that, all of the top promoters in the country were called to a meeting on Long Island. Somebody labeled it the promoters' version of the "Apalachin Meeting" which was an historic 1957 summit meeting of the Mafia in upstate New York that was attended by about 100 Mafiosi from around the world. There were only 32 of us, but it was a powerful group. We represented a combined $150 million in concert grosses that year. Some of the top agents, like Frank, also joined us to figure out what to do about Jerry Weintraub, who was trying to eliminate the local and regional promoters by booking tours directly with venues in all of the cities. For whatever good it was going to do, we voted unanimously in favor of a resolution against nationwide tours that bypassed the local or regional promoters. One of the main reasons this was important, which some of the agents at the meeting finally understood and joined our side, was that cutting off the local promoters' balls would destroy the system that had been established for building new acts. This "What do we do about Weintraub?" discussion would continue for years.

As the meeting was breaking up, I decided to make a quick trip before my flight home and go into Manhattan to spend a little one-on-one time with Frank. Bill told me that he'd arranged for a limo me to take me into the city. I should have known better. The limo took me to a Howard Johnson's in Newark which didn't allow me enough time to see Frank before my plane left. Bill didn't want Frank and me to patch things up. He thought he'd found a crack in my armor and was going to use that to put me out of business.

As the years went by, we were forced to work together. There were groups, like the Stones, who preferred working with me over Bill, but because he was the king, they needed to involve him in the national tours. And, he needed me for the middle of the country because he knew if he tried to go around me, I'd make his life miserable.

In 1983, he tried to interfere with the US Festival (documented in that chapter) and there was another time in the late '80s that he tried to fuck with me and take business away and money out of my pocket. I'd had enough. I snapped and called a guy I'd gotten to know through my gambling named Charlie Blue. His real name was Charlie Blumberg and he was close with, and was protected by, New York mobster Carmine Gallante. Carmine was the Bonanno family boss who met his end while sitting at a table in an Italian restaurant in Brooklyn. Three hitmen walked in and sprayed him and the others at his table. He died with a cigar in his mouth. Just like in the movies.

"Charlie, you still know some people, right? I need to get rid of somebody."

"Yeah, sure, if I have to, I know people."

"I've got to have some guy hit."

"Who?"

"Bill Graham."

Charlie didn't hesitate. "Barry, you know I can't do that." I'd introduced them years earlier. "I like Bill. I won't do it."

I was furious. I couldn't even get a connected guy (one who years later would choose my Denver penthouse as the place from which to jump to his death) to help me get rid of Graham.

I stewed on that for a while and got more and more determined to do something to try to get back at Graham. I contacted the Intelligence Division of the IRS to tell them about his tax evasion. My hatred for him had turned me into a snitch, which I despised. I'd have rather killed him.

It wound up not mattering.

On October 26, 1991 at a quarter of six in the morning, the phone woke me up. It was Frank Barsalona.

"Barry, Bill's dead. He died in a helicopter crash last night."

My grogginess vanished instantly. I felt like jumping up and dancing.

We talked for a while.

Frank asked, "What time are you going to get there?"

"Where?"

"To the funeral."

"Oh, I don't think I'll go."

"Barry, you have to come. You're the next in line; you're the next great promoter."

There was no way I wanted to go to that cocksucker's funeral. But, it was Frank Barsalona asking. So, I got on a plane. Bill's people asked Frank and me to speak at the funeral. Both of us said we couldn't. Frank didn't like getting in front of a group of people like that. In my case, it wasn't because I was too choked up, not at all! It was because I didn't want to be a hypocrite, which is what Bill was; one of the biggest.

At the cemetery, when it was my turn at the shovel and I threw that dirt onto his box, I had to bite my lip to keep from grinning. I probably would have filled up the hole had there not been others waiting for their turn.

This story probably illustrates the dynamic of our relationship as well as any: When we were in Hawaii for the Stones concerts in 1973, we were playing football on the beach at Waikiki. Bill threw a pass and I made a spectacular, diving, fingertip catch. It was so good that people applauded. As I'm basking in the glory of my moment, Graham runs down the beach to where I caught the ball, waving his arms the whole way and yells to everybody around, "Did you see my great pass?"

Pricks*

1. Stevens Weiss
2. Bill Graham
3. Dr. Gerald Aker
4. Former U.S. Attorney Ron Leibowitz
5. Richard Cole
6. Robert Sillerman
7. Bill Elson
8. Marshall Tucker Band
9. Chuck Berry
10. John Bonham
11. Howard Kaufman
12. Larry Melnick
13. Peter Grant
14. Howard Rose
15. Jimmy Buffett
16. Sgt. Kowalski
17. Ed Leffler
18. Miles Davis
19. Bob Zwick
20. Charlie Sheen
21. Randy Michaels
22. Fred Ordower
23. Richard Sherman
24. Howard Gordon

*Not necessarily to me, but pricks nonetheless

Elvis Presley

What can I tell you about the King of Rock 'n Roll that hasn't already been published thousands of times?

How about this: Tom Hulett was partners with Pat O'Day and Terry Bassett in Concerts West and was the point man for Elvis' concerts. When Elvis toured, Tom was his promoter. He managed every performance from 1969 until Elvis died in 1977. He was one of the few people who could manage not only Elvis, but, more importantly, Colonel Tom Parker, Elvis' manager.

Tom told me that in the last two years of Elvis' life, he'd become such a sick man, his bodily functions had become so messed up by all the drugs he was doing, that they had to take extra sheets, blankets, etc. on tour with them, because Elvis could no longer control his bowels. His handlers didn't want the maids or the hotels to know that Elvis had shit the bed.

That aside, Elvis was The King. Don't ever kid yourself.

Truman Capote

After the Denver shows and luau, I took the Stones to Kansas City on June 22nd. That's where I met Truman Capote. He was fascinating from minute one. Truman was covering the tour for *Rolling Stone* magazine. This was about six years after "In Cold Blood" was published but Truman was, and continued to be, a celebrity. He was accompanied by Princess Lee Radziwill, Jackie O's sister. Truman loved to talk, and if you'd ever seen or heard him back then, or more recently saw Phillip Seymour Hoffman portray him perfectly in "Truman", you know that the way he talked was just as fascinating as what he said. He was probably loaded most of the time that I was with him, but we had several great conversations.

If it seems he was an odd choice to cover the Stones, he was. He got bored with the boys and the Stones Touring Party, with whom he never really connected and he left the tour in New Orleans. I don't think the piece he was working on, or was supposed to be working on, ever got published. But, I'd read somewhere or heard that he described Mick's prancing on stage as a "parody between a majorette and Fred Astaire."

For whatever reason, Truman and I became very friendly and hung out quite often; Palm Springs, where he had a home, New York, where he had a home and at my home in Denver. I enjoyed listening to this quirky little guy who was either the smartest person I'd ever met, or who convinced me he was. When we were in New York we'd often go to Trader Vic's in The Plaza for something to eat after which he would always try to take me to Studio 54. I'd go with him as far as the door, but that was it. I had no interest in being part of that crowd. That's where Andy Warhol used to follow him around. Warhol, there was a piece of work! You can read about him in the chapter on Waylon and Willie. But, talk about royalty, Truman knew everyone who was anyone and they knew him. And they wanted to be around him.

With me, it was always a one-way relationship. He wouldn't let me pay for anything, I couldn't do anything for him. All I was doing was basking in his glory. That changed a few years before he died. Around 1980, maybe '81, Truman called me.

"Barry, I'm at the Broadmoor Hotel. I'm trying to kick alcohol, cold turkey. But, I can't do it. I'm going to check in tomorrow to the Mount Airy Hospital. Would it be alright if I stay at your house tonight?"

What am I going to say? "No"? Hell, I felt like hanging a banner outside: "TRUMAN CAPOTE'S AT MY HOUSE!"

"Truman, I'd love to have you stay with me; you're always welcome here." He and his companion whose name I don't recall spent the night and the next day he checked in to Mount Airy.

I still don't know why he wanted to spend time with me. We had not one thing in common except he'd talk and I'd listen. And he genuinely liked me because with all the people he knew and all the things he'd accomplished, there was absolutely no reason for him to spend 20 seconds with me. And our meetings weren't always planned. Cindy and I were at a spa in Palm Springs. I was getting a massage and Truman happened to be on the next table. We spent the next few days together with him doing most of the talking, as usual. But, he liked me and I found him to be fascinating.

After he bailed on the Stones tour in '72, he said that the only real people he ran into on the whole tour were Cindy and Barry Fey. Maybe that's what it was. Maybe that's why he seemed to enjoy hanging with me. Compared to all of the showbiz freaks and sycophants he was around in New York, I was real.

Sometime later, Truman and I were chatting about a trip he took to Folsom prison. He was doing a special on crime and punishment or something.

"Barry, I interviewed Charles Manson."

"That must have been interesting. What did he have to say?"

"I said, 'Charlie, how do you feel about things'"?

"He told me, 'Oh, things aren't bad here, man. I get to go outside, they let me shoot baskets, I play the guitar, the food's okay. The only complaint is that I'm in a cell next to that fucking dingbat (Timothy) Leary.'

"Then, I interview Leary. He told me he was doing reasonably well, too. He said they can't control his mind. 'But my only complaint is that I'm next to that fucking asshole Manson!'"

Freddie Sessler

If you're a casual fan of rock 'n roll you may not know the name Freddie Sessler. He wasn't in a group, but was around a lot of the biggest groups and was one of the most interesting characters I came across in my career.

Keith Richards with his good pal, Freddie Sessler   *Courtesy: Larry Sessler*

My introduction to Freddie was strange. I was with the Stones at their January 18, 1971 concert in Los Angeles, the Nicaraguan Earthquake Benefit. Peter Rudge, the Stones' manager, walked up to me.

"Barry, see that little man over there?"

He was pointing at a small, kindly looking man, maybe in his 50s. Balding; probably Jewish, I guessed. Kind of what your favorite uncle is supposed to look like.

Peter said, "His name is Freddie Sessler. He may or may not know of you, but I need you to take him outside into the parking lot and keep him out of here until I tell you it's all clear. The D.E.A. is after him and they may be looking for him here."

The D.E.A. is after this guy? I walked up and introduced myself.

"BAR-ee, how nice to meet you!"

I suggested that we go for a walk. For some reason, he was willing to go with a complete stranger, so we walked down the tunnel and into the parking lot. For a good two hours, we walked around the Forum parking lot talking about anything and everything. He was hard to understand because his Polish accent was so thick. Freddie was a Holocaust survivor; he had the tattoo on his wrist, so he had stories about that. We talked a lot about the Stones. Freddie was Keith's guy. He's the one who was always around Keith and who Keith always wanted around. Freddie became a bit of a divisive factor because Mick didn't care for him.

Freddie went to Hawaii with us and we gradually became good friends. The only things we had in common were that we were Jewish and liked money. He had all kinds of money making schemes, only one of which was Keith involved in, I think. But, we got involved in the strangest things, like the Snake Venom Clinic.

Freddie was selling snake venom as a cure-all. Or, that's supposedly what he was selling; who knows what it really was. I heard stories that the clinic was mostly a ruse for him to be able to get the pharmaceutical grade cocaine and other drugs that he and his friends, Keith primarily, had a fondness for. But, he had a clinic in Miami that was going gangbusters. People were lined up to get in and enjoy the supposed benefits of snake venom. It was an all-cash business. He invited me down for a grand opening.

"BAR-ee, you have to come for my party. Keith's coming, everyone will be here."

"Hell, yeah, I'll be there."

Freddie invited me to stay at his apartment. He had a car that he told me I could drive anytime I wanted. But, I didn't learn to drive until I was 41, shortly before that, and because I was reluctant to drive his car, I mostly hung around the apartment while he went to the clinic every day.

Before he left for the clinic one day, he said, "BAR-ee, you gotta do me a favor."

"Sure, Freddie, anything."

"Don't let anybody in, but if somehow someone does get in, don't let 'em go to the big trunk in the closet." And he took me to a deep closet and showed me a huge steamer trunk. He didn't tell me what was in it and I didn't ask, because I assumed it was full of drugs. I had a vision of DEA agents showing up with their guns drawn, and I'm telling them they can't open that trunk.

Freddie left. I'm waiting and waiting, watching TV, but all I can think about is what's inside that trunk. I resisted as long as I could, but finally I had to find out. I stood looking at it for a minute. Like an idiot, I looked around to see if anyone was watching. Then, I reached down and popped the latches. I threw the lid open. It was full of cash. There was foreign money and American money. Ones, fives, twenties, fifties, hundreds, I had no idea how much. I closed it and Freddie and I never talked about the trunk again.

Freddie's grand opening party was huge; Keith was there, but more importantly to me, there were piles and piles of delicious shrimp of every type, ribs, chicken, sweet 'n sour this and that; it was magnificent. While everybody else was into the booze and whatever to alter their minds, I just stayed at the table and ate and ate and ate. But, it was all to celebrate Freddie's success in the venom business.

The Snake Venom Clinic had a good run, but the State of Florida decided he was practicing medicine without a license, closed the clinic and threw him out. So, Freddie took his clinic to Jamaica where he was doing a good business—not as big as Miami, because there wasn't as much money in Jamaica. He'd set up shop in a convalescent facility, which was like a hospice. Cancer patients would go there to die. It went under, but with Keith's help, he was able to take it over, including the pharmacy, which was better than the one at the Montego Bay Hospital. His Snake Venom Clinic legally had a license to bring in whatever drugs his "patients" needed. The primary, legitimate patient, was Ronnie Lane, who had played bass with Rod

Stewart in Faces and was legendary in British music circles. He had Multiple Sclerosis and he and Freddie, with the financial support of Keith and other friends, were hoping that they'd find a cure in the snake venom. Ronnie died in 1997.

Freddie was a sweetheart, but he spent a great deal of his day in an altered state. By late afternoon, he was beginning to fade under the haze of whatever he had ingested and, with the exception of evenings when there was something going on, he wouldn't be available for conversation by supper time. Keith owned a house nearby and would occasionally make a trip to check on the clinic.

Somehow, Freddie endeared himself to the Prime Minister, Edward Seaga. In 1981, Freddie called me from the Prime Minister's office.

"BAR-ee, I've told the Prime Minister all about you and everything you've done and he thinks we should have a music festival here."

"Freddie, what the fuck are you talking about? You want to do a music festival...all Reggae?"

"No, we want to bring in the biggest stars from America to play with the Reggae stars."

So, they flew me to Jamaica and Freddie got me into one of the biggest money losing deals of my career.

Freddie took me to a meeting with the Prime Minister and all the ministers of culture and this and that. Seaga had assigned a young lady named Babsy to be my personal assistant and they were all trying to talk me into how wonderful this festival would be.

I was very skeptical, because it was fraught with danger. It was fraught with danger in ways I couldn't even imagine. But, I sent my people to Jamaica and we came up with a plan that we thought would work. I told my financial people to take in partners, form a syndicate, so that Feyline wouldn't lose any money. We were going to put on the first Third World music festival in history.

We built a Bob Marley Performing Arts Center in Montego Bay and booked The Dead, The Beach Boys, The Squeeze (their last appearance), Jimmy Buffett, Peter Tosh, Jimmy Cliff, The B-52s, Gladys Knight, Aretha Franklin, Rick James, The Clash and many more over three nights. What an eclectic lineup. Unbelievable. It should have been one of the greatest fucking shows in history.

But it was a financial disaster. It lost about $900,000, and as much as I had insisted that my people put a partnership together so Feyline wouldn't lose any money, we took a huge hit. There was supposed to be a film made of the concert and I have no idea what happened to that.

The third night of the festival, Rita Marley, Bob's widow, called me on stage and thanked me for getting the pavilion built in Bob's honor and for bringing the wonderful music to Jamaica. She gave me a huge, beautiful handmade basket full of fruit and flowers. I would have liked it a lot more if it had been full of cash.

I did get a bag full of cash, though. The Montego Bay police caught some ticket counterfeiters and I was in the room when they were "interrogating" them. What they were doing was beating the shit out of these guys, who they caught red-handed with the phony tickets and a bag full of cash. The officer in charge handed me the bag and said, "You're the victim, you take this." I took it back to Denver and never bothered to look to see how much was in it, but I know it wasn't close to how much we lost.

On top of that, each time I left Jamaica, I tried to smuggle jerk chicken. And every fucking time, they caught me. I don't know what it is, the pimento leaves or what, but the jerk chicken there is so much better than what you get here. American jerk chicken doesn't come close.

Like I said, Freddie always had a can't miss scheme going to make money. One was "Rolling Stones Commemorative Coins" that he was going to sell during the Steel Wheels Tour in 1989. But, for whatever reason, the coins were delayed and by the time he got them, the tour was over. He brought them to the Stones' Japan shows in 1990, but nobody wanted to buy them. We got there a few days before the boys played 10 shows in the Tokyo Dome and saw Mike Tyson take a beating from Buster Douglas. Freddie took a beating on those coins.

Freddie was friendly with many, many people and was very influential; Keith, Rod Stewart, Steven Tyler, on and on. Guess how he was influential. He got them drugs. That pharmaceutical grade coke that Keith gave me after John Lennon died? Freddie. But, he never sold them drugs that I know of. He was just happy to share.

In August of 1992, I had Metallica and Guns 'n Roses in Phoenix where Freddie lived at that time. I was expecting to see him, because he always seemed to show up. But, he didn't come. I saw his son, Jeff.

"Where's your dad?"

"He's In the hospital with colon cancer."

I called Freddie in the hospital the next day.

"Freddie, are you going to be okay?"

"BAR-ee, if Hitler couldn't kill me, cancer doesn't have a chance."

When I was indicted for gambling, the Fed's case against me hinged on the information they got from wiretaps. So, I went to one of the best wiretap attorneys in the country, Oscar Goodman, who later became Mayor of Las Vegas. Goodman was a very powerful mob lawyer. He repped Spilotro and the others whose stories were turned into the movie "Casino". I remember Oscar telling me that all the wiretaps up to a certain date were illegal, but I was fucked because while all of the other defendants' wiretaps were signed off on by Attorney General John Mitchell's underlings, mine was signed by Mitchell himself. Of course, Mitchell was one of Nixon's most loyal soldiers and was just a bad motherfucker who tried to prosecute any critic of the Vietnam War and, just as bad or worse, dragged his feet on prosecuting civil rights violations. He got his, though.

Anyway, Freddie enters this story years later when I've got the Stones at the MGM Grand. It's November of 1997, after I'd retired, but I had retained the rights to do some shows in Vegas. Freddie was caught scalping tickets in the lobby. I suppose Keith or somebody gave him the tickets. But, scalping them in the fucking lobby of the MGM Grand?! Of course, he was arrested and, of course, the police found drugs in his ever-present briefcase. I called Oscar, who remembered me well from the wiretap days. He must have made a few calls because Freddie was released and he got his drugs back.

It bothered me the way some of Freddie's so-called "friends" treated him. Besides just being a source of drugs to many of them, he got them out of some serious jams. Some took advantage of him and didn't give him what he deserved. Keith seemed to be the one guy who stood by him.

All Freddie wanted to do was just hang around and listen to the music. He was the most fascinating, lovable fucking guy. He had his faults, but who doesn't? He was one of those friends who you didn't need to talk to everyday; you just knew that he was around and felt better because of it.

Freddie died in 2000 on December 18th.

Keith Richards' birthday.

The Aerosmith Intervention

Of all the groups I booked, there were probably no bigger heroin addicts than Aerosmith and by Aerosmith, I mean Steven Tyler and Joe Perry. It got so bad in the later years of their addictions that Tyler and Perry weren't speaking, weren't traveling together and wanted nothing to do with each other. One of my road guys said it got so ridiculous that each would send their own private jets to Boston to pick up heroin from the same supplier.

In January, 1973 when I was at the Stones' earthquake benefit concerts in Los Angeles, I met the band from Boston for the first time. Aerosmith opened the show and, of course, weren't as big as they were going to get yet—*Toys In The Attic* was still a few years away, but they were starting to get noticed nationwide, partly for their similarities to the Stones.

While I was watching them perform, Steven Tyler was prancing around the stage, trying to look, I thought, like Mick Jagger. He was copying Jagger's moves and all this. So, backstage later, I introduced myself to Steve.

"You know, you don't have to do all that Jagger shit. You've got a lot of talent. You should be yourself. You don't want to be compared with Jagger because you ain't gonna win that one." That was my first conversation with Steven. He didn't tell me to go fuck myself, so I guess it went well.

I booked Aerosmith many times in the next several years and we developed as good of a relationship as you can with heroin addicts.

Two of the times I booked them stand out the most. Las Vegas, which I'll get to in a minute. And Denver, on May 22nd of 1988. It was the "Permanent Vacation Tour". "Dude Looks Like A Lady" was the big hit from that one. It was their first tour after Steven and Joe had gotten out of rehab. We had a post-concert party at my house.

Steven was getting married a week later, but that didn't stop him from hitting on my fiancé, Lisa. My teenaged son, Jeremy was standing close enough to hear him say that he'd really like to go out with her sometime. Jeremy said, "Hey, she can't go out with you, she's engaged to my father!" I think Lisa told Jeremy to be quiet.

To this day, Lisa says, "Steven loves me."

Tyler and Perry were known as the "The Toxic Twins" because of all the shit they took. During the '04 tour, Steven collapsed on stage

Notice my right hand in Steven Tyler's pocket.

somewhere; Illinois, I think. In 1986, there was an intervention and they went to rehab. In fact, they'd gone, individually or together, to Betty Ford and Hazleton and wherever. They had t-shirts made up called the "Rehab Tour" listing all of the facilities they'd been in. Finally, Tim Collins took over as their manager and he got them in to a place called the Caron Foundation and a facility called Chit Chat Farms. They, and their wives, went through the rehab program and it seemed to work.

They were clean and sober in 1993 when I had them at the Thomas and Mack Arena in Las Vegas. I remember the year because the movie Casino was being shot and Robert DeNiro came back stage.

After the show Tim Collins called me into a room, where Tyler and Perry were waiting.

It was an intervention. Not for what you might think. As one of the country's biggest rock concert promoters, I had total access to drugs, liquor, sex and any other vice that addiction could serve up. None of that appealed to me.

"You're killing yourself, Barry. Look how fat you are."

"We love you, man. We don't want you to die. You've got to stop eating so much."

They had a guy waiting for me outside the door to whisk me away to a treatment center.

I said, "Look at this fuckin' picture. Three fuckin' drug addicts telling me to stop eating spare ribs?!"

I couldn't believe what I was seeing and hearing.

They kept saying all the things you're supposed to say in an intervention.

I told them to go to hell. And then I probably went to get something to eat. There were nights when I'd eat two servings of prime rib, order a pizza, pick up some Chinese food and then eat a pint of ice cream. My eating was insane. No one weighs 312 pound because they're hungry. Something's broken inside. But, like a lot of addicts, I never looked at food as an addiction.

Despite the failed intervention, I stayed friends with Steven and Joe, but I thought it was terrible, later, when they fired Collins. He saved their lives and made them a lot of money. When the House of Blues hired me to run their concerts in 2001, we had Aerosmith at Fiddler's Green in Denver. I asked someone how much the band was getting paid.

"$600,000."

I said, "For the week!!?"

The drummer heard me and got pissed off but Steven and Joe didn't care. They knew how I was. Joe gave me some of his homemade barbecue sauce. Interesting gift for a compulsive overeater.

There was a second intervention. This one happened in 1994 in Phoenix. My wife Lisa, my son Alan, Frank Barsalona, who flew all the way from New York, Chuck Morris and two of my partners from MCA, Jay Marciano, Fred Ordower and an intervention specialist who Aerosmith had recommended. God bless all of them for trying and Frank Barsalona, what a great friend he had been since the beginning. He was scared to be there because he thought I'd get mad, which I did.

They did the whole, "We love you, we think you're killing yourself, you're hurting us" thing, blah, blah, blah. This time, it wasn't just eating, it was gambling, too. I loved betting on college football and horses. Jay said MCA was going to pay for the whole rehab bill, which was a big deal because it was expensive.

I said, "Hey, listen, I've got no problem with going away."

My willingness took them by surprise. "Great. We'll take you to Cottonwood right now."

"I'm not going now. I'm heading for Vegas. It's the Kentucky Derby tomorrow."

They were flabbergasted. "You're telling us that we're trying to get you off of gambling and food and you're not going to go because you've got to go to Vegas and bet on the Derby!?"

"That's right. The Derby only happens once a year."

I wound up going, finally, in November of 1994. But, before I went, I called Cottonwood and told them there would have to be conditions. I had my own rider. First, I wanted a private room.

"Everybody shares rooms."

"I'm not coming then."

I got my own room.

I also demanded a treadmill, because I was a big walker. Despite my overeating, I walked five or six days a week on a treadmill at a four percent grade at four miles per hour. I was in phenomenal shape. Cottonwood's treadmill was broken, so I walked outside everyday, which worked out okay.

Just because of the guy I am, I created havoc at Cottonwood. I raged and shouted and bitched and threatened to leave for the first few days. Part of the program was that anytime you felt like having an argument with someone, you were supposed to go up to them and say, "I confront you." I was being such an ass, one of the counselors came up to me and said, "I confront you". I said, "Fuck you!" I had a bad attitude and I stuck up for everybody else. I wouldn't let anybody get pushed around. I even got into a big beef with the kitchen staff because I was there during Thanksgiving. They'd thrown all the turkey skin away and I loved turkey skin.

But then, something kicked in. I started to like the place. I got up when they told me, I went to bed when they told me. I obeyed nearly every rule, I went to most of the lectures. I told them it would take an intervention for me to leave. I admitted being a food addict; "Hi, my name is Barry and I'm a compulsive overeater". But, my interveners who had hoped I'd get help for my gambling picked the wrong horse. I refused to admit I was a compulsive gambler and wouldn't go to all of the classes they wanted me to. I gambled for money and because I loved it. I didn't have to gamble. Others, like my wife, Lisa, saw it differently. She's a beautiful woman and there were times when she'd put on her sexiest negligee and I'd have the racing form in one hand and the telephone in the other. I wouldn't even look up. There were Sunday mornings when, instead of taking Tyler out for bagels, I'd go to the Off Track Betting parlor. People who worked with me at Feyline complained that my gambling got in the way of business. I agree that it did in 1970 through 1972, but at that particular moment in Cottonwood, I didn't see it that way. So, I concentrated on my overeating. But, I did all the nature hikes and the spirituality shit and also wrote letters. We were supposed to write hate letters to all the people we were mad at. One I wrote was to my Marine Drill Instructors:

"Dear Sgts. Goldsboro, Kowalski, Alvarez and Verault: I was a scared 237-pound little boy whose father had just passed away and you traumatized me, beat me, humiliated me and made my life a living hell. I lived only for the night when I could lay in my bunk and silently cry. I don't remember praying because no God worth praying to would ever do this to anyone. I know that three of you, all except you, Goldsboro, were busted for cruelty. I hope the rest of you were in the corps long enough to go to 'Nam. I hope you were killed, or better yet, I hope you were one of the MIAs that were tortured. For Kowalski specifically: I hope that if you survived Vietnam, you're homeless and living on the street. And if I walk by, you'll smile and say "Hi" and I'll kick in you're fucking teeth.

If not, let me assure you of one thing. The odds are 1,000 to nothing that my life is better than yours. I have a wonderful wife and family, a wonderful business, a wonderful place in my community and I could buy and sell you many times over.

Still hating you after all these years, Barry Fey, serial number 1615610

I was at Cottonwood for 27 days and lost 12 pounds. On my last day, they gave me a medal. My fellow addicts cried. I cried.

But, I'd lay odds that the staff had a barbecue and party after I left.

The Amnesty International Heimlich Maneuver

Jack Healey, the executive director of Amnesty International and I had big plans. We were going to put together a train, an "anti-torture train" and take it from coast-to-coast. There'd be rock and pop groups on the train and at every stop, some or all of them would play. If it was just a whistle-stop, they'd play from the train. We could turn a couple of flatbed cars into rolling stages. If it was a bigger town or city, we'd unload and go to a venue for an Anti-Torture Concert. Jack wanted all of the flags of countries that were guilty of torture flapping in the wind as we covered the country. And, ideally, as each country succumbed to the pressure and stopped torturing, its flag would come down from the train.

You never heard about the Anti-Torture Train because it didn't happen. We tried; I had my people work on getting the train and the acts, but what a logistical nightmare.

There were two concert tours for Amnesty International in the 1980s. In 1986, I worked with Bill Graham on a half dozen concerts in the United States; "A Conspiracy of Hope" tour. It was A.I.'s 25th anniversary and Jack wasn't trying to raise money as much as he was awareness and to get a new generation of Americans involved in the battle for human rights and dignity.

Graham insisted on selling tickets by mail-order, which was a miserable disaster only two years earlier for the Jackson's Victory Tour. I tried to tell him that it wouldn't work anymore like it might have in the '70s, but he wouldn't listen. I was right. It was dreadful. Graham told others—he'd never have admitted it to me—that the mail order ticketing was a big mistake.

They were great concerts in San Francisco, L.A., Denver, Atlanta, Chicago and the finale in Giants Stadium in the Meadowlands. Big names played: U2, Sting, Bryan Adams, Joan Baez, Lou Reed, Peter Gabriel, the Neville Brothers and the last three shows, in Atlanta, Chicago and New Jersey, included a reunion of The Police.

The concerts worked. The message got through to the next generation. Jack Healey says one month after the tour, Amnesty International in the United States had 45,000 new members.

In 1988, Jack put together another concert tour; this one was world-wide and was titled "Human Rights Now!" Denver wasn't going to be a tour stop and I wasn't involved in putting it together, but I was invited to attend the Oakland concert on September 23.

That was a memorable concert, too. Not only did the show begin and end with Bob Marley's "Get Up, Stand Up", as did every show on the tour, it was Bruce Springsteen's 39th birthday and Joan Baez led the crowd in "Happy Birthday".

Backstage before the concert, there was a dinner for VIPs and guests. Jack was sitting at a table across from Carole Nagengast, who was on Amnesty International's board. I was sitting a table away.

Carole started choking on her food. She was turning blue—literally. Nobody was doing anything. I'd never done the Heimlich maneuver or even seen it done in person, just on TV. But, I got behind her, put my fist under her breastbone, put my other palm on top of my fist and jerked her back as hard as I could. Pop! The fishbone she was choking on fired out of her like a bullet. If anyone had been directly in front of her, they might have lost an eye.

Carole Nagengast is still chairwoman of the Amnesty International board of directors.

1972 Rolling Stones tour ticket: $6.50

2006 value, adjusted for inflation and cost of living: $29.92

2006 actual ticket price: $60 to $450

Tickets and TicketMaster

"Fucking Ticketmaster!" I've lost track of how many times I've heard that. People I run into usually have the same questions: What was so-and-so rock star really like, why have ticket prices gotten so fucking high and why is there such a big service charge?

In 2006, when I had been asked to speak somewhere, I decided to compare the price I charged for the Stones 1972 U.S. Tour, $6.50, with the Stones' current ticket prices, which ranged from $60 for nosebleed seats to $450 for the best seats. I contacted the Bureau of Standards and asked it to factor in the cost of living increases between 1972 and 2006 and inflation to see what the adjusted price should be. $29.92.

$450 for a ticket to one show! I've seen other tours where the prices are double that. How many other shows are you going to be able to see in a year when you're paying hundreds just to see one? That takes away loyalty and the market for small bands. It all stinks.

I'm perhaps as much to blame as anyone for Ticketmaster. I unleashed a monster. In 1983, when I put on the US Festival, I had a choice of using the reigning heavyweight champion in the ticketing business, Ticketron, which had been around since the '60s, or going with the struggling seven year old Ticketmaster. Fred Rosen had just joined Ticketmaster the year before and changed the business model. Instead of charging venues a fee for selling tickets, he tacked on a service charge to the price of the ticket and divided the revenue among the venue, promoter and Ticketmaster. US sold 670,000 tickets. If I had gone with Ticketron, Ticketmaster may never have gotten as big. But, I went with Ticketmaster and several years later, Ticketron was out of business. You're welcome, Fred. (He left Ticketmaster after it was taken over by Barry Diller and last I heard, he was running a Canadian company trying to compete with Ticketmaster.)

If there's one man who killed the rock concert business, it's Robert Sillerman. I never thought that one fucking guy could have that effect on the business that I helped build and all the other promoters, big and small, helped build. Sillerman, who began SFX, started buying up promoters, paying way more than they were worth. And, if you were a promoter who owned an amphitheater, that's what he really wanted to control; the real estate. When he had purchased 60 to 65 percent of what were the best promoters, he wasn't satisfied. He wanted to control all of them. But some promoters wouldn't sell.

So, Sillerman started trying to eliminate them. He was offering groups two, two and a half, three times what they were worth for their entire tours. He would guarantee the groups millions of dollars. And the only way he could pay for that, was to jack up ticket prices. I never let SFX get away with it in Denver, but that was the beginning of the end.

Sillerman sold SFX to Clear Channel Radio and that model should have worked: the synergy was there because Clear Channel owned most of the top radio stations in the big markets, so promotion of its own concerts should have been a snap. But, they started abusing their power and were sued over and over by whatever small promoters that were left. Nobody In Particular Presents settled its slam-dunk case against Clear Channel for unfair competition and that opened up the floodgates to more lawsuits.

Wall Street, which bankrolled Clear Channel's gobbling of radio stations all over the country, didn't like the potential damage to its investment from the lawsuits, plus the concert division wasn't making any money, so Clear Channel spun off its concert business into what is now Live Nation.

No surprise that concert ticket sales are way down, 30 to 40 percent. But in the SFX/Live Nation business model, if tickets didn't sell, they'd heavily discount them or give them away. Their theory was that once people got to the concert, each ticket would be worth exponentially more because of revenue from parking, beer, wine, soft drinks, pizza, hot dogs, pop corn, cotton candy, posters, t-shirts—all of it. They could make money without selling tickets. That's another thing that killed our business.

It's no longer the music business. It's the business of music. You've got two monster billion dollar companies, Live Nation and A.E.G. (Anschutz Entertainment Group) who are running up the ticket prices because they're trying to outbid each other for the big tours. The independent promoter doesn't have a fucking chance.

And, let's say you're a small promoter and you discover a group that becomes big. Don't invest too much time or soul in it, because Live Nation or A.E.G. will wave so much money at the group for a tour offer, it'll drop you in a fucking heartbeat. So much for loyalty and gratitude.

Go ahead; name a promoter other than Live Nation and A.E.G. There's no style, there's no personality anymore. There's no Bill Graham, no Barry Fey. There's nobody like that anymore.

Ironically, two of the main guys at A.E.G. got their start with me. Great guys. Tim Leiweke, who is President of A.E.G. and Chuck Morris, who is President/CEO of A.E.G. Live for the Rocky Mountain region. Tim, who is arguably the most powerful man in the business and Phil's right hand man in entertainment, worked for me when I opened the Starlight Amphitheater in Kansas City. And, Chuck, as I've mentioned elsewhere, was key to the success of Feyline.

Things got even more fucked up when Live Nation and Ticketmaster merged.

Before there was a Ticketmaster or Ticketron or Select-A-Seat, which Feyline ended up buying, here's how the ticket business worked. The promoter would book the show, print the tickets, take them to the ticket outlets and then go back again and pick up the money. When my first son, Alan was a baby, we put him in the car—I don't remember if we had car seats then—and Cindy and I started dropping tickets at 8 am in Colorado Springs at Miller Music, then head north and hit all the outlets in Denver, then to Boulder where we had three outlets on The Hill that were within 50 yards of each other, but each had different clientele: University Records, Phantasmagoria and The Brillig Works. Then, we'd continue north to Longmont and finally, by 6 pm, at Bach or Rock in Fort Collins. Easily 300 miles during the day. People who were working with us in those days, including Leslie Haseman and Cathy Millward, would learn where the best seats in the venues were and make sure the tickets were divided up so that each ticket outlet would have the same number of great seats. Then, in the days leading up to the show, we'd be on the phone, finding out how tickets are selling and if they weren't selling at one outlet, we'd have to drive to pick them up and take them to an outlet where they were selling. Then, on the day of the show, we'd have to drive around and pick up the ticket money and take it to the concert hall where the band would get its share.

When computer ticketing became widely used, that certainly cut down on our driving. But, it didn't stop promoters from trying to screw the bands and the bands from trying to screw the promoters. He probably wasn't the first, but like pretty much everything he did, Bill Graham took it to the extreme. As I mentioned in his chapter, Graham would tell the band that the hall held only so many people—way short of what it actually held—and he would resell tickets and keep the extra seat money.

The formula of the day—$X amount for the band and the promoter would keep everything above that, if there was anything above that—worked for a while. But, some of the bands were getting shafted, badly. Even with the amount of risk we were absorbing, we were often taking advantage of them.

When I started in the late '60s, I'd give the bands $5,000, $10,000, whatever it was and that was that. I'd keep everything over that, if there was anything. Then, the bands got wise to that and it became, say, $10,000 guaranteed plus 50% of the gross over $50,000. They wanted a piece of the backend. Then it went up to 60% and 70%. Eventually, it got to where the big bands wanted no guarantee, but they wanted 80% of the net after expenses. So, if you grossed $300,000 and expenses were $100,000, there's $200,000 left, they got $160,000 and I got $40,000. But then, they decided they wanted a guarantee against the 80%, which soon grew to 85%. And then to the dreaded "90-10".

That's where the bands and their managers started getting abusive and wouldn't allow us to earn a living. They became unconscionable and insulting. They turned us into thieves. We had to invent ways to make money, like phony ticket commissions, phony insurance and phony whatever to increase expenses because the split on the net had gotten so ridiculous, which brings me to Jimmy Fucking Buffett. By the way, I respect Buffett for one reason. He never professed to have talent. He'd always say, "I don't know what I'm doing here." He found a hook, a formula, and played it to the hilt. He still is. But, here's the thing about Jimmy: 90-10 wasn't good enough for him. He started demanding 105%! All of the gate plus five percent of the gross. It worked out for me and the other promoters because of beer sales. Buffett's fans, which included uptight accountants and lawyers who showed up wearing Hawaiian shirts and had balloons, parrots and whatever else on their heads, drank beer until they puked, like there was no tomorrow. That's the only way we could make any money on Buffett concerts.

And those Ticketmaster service charges that kept going up and up and in some cases got to 50% of the ticket price? Promoters were getting part of that kicked back. I'd get 35-40% of the service charge.

Michael Cohl was the smartest promoter I've met. He was a debating champion, a math champion and he could figure deals quicker than anybody I'd seen. *Fortune Magazine* labeled him the "Howard Hughes of the entertainment business." I think that was meant as a compliment. He was the first one to tell me that I needed to charge more for tickets.

"Barry, you aren't charging enough. Charge more. The people will pay it."

He was right, but I never thought it would get this crazy.

But, what Michael did to Bill Graham, while a thing of beauty in one sense because I enjoyed seeing Graham get fucked, ten years later led to the tour guarantees that Sillerman used to put the smaller promoters out of business, which was a larger play on what Jerry Weintraub and Concerts West tried to do decades earlier.

Cohl had gotten involved in the Jackson's Victory Tour about halfway through and, because of his genius, made it less of a financial debacle.

About four years later, he used a similar formula to put together a group that would BUY the Rolling Stones tour. Now, Graham had been involved in the Stones tours, as had I, in '72, '75, '78 and '81. They hadn't toured since '82 and Cohl had a plan to get them back on the road with their Steel Wheels album in 1989. Graham assumed that he was going to get Steel Wheels. But, he was blindsided by Cohl, who'd already been working for months to put together the deal. After he had it all but finalized by the Stones, Bill was given a chance to beat it, but there was no way he could.

Michael continued using and expanding his formula and after Clear Channel spun off Live Nation, he invested hundreds of millions in acts like Madonna, Jay-Z, Shakira and Nickelback. Huge guarantees: $120 million to Madonna; $150 million to Jay-Z, in exchange for a large back end percentage on nearly every part of their business, from touring to t-shirt sales to recording deals. Then Live Nation and Ticketmaster were allowed to merge and look who's at the helm! My old pal Irving Azoff (more about him in the Eagles chapter). There is no middle man, no local promoter, who has a chance to make a big score on a big concert anymore. It's a fuckin' quagmire and that isn't sour grapes. Feyline couldn't exist in this environment. Graham couldn't have either. When your product and your venue are taken away from you, there isn't much you can do.

Of course, another element to the ridiculous ticket prices came courtesy of the Internet. People don't buy CDs the way they used to. Why should they? If they aren't getting it for free on the Internet or from friends, they're buying singles for 99 cents on iTunes. The groups can't make money if they don't tour. Another result is the impact on new artists, developing artists. Take a listen to Classic Rock stations. The music they're playing will be the same in 20 years from now because there aren't any "new" Stones, Who, Zeppelin, Beatles, Skynyrd and ZZ Top. The pipeline has dried up.

There've probably been scalpers since the beginning of ticket sales. It's human nature, at least American entrepreneurial nature, to figure out a way to make money on someone else's product. Buying tickets for $X and selling them for $X+ will continue and there isn't a lot that anyone can do about it. I thought the $450 tickets would end scalping, but there are people willing to pay a premium on those, too.

I also thought that charging only $5 a ticket for U2 concerts at Sun Devil Stadium during the Joshua Tree Tour would eliminate the scalpers, but they outsmarted me.

Before computerized ticketing, the scalpers would take buses around cities, picking up vagrants or whoever wanted to make a few bucks and put them in ticket lines. At one of my Neil Diamond shows, I got a call from a security guy who said the lines were unusually long. So, I went over to take a look and picked out a guy who didn't look at all like a Diamond fan.

"What's your favorite Neil Diamond song?"

"I don't know any of his fucking songs, I'm here to buy tickets for my mom."

"Oh, really? Let's go call her." So I dragged him out of line to a payphone and made him call his mom.

"Yes ma'am, my name is Barry Fey and I'm promoting the Neil Diamond concert. This young man says he's here buying tickets for you. Is that true?"

She confirmed it. I took the kid back and put him in line.

The first time I heard of bands scalping was Rod Stewart. His managers, Arnold Steifel and Randy Phillips were scalping their own tickets, but it's gotten to the point where nearly all of them are.

As for why you can't often can't get the best seats no matter how quickly you get on the computer when tickets go on sale, the bands are often as much to blame. In 2007, the *Wall Street Journal* broke the story that Van Halen was sending premium seats directly to scalpers before the regular fan had a chance to buy them. The *Journal* said Irving, who managed Van Halen, was behind that, and Van Halen took in an extra million dollars on its tour from the scalped tickets. It isn't just Van Halen. Neil Diamond, Madonna, Bon Jovi, Celine Dion, Billy Joel/Elton John and others were or are doing it. Even sports teams got in on it with a Ticketmaster scalping competitor, StubHub. All of Major League Baseball, several NFL and NHL teams and many college teams scalp their own tickets through StubHub.

There are some notable exceptions among rock groups. When Springsteen found out in 2009 that on the same day his tickets were going on sale at Ticketmaster, they were also going on sale at Ticketmaster's scalping site, TicketsNow, he blew a gasket. Years earlier, the Grateful Dead essentially told Ticketmaster to shove it and demanded that it be allowed to sell 50% of its own tickets. That way, it could take care of the Deadheads. Other bands have tried to reward loyalty with similar fan club setups that gave preferential ticket treatment.

Springsteen and a few others should also get credit for doing the best they can to keep prices down. He's big enough that he can do it. His ticket prices are well below the average. While similar groups, in terms of popularity, are over $100, he'll be at $65. Tom Petty and a couple of others try to do the same.

But, here comes Jimmy Buffet again. His agent, Howard Rose, required me and every promoter in the country to send 150 to 200 tickets to his office in Hollywood for each concert. Then, Howard would send the tickets to Howard Kaufman, who was Jimmy's manager. Kaufman would then sell the tickets to Sandy Simon, a big L.A. ticket broker who would pay Kaufman $50 a ticket over the face value. Simon would then send them around the country to ticket brokers who would mark them up again.

A Rolling Stone reporter got wind of this arrangement and called me and several other promoters. He had it all sourced out and was going to run a story on it, but somehow, it never showed up in the magazine. I was told that Irving called Jann Wenner and the story was killed. Rose and Kaufman later said they'd always intended for the $50 to go to charity.

Speaking of charity, many groups are pledging $X above face value per ticket sold to charity. That has a warm and fuzzy feel to it. But, personal experience suggests there's too much opportunity for that money to get diverted to other pockets. Petty's manager agrees. Tony Dimitriades has said that if a group wants to give money to charity, then just give to charity. He said "anything that encourages tickets to be sold for above face value isn't good. Even for charity, it's still giving these tickets to the elite. We prefer to save some front-row tickets and other good seats each show and go to people with bad seats and give them these for nothing."

I am standing and applauding.

But, for the most part, greed has sucked the heart and soul out of the music business.

Muhammad Ali

August 12, 1981, I was working in my office when I heard a commotion in the lobby. Commotion in my office wasn't unusual, but this had a different sound to it. I walked out to see what was going on and there was Muhammad Ali playfully sparring with my 14-year-old son Alan. Everyone in the office had dropped what they were doing and had gathered around. Muhammad Ali was in our office!

A month earlier, the office had given me as a birthday present an Everlast punching bag. Each of them signed it with something clever like, "Punch this instead of me, Barry".

Ali signed it "The Greatest" and dated it for me. Then, he walked into my office accompanied by a very pretty young white lady from Memphis. He was being honored in Denver the next night with a big to-do at the Regency Hotel. Everyone was going to be there—politicians, civic leaders, athletes—and, most importantly and the reason he was in my office, his wife. He asked me to "make a new friend" of this woman and be her date to the event. Ali wanted me with her all the time that I could while she was in Denver, *except* the times that he could steal away and be with her. In other words, I was going to be his beard so his wife wouldn't be suspicious. What could I say to "The Greatest"? Of course I did it.

We went to the Regency for the gala. People were falling all over themselves to get close to Ali. My "date" and I sat at the same table with Muhammad and his wife and a few others. The evening went well and, as far as I know, our "rope-a-dope" ruse worked as Muhammad had planned.

Here's the weird thing about that experience: I'd never talked to or met Muhammad Ali before his visit to my office. I never found out why he chose me. I was so stunned by his request, I never asked. Maybe I didn't really care because I got to spend time with him. And with a very pretty woman.

Saving The Symphony

In April of 1989, I was reading "The Denver Post" and in a headline box at the top of the page it read, "Board to Decide Fate of Symphony Today". Symphonies all across the country were failing because they were doing the same thing the Denver Symphony was doing, which was running it like a private club, basically saying, "Give us your endowment, give us your money, but we don't want you coming". I called my columnist friend at the Post, Dick Kreck, and asked him what was going on. He said the board, headed by John Low, was going to decide whether to declare bankruptcy and shut down the symphony. Denver would not have a symphony. I said, "Who the fuck are these guys to decide whether Denver has a symphony orchestra or not?"

"That's just the way it is, Barry."

"What can I do about it?"

"Well, let me have Lee Yeingst call you. He's the president of the Denver Symphony Orchestra."

Lee called me. "What can I do for you?"

I said, "Well, it's just not right."

He said, "We can't continue. We haven't been paid since March" and this and that.

I said, "Why don't you get together with the orchestra and see if they want to work out a deal where I'll take them over, go on a show by show basis and pay our bills after every show?" He said he'd take the idea to the symphony and get back to me.

They called me down to a meeting and I pitched my idea. Some of them liked it, some of them didn't. The Denver Symphony was threatening this and that. But, a few months later, three days before Lisa and I were to be married, the majority of the musicians voted to go with my plan. We organized a big comeback show in October at McNichols Arena for the new Colorado Symphony Orchestra. Every television and radio station got behind it—even the sports radio show of "Irv and Joe", which sent three buses full of people. Over 13,000 people showed up. As I did with so many of my rock shows, I stepped to the microphone and did the intro: "Ladies and gentlemen, please welcome your Colorado Symphony Orchestra". By the time that night was over, I was crying, because those gutsy musicians, 99% of them, had held out and it had paid off. It has continued

Rock promoter Barry Fey, at right, bankrolled the Colorado Symphony's first concerts, including one at McNichols Arena.

ROCKY MOUNTAIN NEWS/198

to pay off over the years. There've been ups and downs, and the so-called elite of Denver society boycotted the "people's symphony" for a while, but it's still going.

They gave me a plaque:

> *"The Colorado Symphony salutes Barry Fey, the*
> *man who lit the fuse and ignited the rocket*
> *that is now known as the Colorado Symphony."*

The appreciation dimmed. On the tenth anniversary of the Colorado Symphony, I called and said, "Listen, let's do another show. I'll promote it for free, I don't want any money. We'll do a big show to celebrate ten years." They came back and said, "No, we don't want to be reminded of the bad times." They could have made another quarter million dollars.

Lisa lost her honeymoon because I had to get the show ready. But, it was for a good cause. I'm not bragging, but I saved the symphony. I really did. And I also saved the Paramount Theater, later, when a guy had gotten around the historic designation, declared a hardship and was going to tear it down. I negotiated with him and came away with a ten-year contract that saved the Paramount. In

1994, we donated 50 cents from each ticket sold during the summer at Red Rocks and Fiddler's Green, raising money to keep metro Denver recreation centers open longer during the summer so kids would have somewhere safe to go. Despite all of my bravado and madman act, I've done some really good shit for the City of Denver.

Mikhail Baryshnikov

In 1985, we sold out two shows at Red Rocks for ballet legend Mikhail Baryshnikov. He never made it on stage. He travels with his own wooden dance floor to put down on the stage, but it was raining, so we had to move it indoors at McNichols Arena.

The seating footprint was much different at Big Mac. For example, there were no side view seats at Red Rocks, but there were thousands at Big Mac. Hopefully, those people enjoyed their peeks into the stage wings where Misha was doing his warm-ups between numbers. We were meticulous in making sure that the people who would have had the front rows at Red Rocks would have the front rows at McNichols. Nice try. We were bombarded with complaints because the stage at Big Mac was high enough that people sitting in the front few rows couldn't see Misha's feet.

Scared To Death in Sarajevo

My phone rang in late 1995. It was the U.S. State Department asking if I'd like to book a concert.

I still don't know why they called me, but that was during the Clinton years and I'd been to the White House a few times and Pat Schroeder had a lot of clout as Denver's Congresswoman.

"Where do you want to hold a concert?"

"Sarajevo."

"Really!"

"Yes." And they wanted me and one of my employees to go there to scope it out and see what it would take to make it happen.

Now, the truce in Bosnia was only a couple of months old and I had no idea how to prepare. We didn't know what we were going into. My production manager, Nick Williams, and I decided that we needed to be ready. We decided that taking bulletproof vests were a waste of time.

"Nicky, we need to take guns."

"What are you talking about? They took all the guns away from the troops. You think they're going to let us bring guns?"

He bought a .45 and I bought a .38. When we got to customs in Zagreb, they were confiscated.

On January 3, 1996, a guide picked us up in a van. Along with Nicky and I, there was a news crew from a Denver TV station and two people from the State Department.

As I said, the truce was still fresh and apparently not all of the Serbian rebels got the message. On the highway to Sarajevo, there was a Serb road block. Now me, with my big mouth, wanted to give them the business and tell them to get the fuck out of our way, there's a truce, there aren't supposed to be any roadblocks. But, our driver pleaded with me to be quiet because he was on a Serbian hit list and was afraid I'd get him killed.

So, instead of going the rest of the 30 miles to Sarajevo on a modern, paved highway, the Serbs ordered us to take a left and go over a rugged mountain trail to get to Sarajevo. It's the dead of winter, it's snowing hard and at the top of the mountain pass our van got stuck. I think that was the most afraid I'd ever been, including when I was in the Marine Corps.

"Nicky, I think we're going to die."

"Barry, you know that I always try to cheer you up..."

"Yeah?"

"But this time I think you're right."

After about an hour or so later of digging, pushing, putting things under the tires, the van started to move. We were on our way down the other side of the mountain.

But, the van skidded to a stop. For some reason, the driver sensed something was wrong. Just before we were about to cross a bridge, be brought the van to a stop. We all got out and looked. There was no bridge. It had been bombed. The driver turned around and found another way to get to Sarajevo, but we didn't arrive at the hotel until about 3 in the morning.

At daylight, I looked out the window of the hotel and I couldn't believe what I was seeing. Every building was damaged. Most of them looked like the Murrah Federal Building in Oklahoma City after Timothy McVeigh got done with it. Incredible damage. The hotel we were in had been heavily damaged; part of it was gone, there were sections of the floor that were missing and the walls in many of the rooms were pockmarked with bullet holes and mortar damage. And they wanted me to put on a concert here?

I went for a walk one day—there were areas where it was safe to walk without fear of being picked off by a sniper sitting miles away in the mountains. And, IFOR troops were stationed at nearly every corner, so I felt fairly safe. There was a girl, probably 17 or 18, standing on a corner.

"You're American, aren't you?"

"Yes, I am," not sure where this was going.

She started crying and told me a story that made me cry. Made me sick.

Less than a year earlier, she and her 15-year-old sister were living with their mother and father. On a Friday afternoon, five Serbian rebels broke down their door, shot and killed their mother and father and over the weekend, took turns raping the girls. On Monday, the soldiers left the girls with their dead parents.

She's crying. I'm crying. I just don't get it. The "ethnic cleansing" as they called it; the Holocaust; the genocide in Rwanda; how can people do that to other people?

We said goodbye. I went back to the hotel and told someone that I was going home to hug my wife and children.

Before we left, I made arrangements for the concert. We went to Kosovo Stadium, a soccer stadium, which would hold about 30,000. It had been used as a morgue during the attacks on the city and was one of the only big spaces left. Most of the soccer fields had been converted to graveyards. So many people were slaughtered that the graveyards ran out of room. Nicky and I surveyed the stadium and decided where we'd put the stage.

Back in Denver, one of the first groups I called was Metallica. They couldn't believe what I was asking of them.

"They're still shooting people over there, aren't they?"

"Yeah."

"And you want us to go?"

Metallica said no and, as it turned out, I didn't finish the concert plans. A charity group that was involved was making it too political and I didn't want to be in the middle of a no-win situation. But, my team and I laid the groundwork for a U2 concert that was held there about a year later.

Hey, Mrs. Robinson, We Found Joltin' Joe!

"Where have you gone, Joe DiMaggio,
Our nation turns it's lonely eyes to you.
What's that you say, Mrs. Robinson.
Joltin' Joe has left and gone away,
Hey hey hey."

—Paul Simon

Without a doubt, the finest thing I've ever done as a promoter was on September 30, 1983. Mile High Stadium in Denver was packed with fans for "The Denver Dream".

There was no stage. There was a pitcher's mound and a batting box. Instead of guitars and drums, there were bats and balls. Instead of Jagger, Richards, Hendrix, Morrison, Daltrey and Townshend, there were DiMaggio, Mays, Aaron, Banks, Ford, Marichal and many others.

When I was putting it together and was promoting it even though I didn't have the players confirmed yet, I held a news conference. A reporter asked me, "How many tickets do you need to sell to break even?" I said, "A little less than 30,000". The gathered press shook their heads at this fool who thought Denver baseball fans would turn out in those numbers. They laughed when I predicted that we'd come closer to selling out than losing money. We drew over 58,000 and it started people thinking about Major League Baseball in Denver. People were standing with tears in their eyes an hour after the event.

In 1983, Zane Bresloff, a friend of mine from Chicago, who I'd brought here several years earlier to work for me at Select-A-Seat and went on to promote wrestling for Vince McMahon, introduced me to Ernie "Let's Play Two!" Banks, "Mr. Cub" and his agent at the time. I told them that I'd always wanted to put on an Old Timer's Baseball game in Denver. Ernie helped me contact and line up the rest of the legends. I brought in Jack "Hey, Hey" Brickhouse, a legend in Chicago sports broadcasting with the Cubs, as the emcee. He introduced the players and they lined up on each base line, the way it's done before MLB All-Star games and such. And when Joe DiMaggio came out of the dugout, even though he was wearing a suit—he wore his uniform the second year—the place went wild. Joe was majestic, regal, a god. He hit in 56 straight games and slept with

Marilyn Monroe. What more could a mortal do? I was standing with my sons, Alan, Geoffrey and Jeremy, all of them in their baseball uniforms and I started crying. I'd been telling them for so long about my love for Major League baseball as a kid, loving the Cubs, and I was finally able to give them a glimpse of that.

After the game, people were still hanging around outside the stadium an hour later, reminiscing about baseball in their childhoods and crying. No event I promoted had a bigger emotional impact on the audience. It was after midnight and people were still hanging around. I didn't want to leave the ballpark. The radio station that broadcast the game, KOA, was putting callers on the air for hours after the game, each of them telling how special it was to them.

Who won? Billy Williams, the Cubs legend, hit a home run over the center field wall, 400 and some feet, in the ninth inning to win it.

Fans who got there two hours before the game could line up on the field where the players were sitting at card tables and get autographs, for nothing. This was before players' signatures became a big business. Mickey Mantle was there for the second year and there was a huge line for him, snaking through the stands.

That second year, Joe DiMaggio left his "number five" Yankees uniform in the clubhouse. Someone from the stadium called a couple of days later and asked what they should do with it. I had them send it to me, and I sent it to Joe. I didn't even check to see whether he wanted it back, I just sent it. I should have called. Maybe he would have told me to keep it. Others have told me that it would have been worth a fortune. But, to me, it's priceless and wouldn't have been for sale.

The only player I tried to get and couldn't was Ted Williams. The Splendid Splinter told me that he only played in those kinds of games for Mrs. Yawkey, the Red Sox owner.

The players who'd accepted my invitation in 1984 wanted the vice-president at that time, George Herbert Walker Bush to play. He was a baseball player at Yale, quite an athlete and he got a hit. (So did I, in batting practice. Whitey Ford was pitching and I connected. Earlier, during the press conference announcing the game, Ernie Banks was there and lobbed me a ball that I hit over the left-field fence, which was short because of the football field configuration. But still, Barry Fey went deep!)

Before the game, when George is still in the dressing room getting ready, the Secret Service wouldn't let me on the field.

"We're sorry, sir, you can't walk on the field until the vice-president has left the stadium."

I looked at them and said, "I rented this stadium. Mr. Bush is here as my guest. If I say he doesn't play, he don't fuckin' play. Now, if you don't get out of my way, then you can have the pleasure of going into the clubhouse and telling him that he can get dressed and get the fuck outta here."

They were stunned. I don't think they'd ever been talked to like that. They glanced at a couple of Denver cops standing nearby, who nodded at them as if to say, "he's serious", or maybe, "save yourself some brain damage and let him in", and they stepped aside. I could be such an asshole and I don't know where along the line I got the idea that I could talk to people like that, but it worked.

I did two more Old Timers Games, which many believe, including me, showed Major League Baseball and the rest of the country that Denver could support a franchise. When the Colorado Rockies arrived in 1993, MLB attendance records were set that may never be broken.

The baseball games were so successful, I decided to give football a try. On July 22, 1988, I sold air. I sold ice to the Eskimos. I mean, who in their right mind would pay $15 to watch a flag-football game featuring former stars who were long past their prime. 31,000 people did. And what a show they got! The Broncos All-Stars vs. the Raiders All-Stars. Lyle Alzado played for the Broncos in the first half and for the Raiders in the second. The Broncos won, 62-54.

The second game was on September 15, 2001: "Say Goodbye to Mile High" the last event before the stadium was torn down. It was the Broncos All-Stars vs. a group of NFL All-Stars. The legendary John Elway, whose dozens of come-from-behind game-saving drives kept Denver cardiologists in business, called the plays for a "Who's Who" of former Broncos: Otis Armstrong, Floyd Little, Louis Wright, Rick Upchurch, Vance Johnson, Randy Gradishar, Karl Mecklenberg, Haven Moses, Dennis Smith, Steve Atwater and a dozen more. The All-Stars had Joe Montana at quarterback, backed up by a Hall of Fame lineup including ex-49ers Roger Craig and Ray Guy, ex-Raiders Jan Stenerud, Dave Casper and Ted Hendricks, and Marcus Allen, Herschel Walker, Tony Dorsett, Willie Lanier, Ed "Too Tall" Jones, Lawrence Taylor, Bob Lilly and William "The Refrigerator" Perry.

I didn't make much money on that game because the big-name players were expensive. Elway got $100,000. Montana cost me $80,000.

Music was my occupation. Sports were my true love.

Axl Rose and My .357

In 1992, I booked stadium shows for Guns N' Roses and Metallica, including one at Mile High Stadium in Denver. We sold 48,000 tickets for a warm September night. It was going to be great.

But, I'd been warned that in Toronto a week earlier G N' R's front man, Axl Rose, had walked out on the concert, started a riot and people got hurt. I wasn't going to let that happen on my watch.

So, things are going okay. Metallica does its set. The place is rockin'. Literally, the steel stadium seats would sway a little when everyone was standing and stomping and yelling. The rumble of the metal stands being stomped on is what became known as "Rocky Mountain Thunder" during Denver Broncos NFL games.

G N' R comes out and starts to play "Welcome To The Jungle". Man, that's one of the greatest concert opening songs ever!

I'm out in front watching the crowd, checking the sound, just like I do with every show. They're crankin' along, things seem perfect. As I go back stage, one of my guys runs up and says Axl has left.

"What do you mean he left?"

"He's gone, he got in a limo and left!"

I walk backstage and find Big John, who was in charge of the limos. I told him, "You don't work for Axl Rose. You work for me. If you ever want to see another fuckin' dime of my money, you get that fuckin' car back here! And make sure the only way Rose gets out of that car before he gets back here is if he jumps out on the street."

In the meantime, the rest of the band is up there jamming. 25 minutes goes by and the crowd's getting restless and is starting to boo. People were even taking the t-shirts they bought for G N' R back to the stands and demanding a Metallica shirt instead. G N' R didn't know what to do. They sent someone to Metallica's dressing room and asked them to come back on stage.

Lars Ulrich of Metallica's message was something like, "You bozos don't have enough money in your collective bank accounts to get me back on stage." I didn't know what to do, so I went to my car and got my .357 and stuck it in my back pocket.

The limo came back, Axl trudged back on stage and the concert goes on. I put two big security guys at the bottom of the stage steps along with a couple of Denver cops. The only way he was getting off that stage was to go through the audience. And if that happened, I would run on stage and announce that Axl decided he didn't want to play for you nice folks, so please give him a nice farewell.

The show went on pretty much as planned and afterward, I found out that Axl had an argument with Slash and that's why he walked out. But he was a manic-depressive heroin addict. No shocker that he was unreliable.

Would I have shot him? I don't know. There's no percentage in talking to a fuckin' madman who would walk out in the first place.

That was the same night of Slash's bachelor party at the Embassy Suites. All the guys who went were handed tickets, like you'd get at a raffle. If you took a blue one, that meant you wanted to get laid. A yellow one meant you wanted a blow job. A red one got you both.

But that gun thing has followed me. Ever since then the first thing Lars says when he sees me is, "Hey, Barry...you packin'? You packin' today man?"

You never know.

And I'm the Queen of England

My business relationships with the groups I booked occasionally turned into social and personal relationships: Bono and U2, Truman Capote, Roger Daltrey, John Denver, Jerry Garcia, Jimi Hendrix, Mick Jagger, Sam Kinison, Steve Miller, Jim Morrison, Willie Nelson, Ozzy and Sharon Osbourne, Robert Plant, Keith Richards,

David Lee Roth, Pete Townshend, Lars Ulrich, Ronnie Van Zant and Ronnie Wood. I included Truman in that group because I met him through the Stones.

All of them became good friends over the years. Most of them were at my house, more than once. But, just for perspective, the ones who are still alive have, for the most part, continued being among the world's most famous people. Me? I'm just Barry. The only one who I can say crossed over from friend into best friend territory was Ronnie Van Zant. We'd talk frequently about nothing and every-thing. Our loyalty to each other was unchallenged and what he did for me when a manager tried to take some of his tour away from me, man, I loved him for that.

The others didn't call as much as Ronnie, but they'd call now and then. When I was in Los Angeles once, my first wife Cindy was at home when the phone rang.

"Is BAR-ee there?"

"No, he isn't. Who's this?"

"This is Mick Jagger."

Cindy said, "Yeah, and I'm the Queen of England."

Luckily, she didn't hang up and Mick was able to convince her who he was and she gave him my hotel number in L.A.

Part Seven

IN THE KEY OF G

- ○ **Groupies**

- ○ **Goon Squad**

- ○ **Gambling**

*Winner of the 1983 Caesars Palace Handicapping Contest.
That's $104,000 in my hand.*

Groupies

I was anti-groupie. To me, they were interfering with my business. They were always hanging around hoping to get invited backstage and into dressing rooms and wherever and I had no patience for any of it. I knew of other promoters who would take advantage of the girls, but I didn't have any time or interest. But, they'd always get in because a roadie or manager or doorman would let them backstage. If I caught them, my standard greeting was, "Get the fuck out of here!" And it wasn't because they weren't offering me any of their special kind of friendship.

There was the time when I had The Who and Lynyrd Skynyrd in St. Louis, under the Arch at the Arena. I was backstage when I got a page. I picked up the phone and the operator said, "There's a young lady here to see you." So, I walked to the front and met this girl named Connie. Connie Hamzy.

"Joel (Brandes, one of my national tour guys) told me to come and see you at the show and you'd make sure I got in."

God damn Joel, just what I needed! I reluctantly told her to follow me. She was kind of pretty in a girl-next-door kind of way. She had a little camel-hair coat on and knee socks; you know, like she was in school.

As we're walking down this long corridor toward backstage, she put her arm around my neck and whispered in my ear, "I want to lick your balls and I want to suck your cock."

A guy doesn't get that kind of offer everyday, but I was so shocked and, as intriguing as it was, I told her that I wasn't interested. What I said exactly was: "Wait a minute. There are two rules. You keep your filthy mouth shut and keep your fuckin' hands off me!"

This is the same Connie—from Little Rock—who was memorialized in "American Band" by Grand Funk Railroad.

> *Out on the road for forty days*
> *Last night in Little Rock, put me in a haze*
> *Sweet, sweet Connie was doin' her act*
> *She had the whole show and that's a natural fact*

So, we were backstage in St. Louis while The Who performed. The two managers of record of The Who were Chris Stamp and Kit Lambert. I went in the dressing room to get one of them because there was a problem and there was Sweet, Sweet Connie doin' her act, giving one of them a blow job while the other one was giving it to her from behind. I just turned around and left and a few minutes later, Connie comes out of the dressing room and walked up to where I'm standing with my wife Cindy, my assistant Leslie Haseman and Mina Low, who was regarded as the head groupie among the Denver girls and who I'd kicked out of many shows. She'd apparently been invited by somebody in the band to make the trip to St. Louis.

Connie, slurring her words as if she'd had a stroke, asked, "Do you know where I can rinse out my mouth?"

The ladies were so embarrassed and you can imagine the looks on their faces. One of them directed her to the drinking fountain.

That night backstage, there was a huge argument over some missing money among The Who and its managers. I heard Roger Daltrey yelling at Chris and Kit, "We don't need you anymore and get the fuck away from us." And that's the last I saw of either of them. But, I wasn't sure what the Who's management arrangement was at that point. Like I said, Stamp and Lambert were "managers of record", but there were also Bill Curbishley and Peter Rudge. Rudge is long gone and doing something else. Curbishley, a great guy and talented producer who also resurrected Robert Plant's and Jimmy Page's careers, remains as the Who's manager.

Back to Connie: She was the one who showed up the most at my shows. For years—spanning both of my marriages—I'd get homemade Christmas cards from her. She'd go somewhere, say New York, and pose nude in front of a landmark, a statue or something, and send it to me as a card. Neither of my wives liked that for some reason.

Another Who groupie story was in 1971 when the band played in Miami in November. The roadie for John Entwistle—each of the guys had their own roadie—picked up a real pretty girl in Miami and took her on tour with him. A couple of weeks later, they arrived in Denver. The roadie couldn't find his girl and started looking around the hotel—I think it was the old Radisson downtown—and found out that she was in Roger Daltrey's room. The roadie's livid, fuming, but doesn't do anything then. I mean, come on, he's the roadie for the bass player and how's he going to compete for a groupie with the lead singer? That night at the Coliseum, I was backstage before the show and from one of the other rooms, I heard screaming. I ran to see what had happened and Entwistle's roadie had Daltrey by the throat—of all the places to grab the lead singer! —and was trying to strangle him. My security guy, L.C. and I, ran over and grabbed this guy, tore him off Daltrey, started banging his head against the wall and told him, "Don't you ever touch Daltrey again! Settle this after Denver if you want, but leave him alone here."

Some of the groupies adopted gimmicks to set themselves apart from the crowd. There were the "Plaster Casters", led by a woman from Chicago named Cynthia. She and her fellow caster would—if they could get the guys to cooperate—make plaster casts of rock stars' cocks. She claims to have gotten Jimi and Noel Redding, but most of the others on her list are roadie-level guys.

Another of the more noteworthy groupies was a woman who called herself The Butter Queen. Barbara Cope of Dallas. She decided to spend the summer in Denver and gave me a call.

"You're the promoter, right?"

"Yes, I am."

"I'm the Butter Queen. Have you ever heard of me?"

"Yes, I have." What I had heard about her was that once she got a guy's attention, she would use a stick of butter in creative ways.

"This is just a courtesy introduction. I'm not going to bother you. I never have trouble getting in to shows."

The Butter Queen was immortalized by Jagger and Richards in one verse of "Rip This Joint":

From San Jose down to Santa Fe
Kiss me quick, baby, won'tcha make my day
Down to New Orleans with the Dixie Queen
'Cross to Dallas, Texas with the Butter Queen

I'm sure the dairy industry was quite proud.

My resistance and dislike of groupies pretty much ended in January of 1973. I was with the Stones in Hawaii for three shows after the Nicaraguan Earthquake Benefit Concert scam in L.A. It wasn't a total scam because hundreds of thousands of dollars were raised, but the reason for the concert was a scam, as I explain in the Rolling Stones' chapter.

I was walking by the pool one afternoon about a week before the concert at the Hilton Hawaiian Village and I heard someone shout my name. Nobody knows me in Hawaii, so I figured I must have been hearing things and kept walking. But, again, "Barry!"

I looked again and saw Mina Low, the aforementioned number one groupie from Denver.

"What are you doing here?" I asked.

"I'm down here with some guys." She was a very pretty girl and had befriended a few fellows who appreciated her company on a trip to the islands. I was polite to her; I mean, the Hilton wasn't my venue and I couldn't kick her out.

"How long are you going to be here?" I asked.

"Tomorrow morning, but I understand the Stones are coming. Are you doing those shows?

"Yes."

"Is there any way I could see them?"

"I tell you what, Mina. The day after tomorrow, I have to go to L.A. to do the Stones earthquake benefit show there. I've got an office adjoining my suite. If you wouldn't mind staying there and taking calls, taking messages so I don't miss any business calls, I'll let you see the show."

"I'd love to do that."

After letting the other gentlemen know that she wouldn't be going back with them, she came back to the hotel with me. I showed her where she'd be staying; the office, which is actually a bedroom. The door between the rooms was unlocked. She asked if she could move her bag into the office. Sure, go ahead.

Several minutes later, as I'm sitting on the bed, watching TV (which is pretty much what I do most of life) the door opened. Mina walked in wearing a silk robe. She stopped in front of me and opened the robe and she had nothing on. Now, did I mention that this girl was beautiful? I lost my breath. She seduced me. I'd never done anything like that. I spent the next couple of hours living like a rock star, but, as always with me, I got hungry. We went downstairs to the, I think it was called, "The Golden Dragon", a bar-restaurant in the hotel. After we ate—absolutely great Chinese spareribs—we went for a long walk on the beach, having a lot of fun and on our way back, we did it again in a park. Wow.

After the L.A. show, I flew with the Stones to Honolulu and we had dinner for the boys. I invited Mina. That was the end of that. Jagger laid eyes on her and just like that, it was back to watching TV for me. I didn't care, I wasn't jealous. Come on...he's Mick Jagger, I'm Barry Fey. If you're a girl, there ain't a lot of choice. Besides, it gave me something in common with Eric Clapton. In the late '80s, he told CBS's "60 Minutes" that Jagger stole his girlfriend, an Italian model, which set off homicidal fantasies.

So, after Hawaii, my policy toward groupies was different.

The Goon Squad

One thing was made crystal clear at the Denver Pop Festival: the cops weren't good at rock concert crowd control. At nearly every concert all over the country, crowds didn't need much to get rowdy and their was plenty of fuel: the civil rights tensions, Vietnam protests, a huge generation gap and a general hatred and distrust of authority, of which the "pigs" were the point men. The uniformed police with their riot helmets and clubs only made things worse. We had confrontations every night. I'd book a show, then live with the anxiety of it for 30 or 40 days and then dread it when it would come, because I knew there would be problems. Somebody was going to do something stupid which would get in the way of the audience enjoying the music. I hated that. The most important thing to me was the audience, keeping the audience safe.

So, to try to keep the cops out of the arenas and eliminate that source of tension, we formed our Peer Group Security, what some people called the Goon Squad. They were guys who looked like most of the many of the rest of the fans, long hair and all that, but twice as big. Huge guys. Our "front line" was bigger than those on most pro football teams.

Tony Funches had worked security for the Stones and was Jim Morrison's body guard until the end. When The Doors came to Denver, Tony was there. I liked how he operated, a real smooth guy who was tough as nails and put up with zero bullshit. I tried to hire him several times. Finally got him. He became the head of my concert security. Tony was about 6'7", 275 pounds. I asked if he could find other guys like him, so he scouted around and found some beef loaders at a packing house. They were monsters who muscled sides of beef around for eight hours a day. John Suzey weighed about 325. Ernie Kaiser was 350. We had Larry and Jerry McKim, "the Twins", that's how they were known on the street. "Oh, you don't want to mess with the Twins, man." One of them was 295 and the other was 305. And their brother, Big John, was 320. L.C. Clayton, who Tony brought in was a little smaller, 6'3", 240, but he was the toughest of them all.

We made up yellow t-shirts with crossed tennis shoes on the front, because I always wore tennis shoes and on the back, it said: "May I Help You?" The irony of that was that they had a terrible reputation and, actually, weren't very nice guys. But, you needed tough guys to keep the people safe. If some idiots started trouble, they may have gotten roughed up a little, but my guys kept the innocent fans safe and for the troublemakers, dealing with my guys was better than being shot or tear gassed or thrown in jail. When we did out-of-town shows, the halls wanted me to bring our security, because they knew how to keep the peace.

One newspaper guy told me once, "The reason you have security is to protect the crowd from you." True, to some degree. They stopped me a few times when I wanted to run up into the stands and get into it with some idiot. It was a rough and tumble business back then.

After the violence pretty much ended in the early '70s, they became glorified ushers. Those big guys were good at clearing aisles, I'll tell you. And, they were smart. They could see bad situations developing and would prevent them. I can guarantee you this: If my guys had been in charge of security for the 1979 Who show in Cincinnati where eleven people died in a stampede, there would never have been a problem. It was general seating and, as is usually the case when you have first-come-first-in, fans arrived hours early. It was bitterly cold, which is the first thing my guys would have addressed. Rule number one: you make sure your customers are safe. It wasn't safe out there because of the cold. Aggravating the problem was that The Who had a late sound check; the thousands waiting outside heard it and thought the concert was starting and tried to rush the locked doors. Eleven kids at the front, most of teenagers, were crushed, trampled and suffocated. There's no excuse for that happening.

Four Dead in Ohio and West Virginia + 6 ½

Most of my life has been a gamble, basically. I mean, just look at the business model of being a rock concert promoter. You send thousands of dollars—tens or hundreds of thousands of dollars—to a bunch of guys on the promise that they'll show up so that you can send thousands of dollars to a venue to reserve a date and spend thousands of dollars for ticketing and security and set up and do it all on the bet that the weather will be good, if it's an outdoor show, and that enough people will buy tickets so that you can recoup your investment and then some.

But, I was known to do some actual betting—on sports and horses, mainly. Casino gambling never really interested me. I was smart enough to figure out that those big, glittery casinos and hotels weren't built with gamblers' winnings.

I loved gambling. It started early in my life and I quickly learned the down side of losing. I remember my first bet on a horse. It was the early '60s. I was working on the docks in Chicago after I got out of the Marines and there was a horse track called Washington Park about 20 miles south of The Loop. It isn't there anymore. I bet $6 on a horse called Qudel. He paid $90. I'd never had that much money in my pocket. I was hooked and before long, I was bumming around, and I mean bumming around and taking money from loan sharks just to get money to bet. I'll never forget this one guy, Budy. He hung out in a pool room on the South Side of Chicago.

"Budy, I've got to have $5000."

He said, "Well, you come with good references." I knew a lot of the "right" people. Then, he put a gun to my head, right to my temple.

"Don't take this money. You're a nice Jewish kid and I don't want to have to kill you."

I don't know where I got the balls, but instead of thanking him and getting the hell out of there, I said, "Give me the money".

I thought I was a good gambler, an excellent gambler, smart. But, I lost it all. $5000. And, I missed some payments to Budy. I'd paid most of what I owed, but couldn't come up with the rest. The only assets I had were my Cubs' tickets.

Every year, my sister Sheila would buy me season tickets as a gift. Box 65, Tier 1, Seat 1. A great seat. It was between home and first base. One Saturday morning, I took all my season tickets to the Wrigley box office. The Cubs ticket manager, Jack Maloney, said, "Barry, these are great seats. You sure you want to sell them?"

"I don't want to. I have to." I saw Sandy Koufax pitch for the Dodgers in those seats. I saw Henry Aaron hit for the Braves in those seats. It broke my heart to sell the tickets.

I took the money down to the South Side and paid off Budy.

Taylor Street in Chicago, where all of the great Italian restaurants are now, is where another shark hung out at a bar. I was there to confess to him that I didn't have his money when a guy came in who was late on paying his juice. They sat him down at the bar and he was going, "Hey man, I'm sorry I'm late", blah, blah, blah. "I won't be late again". They took him out the back and beat the shit out of him. As I slunk out the door, I learned from that not to show up unless you could pay your juice.

But, I was a slow learner. I got into another guy for about three grand. One night, there was a knock on my apartment door, I opened it up and, POW! He punched me in the face. No "Hey, you owe me money", or "Give me my money", he just popped me. Then he said, "You'd better get me my fucking money." And left.

Message received.

But, that didn't stop me from gambling. I loved the horses. And I still do, although I stopped gambling in 2003. But, I was good at it and I won hundreds of thousands of dollars. I was so good at handicapping that many bookies didn't want to handle my bets. There was a bookie in Denver, Paul Villano. He was more than a great bookie who paid on time, he was a great guy. Anytime I needed anything, he'd help. But, he'd also take my bets and I usually won. One time, in the early ''70s, Paulie took my bet on the three Big Eight football teams who were in bowl games: Nebraska, Oklahoma and Colorado. I bet $10,000 on each team and a $5,000 three-team parlay, so Paulie owed me $60,000. As promised, Pauley shows up with his money, but there's an older guy with him.

"Hello Barry, I'm Chauncey Smaldone."

Everybody in Denver had heard of the Smaldones. Brothers Clyde, Checkers and Chauncey were Denver's version of the Chicago Outfit, but on a much smaller and less violent scale. They weren't Mafia, but if there was small-time stuff like loansharking, prostitution, drugs and bookmaking going on in Colorado, they probably had their fingers in it. I'd never met any of them. The only guy I knew was Paulie, who was the Smaldones' nephew. Anyway, Chauncey shows up and watches Paulie pay me my winnings.

Smaldone said, "I didn't believe anybody could beat Paulie so much and on such a regular basis." He must have thought Paulie was fucking him, that I was just some sort of make-believe account. But, he saw me get paid, we shook hands and I never saw him again.

Paulie died in 2003 at the age of 76. I went to his funeral and person after person got up and told stories about how good he was to them and how he'd get them free tickets. Something compelled me to get up and speak.

"All those tickets Paulie was giving you, where do you think they were coming from?" They all laughed. "Let me tell you something about Paul Villano. You look in the dictionary under friend, his picture's there." He was great to me. If I needed cash, if I was short and needed several thousand for a few days, he was right there with his rubber band. He always carried his cash rolled up in a rubber band.

Betting on college football led to me being indicted with a dozen others after an FBI investigation. The rest were all bookies; all I was, was a bettor. I needed an attorney and went to see Melvin Belli, who'd made a name for himself by representing celebrities, including the Stones and Chuck Berry. He told me there was an Article 1952, or something like that, stated that a mere bettor shall not be construed to be in violation of the law.

"You're absolutely innocent and we'll make such a big case out of this...."

I didn't really want the notoriety that came with Belli, so I went to see Morris Schenker, who was Jimmy Hoffa's attorney. The reason I was able to get an appointment with him was because of a guy I knew named Kenny Lipsitz, whose grandmother helped raise Morris when he came to the U.S.

"You don't have to worry," Morris told me. "They'll try to get you for aiding and abetting, but they won't get you." But, the federal charges against me were filed in California and I had to defend myself there. I hired a California attorney named Richard Sherman, who turned out to be worthless to me.

The other 12, who all had priors for interstate gambling, theft and racketeering, pled guilty and got probation; no jail time, no fines. I wouldn't plead guilty.

The prosecutor was a guy named Ron Leibowitz who pronounced it LEB-owitz; maybe he didn't want people to think he was Jewish. I asked him why he was charging me, I was just a bettor. He said, "I don't give a shit about you. You're just a statistic. If I can nail you, our numbers look better and we'll get more appropriations." I went for him. Other people had to pull me off. I mean, how dare he so casually throw my life away to make his "numbers" look better!

They were going to drain me dry. Leibowitz told me that if I didn't plead guilty, they would keep me in court forever. They had

150 yards of telephone transcripts from the taps on the bookies' phones and they were going to read every line in court. I wasn't going to win. That's what the feds can do to you; they make it so you can't go on.

On top of it all, I was busy as hell with concerts. Between June 14th and June 30th I had ten shows with the Rolling Stones, four shows with Led Zeppelin and one show with Jethro Tull. And that fuck Leibowitz was messing with me just because he could.

When the feds summoned me to Los Angeles, there'd been a shooting on Spring Street in downtown L.A. and for some reason, two of the suspects were brought to the Federal Courthouse where I was waiting and they put them on the bench next to me. I remember saying, "Jeez, look at me. All I wanted was West Virginia plus 6 1/2 and I'm sitting on the bench next to two murderers."

Sherman talked me into pleading guilty to one count of conspiracy to commit interstate gambling. I got no probation and a $10,000 fine.

No one else got a fine. I asked the judge, "Why am I being fined?"

"Because you can afford it."

The court transcript read like I was getting an honorary degree. "Mr. Fey's a prominent member of his community. He's not involved in organized crime in anyway", blah, blah, blah.

In fact, the FBI complimented me on my gambling. Here's the text of a letter from William Malone, a retired FBI agent who worked on my investigation:

> *"Through bookmakers and the gambling element in the Denver area, I learned of and became acquainted with Barry Fey who was involved in betting on college football games and thoroughbred racing. Mr. Fey was not, and is not, an organized crime member.*
>
> *"I learned that several of our local and national bookmakers eventually were reluctant to handle his betting action. Those who did handle Mr. Fey's betting activities would attempt to lay it off.*
>
> *"I know first hand as a qualified gambling expert that Barry Fey is, and enjoys a reputation as, one of the top thoroughbred handicappers in the nation."*

How about that? I get indicted, then praised.

But, I couldn't figure out why the Feds were doing this to me. I was small potatoes. I found out later that it was because I was on Richard Nixon's Enemies List. I never saw the list, but an FBI agent told me I was on it.

Being on Nixon's list was a surprise to me. I was kind of a narrow-minded Hawk when I moved to Denver in 1967. I'd see these real pretty girls with these hippies, these ugly guys, and wonder, "What don't I know?" But, after I went to San Francisco later that year and experienced Haight-Ashbury and the Summer of Love, I was adopting a more tolerant view. Things changed radically for me on May 5, 1970. I'm sitting in Straight Johnson's, a pizza place, and the afternoon paper came in. The headline said, "Four Killed at Kent State". I was so enraged; I called my sales people at the papers and I ran full page ads in the *Denver Post* and the *Rocky Mountain News*. They ran in the Friday papers. The next day, there was an anti-war march up 16th Street from the Federal Building to the Colorado State Capitol. I didn't organize it, but I was one of the leaders. Thousands showed up, many of them were waving my ad.

It was a crazy day because even though it started as an anti-war march, everybody who had any kind of cause or agenda showed up. I remember signs for "Free Bobby", for Bobby Seale of the Black Panthers. Anyway, that anti-war newspaper ad, which I guess Nixon and his people figured was anti-Nixon and anti-America, is what made me a marked man. Besides the indictment, I was audited by the IRS. My life was turned upside down. Even after Nixon left office, the IRS was still hounding me for no other reason than to harass me. My accountant and I were in a meeting at an IRS office in southeast Denver at Tamarac and Hampden. The agent was being a bureaucratic prick. I reached over and grabbed his phone and started dialing.

VIETNAM 41,610*

CAMBODIA 27*

KENT STATE UNIVERSITY 4*

THE KILLING HAS GONE TOO FAR

WE MUST STOP!

PLEASE!

* *These Figures Subject To Change*

This Message Sponsored by Barry Fey,
and the People of Feyline, Inc.

"What are you doing?"

"I've had enough of this. I'm calling Pat Schroeder (the Denver Congresswoman who'd become a good friend) in Washington. I'm going to bury you at your desk."

She was on the House floor, so I left this message: "Will you please tell Pat that I'm being harassed by the government, by the IRS" and blah, blah, blah. The guy sat dumbfounded.

Not long after that, lo and behold, they cancelled everything and let me go. But, being on that list cost me a fortune.

The Denver vice cops had their eyes on me for awhile. Sgt. Gray showed up at my office and opened one of my drawers and found notes reading: "Chicago, $600,000" and similar notes with other cities and large amounts on them, he proclaimed, "We've got the biggest bookie between Chicago and L.A.!" They were my notes about the Rolling Stones tour grosses.

Colorado Congresswoman Pat Schroeder told this story at my roast in 1992:

> *"I have always liked him because he's like me. He's a liberal and he thinks the Seven Deadly Sins are really just misdemeanors, and that we should all be compassionate and humorous. I know there are a lot of you from out of town and we hear all these Barry Fey horse stories, but I'll bet you haven't heard the best one. When he came here as a kid from Chicago, and a kid who was born in New York, obviously he's a city kid. But out here, this is Marlboro Country; you know, testosterone, the Broncos...you've got to be kind of a cowboy. So in one of the parades Barry decided to ride a horse. They found him a great white horse to ride, and it was really quite an awesome sight of Barry on this large white horse going down the street. People were chanting as he went by. Well, a year later the same parade was going on and Barry said that it went so well last time, that he wanted the same horse. 'I want that horse back. I want that white stallion.' They told him, 'Barry we can get that horse, but that wasn't a stallion, that was a filly.' He says, 'No, no, no, I know it was a stallion. It was a white stallion from the Smith Ranch.' 'No, Barry,' they said, 'it was a filly.'*

Barry insisted again, saying, 'I know it was a white stallion because as I rode down 17th Street people were cheering and saying, look at the big prick on that white horse'"!

I loved horses. I was really good at betting on them and won hundreds of thousands of dollars.

I'll begin with the highlight of my horse racing career. Reraise. I had never owned a horse, but a horse buyer friend of mine, James Sternberg, came across a two year old that he thought I should get involved in. "Barry, I saw this horse run and he was amazing. He started slow and had to run wide and he finished nearly up against the grandstand, but he still won." He had talked to the trainer and he wanted to sell the horse because his knees hadn't developed the way he wanted them to. Apparently the knees didn't knit together the way he wanted them to. He wanted $170,000.

"I don't know if I really have that much, James. Let me see if I can get someone to go in with me. I had become pretty friendly with Bud McLarty, the brother of Mac McLarty, President Clinton's chief of staff. Bud told me he was in. I picked up a few other minor investors and told James it was a go. We're buying Reraise.

When it came time to write a check, Bud changed his mind. So, I ponied up his share, which gave me 60% of Reraise for $102,000.

What a magnificent horse! After I saw him run for the first time, I wanted to call him Michael Jordan because he ran with his tongue out. But, he didn't race for five months because his trainer, Craig Dollase, said he wasn't ready. When he finally ran his first race for me at Hollywood Park, he won. In late October of 1998, we had him entered in the Breeder's Cup Sprint at Churchill Downs. That was a great moment. My sons Alan, Geoffrey, Jeremy and Tyler were there along with my wife Lisa. Reraise took the lead early and held it all the way, winning by two lengths. NBC carried it on TV and showed Geoffrey, so excited, holding Tyler, jumping up and down, yelling and throwing Tyler in the air...you should have seen the look on Tyler's face, he was so scared. We were in the Winner's Circle, then we were taken to the media tent where I bragged that "they could have gone around again, they weren't going to catch this horse." I was so happy. The family was so happy. The Breeder's Cup trophy is more special to me than any of the rock 'n roll memorabilia I've collected. Reraise was Sprinter of the Year in 1998. It was just wonderful...such a perfect moment. It was nearly as perfect as when I was playing third base at age 11.

But, just like when I was 11, it all changed.

The next year, June 23, 1999, I was staying at the Beverly Hilton Hotel. Two bad things happened there and I'll never stay there again. I got a call telling me that Charlie Lyons, who was orchestrating the sale of Ascent Entertainment, owners of the Nuggets, Avalanche and Pepsi Center, had been dismissed by the board because of an alleged conflict of interest. In setting up the sale to a partnership controlled by Bill Laurie and his wife, Wal-Mart heiress Nancy Walton Laurie, Charlie made a deal for himself to become president of the partnership and part owner. The Ascent board didn't like that and canned him. I love Charlie and not only did I feel bad for him, truly one of the nicest guys I've known, but also because my $25,000 a month consulting fee with Ascent was going out the door with him.

The next morning, about 6:30, I got a call from Delosse. "You'd better come down to the barn." Reraise was hurt and we had to pull him from the big stakes raise at Hollywood Park in two days. I went to the barn, hoping that it was just temporary soreness. But, Delosse said, "No, he's walking lame, he can't run." I went over and petted Reraise and then Tyler and I walked to the far wall of the back stretch, sat down and I cried. I was so upset. I went back later in the day to pet him again and he bit me on the arm. Hard! He still had the spunk and I was sure he'd run again.

He didn't run for most of the next year. But in his first race after rehab, Reraise ran at Hollywood Park and won. He was back! Then, I got an invitation to run him in a $2 million race in Dubai. But, Delosse didn't want to send him, he wanted to wait. I fired Delosse and hired a trainer named Tom Skiffington, who specialized in rehabbing injured horses. I asked Skiffington what he thought about Dubai. He said Reraise was looking really good, getting stronger and that he should go. We got all the plane tickets and transportation of the horse set up. Skiffington called me one morning not long before we were scheduled to leave and told me, "His ankle swelled on me today. I can't send him to Dubai."

Reraise never recovered and we gave him away, to a farm in Virginia. He didn't owe us a thing, he made us a lot of money.

Not to brag, but my horse betting skills are legendary. I was in Omaha with Willie Nelson one year and on our way to the airport in a taxi, I wanted to stop at the Ak-Sar-Ben track and make a few bets. Jeff Krump was with us. Our stuff was in the cab, so I paid the cabbie to come in with us. I picked the first six winners before we had to get to the airport. Willie, Krump and the cabbie were pretty impressed.

I won hundreds of thousands of dollars playing the horses. Here's a story from Las Vegas, where Barbra Streisand was playing at the gala grand opening of the MGM Grand in 1993. Janis Joplin was the greatest female singer in rock 'n roll. Streisand was the best pop music singer, best pure singer. Her phrasing, that voice, my God, she was incredible. Which is why I was so disappointed when Barbra came backstage at the 1973 Stones' Nicaraguan Earthquake Benefit in Los Angeles. It just seemed so beneath her. Come on, Barbra! What are you doing backstage at a rock 'n roll show asking to meet the Stones? You're the queen...that's beneath you!

Anyway, in 1993, I took Lisa to see Streisand at this gala grand opening of the MGM Grand. Anybody who was anything in the entertainment business was going to be there. Tickets were impossible to get, unless you knew somebody. I did: my old pal Richard Sturm. Together, he made a name for himself and I made a lot of money with the Stones and all of the other big groups I brought to Vegas. He runs the MGM Grand.

A few hours before the concert, I was sitting at the Mirage betting on horses. I bet on a Pick Six, which is where to win your bet, you have to hit six races in a row. Well, the first horse wins, a 60 to 1 long shot that paid $121.60, which is a helluva way to start! Then, I won the next one. Then, the third one. And, the fourth one. But, there's about a half hour between races and it's time to go to see Barbra. I hurried back to Bally's and got dressed in my tuxedo and all that. Lisa was in her gown looking gorgeous and getting impatient. I told her that I'd won four out of six races. She couldn't have cared less. She didn't want to be late for Streisand. My son Alan and his fiancée and a few other people were going with us, too.

On the way down to the cab I peeked into the horse book and saw that I won the fifth race! Now, there's no way I'm not going go see how the sixth race finishes, so I told Lisa, "I'm sorry, but I can't go to Streisand until I see how this ends." She's furious, but I'm not budging. The others had gone out to get in the cab line. Coming into the top of the stretch, my horses are running one-two-three. One of my horses wins.

Lisa says, "That's nice. Can we go now?"

I said, "Just wait a minute to see how much it pays."

The screen flashes, "One winner, $135,000". Even Lisa got excited, but she still didn't want to be late. I told her I needed five more minutes to run the winning ticket to the safe deposit box because I didn't want to carry it around and risk losing it. When I got back downstairs, we pissed dozens of people off by jumping the cab line and I gave the cabbie a fifty to break the law and take an over-loaded cab—seven of us—to the MGM.

We made it in plenty of time because Barbra was fifty minutes late coming on. Fifty fucking minutes! What possible reason could there be for her to keep us waiting that long? The only good to come out of it was that Philadelphia Eagles quarterback Randall Cunningham and his wife were sitting in front of us, so I got to talk a lot of football.

The next morning, I went to the Mirage and cashed in my ticket, which counting the Pick Threes and Pick Fives, totaled over $150,000.

"Memories, light the corners of my mind...
If we had the chance to do it all again,
Tell me —would we? Could we?"

Damn right Babs, but I wouldn't have been in such a hurry to get to your show.

With apologies to Jimmy Breslin, the following story is worthy of being filed under "the gang that couldn't shoot straight". Until the 1970s, Las Vegas casinos didn't have sports books. There were "turf clubs" that were run independently from casinos. One thing keeping casinos out of the sports book business was a ten percent tax the city of Las Vegas imposed on sports bets. You had to pay it up front when you made the bet. Win or lose, you paid the tax. In 1974, the tax rate was lowered to two percent, which made it more desirable for casinos to have their own sports books and in 1975, the law was changed to allow casinos to run sports books and that was the death of the turf clubs. The one I bet at was Churchill Downs, which was where the Paris casino and hotel are now.

I was sitting with Tony Hegler in his office at the Barbary Coast. Tony's an old friend who was Feyline's banker for a while when he worked in Colorado and he went on to a long, successful career in Las Vegas. A guy came into his office, an acquaintance of Tony's. We started chatting about horse betting and also about the stupid tax that Las Vegas had. He said, "I can help you out because I know the guys at Churchill Downs really well".

Well, he's in my buddy Tony's office, so he must be legit. I gave him $2000 and he comes back with a betting slip. It says $200, but there's a little curly-q scrawled under the number. He said the curly-q means that if I won, they'd know at Churchill Downs that my real bet was $2000. I didn't have to pay the tax that way. Fine.

Naturally, my horse comes in and I go to collect my winnings. The guy at the Churchill Downs window gives me $200. I said, "What about the curly-q?' He said, "What are you talking about?" So, the guy in Tony's office conned me out of $2000. I went back to Tony and told him what his "friend" had done.

Tony was livid. He talked to him, I talked to him. He didn't have the money, blah, blah, blah. Well, since gambling is legal in Las Vegas, I called the police to swear out a warrant for theft. I told a detective what had happened. He said, "Done. I'll issue the warrant."

Time goes by and nothing's happening and I wasn't going to let it go. So, I sent two of my security guys, L.C. Clayton, the baddest of the bad and Tom Smith, a real nice guy, but a martial arts expert. I gave them a picture of the guy and told them where he usually hangs out. I told them there's a warrant out for him, so find him, make a citizen's arrest and take him to a police station.

Little did I know that the detective who I spoke with knew the guy's wife. He called her to give her a heads up and she begged him to wait on the warrant; that she'd make sure he turned himself in.

So when Tom and L.C. grabbed him, there was no warrant. He's screaming like crazy in downtown Vegas, attracting a crowd and the police come and arrest my guys! I got them bonded out, but the prosecutor called for a grand jury and I had to testify. I flew to Vegas and checked in to a casino hotel across the street from the courthouse. I testified, the charges were dropped and we all went home. I never got my money from the bastard, but I did win $3,000 playing craps in the hotel where I was staying.

Unfortunately for him, I wasn't the only one he screwed over. About a year later, he was murdered.

Part Eight

THE LEGENDS

Nearly everyone to whom I've devoted a chapter is a "legend", but I wanted to separate several into this section so that I could give them a little extra, and well deserved, time in the spotlight.

David Geffen

David Geffen is a monster in our business. I mean that in terms of importance, not temperament. David began in the mailroom at William Morris and had just started as an agent when he put together Crosby, Stills, Nash, Young. He wanted me to book them as part of the Denver Pop Festival in 1969. I refused to give them their first big concert because their album was delayed and wouldn't be out before the concert:

"David, I ain't paying $10,000 to a group with no record!"

He wasn't happy, but said, "That's okay, Barry. We'll work together again." And we did, many times, but I paid a lot more for CSNY the next time and every time after that.

From that to everything he's accomplished since—Asylum Records, Geffen Records, Geffen Films, DreamWorks SKG with Steven Spielberg and Jeffrey Katzenberg— David's a winner.

In 2007, he called me three or four times. Each time was about politics.

"Barry, get yourself next to this Obama, I'm going to make him president."

"Well, wait a minute, David. Aren't you really close with Bill and Hillary."

"Barry, I love them, but they're both fuckin' liars."

Before the general election in 2008, I called David to see if he wanted to partner with me on a project that was too big for me to handle by myself.

I began with, "David, you were right, it looks like your guy's going to win. Congratulations!"

He seemed so down. I know a lot of people despised him, but he's always seemed to me to be a very sensitive guy.

"What's the matter, David?"

"Aw, nothing, Barry... I don't know what the hell's going on, I don't feel good about anything I'm doing and I'm just not in any mood to make a deal right now. I kind of don't want to go into business with friends anymore because I lose them so quickly."

I knew that, even though he always took my calls, talking to me at that moment wasn't what he wanted to be doing.

"David, let's talk later. It's not that important."

Three days later, David left Dreamworks. Just walked away. How the fuck do you walk away from that? "Sorry, Steven... gotta go"?

With all of his quirks, I have nothing but respect for David. Years ago, I think it was 1992, he was part of a benefit at the Universal Amphitheater for the L.A. AIDS Project and Barbra Streisand performed. Because I was partners with Universal at the time, they gave me tickets. Streisand was my wife Lisa's favorite act. Huge fan. I worked out an elaborate ruse to surprise her with a trip to L.A. to see Barbra...lied to her about me being chosen to be on "Jeopardy" and her friends were all in on it. But, that's away from the point. David was being honored for his support of the L.A. Aids Project. It was certainly no longer a secret, if it ever was much of one, that David was gay.

In one of the most touching moments I've ever seen, he stood at the microphone and held up a business card.

"I was sitting in my office one day and I got a call that this man had died from AIDS. I was very sad and flipped my Rolodex to where his card was. I took it out and was going to tear it up and throw it away. But, I didn't. I put a rubber band around it and kept it."

Then he held up a three-inch thick, rubber-banded stack of cards that had been in his Rolodex, all with the names of people who'd died from AIDS.

What's the first thing you do when you meet David Geffen? You bow. That's how I feel about David. He's the best product of this business. He was special at everything he did. He worked hard for everything he has.

The Eagles and Irving Azoff

If you bow when you meet David Geffen, you duck when you meet Irving Azoff. I was sitting in his Hollywood office in the mid-'70s and he was yelling at the top of his lungs into the phone, reaming somebody about something. "Motherfucker" this and "motherfucker" that. I was sitting a few feet away, finding it shocking and amusing that someone besides me would actually speak to another human being that way. In the middle of his tirade, his secretary buzzes in:

"Don's on the phone."

Immediately, Irving ends his harangue, pushes a button on the phone and in the calmest, friendliest voice says, "Hi, Don, what can I do for you?"

Don Henley ran the Eagles, despite the efforts of Glenn Frey and Don Felder.

It's like the old joke; when Henley said "jump", Azoff's only response was, "how high?"

Irving and I go back to when he was a small agent in Champaign, Illinois. From my first dealings with him, he was difficult. You know how some people are nice when they're small and just getting started and then turn into asses when they become successful? Irving was an ass from the beginning. I admire that.

But, he was always good to me.

He started a company called Frontline Management. He ended up managing Jimmy Buffett, The Eagles and many other big acts, but it seemed everybody he managed was booked by Howard Rose. Irving worked with two Howards: Rose and Kaufman. Kaufman was the manager. Rose was the agent and would handle most of Kaufman's acts. He was sharp, knew talent and did a great job. Elton John thought so, too, and gave him a Rolls Royce. But, Rose was so nonchalantly harsh and would drive promoters nuts because he'd already decided how many tickets a group was going to sell in whatever city, how much the gross and net should be and when he quoted a price, if you didn't like it, "fuck you". Rose was so universally disliked in the business, a bunch of us would take bets on whether they could find six people who'd carry his coffin. We came up with five: Irving, Kaufman, Elton, Buffett and Steve Smith, his brother-in-law who worked in his office. "The Howards", which is how Irving describes them, were in a syndicate with me when we owned some race horses. That dissolved for one reason or another, but when I was buying Reraise, I called Howard Kaufman and offered him a piece. I told him he needed to get in on this one, that this one wasn't just a horse, he was a freak. He said no, and said no each of the several times I tried. After Reraise won the Breeder's Cup and earned the Eclipse Award for Sprinter of the Year, Howard was never the same with me. He became very cold, and I think it was because he was jealous of my success with Reraise. He had the same kind of big dreams I had; he was a gambler, he wanted to own a big horse. Despite all of that, "The Howards" and I got along fine. Maybe it was a kinship of meanness.

When I was diagnosed with prostate cancer in 1997, *Pollstar Magazine* did a piece on me and asked me about the cancer and the prognosis.

"If dealing with Howard Rose and Howard Kaufman for 25 years didn't kill me, cancer doesn't have a chance." Irving's public relations guy in Los Angeles, Larry Solters, clipped that out, blew it up and put it on his wall.

Early in our career together and by "our" career, I mean Irving, Chuck Morris and me; Chuck pissed off Irving so badly that Irving put him in what he called his "penalty box."

After a while, it was getting in the way of our business, so I told Chuck to fix it. We were doing too many deals with Irving and I needed Chuck to get out of the penalty box. So, Chuck went to see Irving at a hotel in Florida where he was staying. Chuck sat in the lobby for three days waiting for Irving to see him. Irving made him wait. He wouldn't talk to him.

One of Irving's most famous lines was, "I'll take care of you, Barry. If you lose money on one of my shows, I'll take care of you." And, we did lose money on one of the Eagles' stadium shows in the late '70s. About $30,000. Irving said, "I'll get you back $25,000." But, a little time goes by and we get nothing. I called Irving.

"What the fuck's going on, Irving?"

"Barry, I wanted to give you the money but the band won't let me. And, after all, it's their money."

I didn't believe that. So, I called Joe Walsh. He lived in Colorado and Chuck had his home number. I explained what Irving said.

"Barry, what the fuck... we don't know anything about that."

The next day, Irving called me.

Screaming, he said, "Don't you ever talk to my acts! You talk to me!"

"Fuck you", I said.

Two days later, a cashier's check from Irving arrives for $25,000. Irving had his ways of doing things, but he always kept his word.

In 1994, I did a bunch of Eagles stadium dates on the "Hell Freezes Over Tour". I made a bunch of money on all of those dates, except Albuquerque where we took a beating. When I told Irving, he said, "Barry, I'll take care of it. I'll take care of it somehow."

When I brought the tour to Mile High Stadium, I could sell the suites separately if the suite holders didn't want them for the show. Irving said, "Here's what you do. Since the contract says you can't sell them without the owner's permission, tell my accountant, (Bob

Hurwitz) that you couldn't sell the suites. Then sell them and keep the money. That'll make up for Albuquerque."

One sidebar about Bob: He'd been with Irving for a long time and many years earlier, we had a woman working for us who was large breasted and Bob couldn't keep his eyes off her chest. So, we'd send her in during the show settlements. Bob would be looking at her boobs, trying to get her to go out with him for drinks after the show. We had some good settlements with Bob.

Anyway, during the show, Bob walked up to me.

"Barry, look," and he's pointing toward the suites. Their lights were on. "I thought they weren't sold".

"They weren't," I lied.

"Then what the fuck are the lights doing on?"

"I don't know, man, ask the stadium manager."

But, Bob runs to find Irving and drags him out.

"Look, Irving. The suites are being used. I think we're being ripped off."

Irving looks up at the suites, turns around and tells Bob, "Don't fucking bother me when I'm busy" and walks away. Bob was left stammering, "But, but, but...." I never heard another word about the suites and the money from them more than made me whole.

A lot of people were scared to death of Irving, or hated him, but he and I always got along well.

I had a ton of dates on that tour, including one stadium show near the beginning in San Diego. Everybody was so happy: Henley, Frey, Walsh, Felder and Schmit. They were all getting along so well. But, by the end of the tour, they were riding in separate vans; they would barely talk to each other. Walsh and Schmit were never problems; Joe was real mellow and didn't give a shit about much of anything and Timothy was just happy to be making all that money. It was the other guys who weren't getting along.

The Eagles' first appearance in Colorado was over Christmas break 1971 at Tulagi's in Boulder. It was before their first album, *Eagles,* came out. This was when Chuck Morris was booking Tulagi's. He didn't work for me yet and I had nothing to do with it. He told Irving that it was a bad time for the Eagles to play; the University of Colorado was on break; the town was empty; nobody would come. But, Irving insisted because he had some producers who wanted to see the band. So, Chuck did it and didn't lose any money, but didn't make any, either. And—this may be the only time I know of that Irving broke his promise—Chuck says Irving promised him that if the Eagles caught on, he'd book them in Colorado through Chuck. A year or so later when the Eagles came to Colorado, Irving booked them through me and they always played for me after that.

There were only two groups that always sold out for me. Never an unsold ticket. The Stones and Eagles.

Managing the Eagles had to be a handful. Irving said to me once, "You know how crazy these guys make me, Barry?" And he went on to tell the story of how he was negotiating with Budweiser to be the sponsor of the 1994 "Hell Freezes Over" tour. He said it took weeks to put a deal together, very difficult negotiations, but he finally got Bud to agree to pay $13 million. He said they were all in an attorney's conference room somewhere and everybody for Budweiser was happy with the deal and everybody with the band was happy and just before the papers were signed, Henley said, "One more thing...you've gotta let the whales go from Sea World", which Anheuser-Busch owned. Irving said the big shots for Budweiser didn't say a word; they just packed up their briefcases, got up and left. The tour went on without a sponsor.

In 1996, Henley was at my house for a political fundraiser. Tom Strickland was running for the U.S. Senate from Colorado. Henley was so grumpy. People had paid thousands of dollars to mingle with him, but all he did was sit in my living room in a chair. Maybe he wasn't feeling well, or maybe he was just being his naturally wonderful self, but he wouldn't move all afternoon. However, when it came time for him to perform—we had a stage set up in a tent on my lawn—he went out and played a great show.

Henley had a good line about Irving. During the Eagle's 1998 induction to the Rock 'n Roll Hall of Fame, Henley said of Irving: "He may be Satan, but he's our Satan".

Irving has had incredible success, managing several other big acts (Van Halen, Journey, Neil Diamond, Steely Dan, REO), moved into movie producing ("Urban Cowboy", "Fast Times At Ridgemont High") and then he became CEO of Ticketmaster and, after the merger, the CEO of Live Nation. He still manages acts and may be the most powerful man in the music business. I have nothing but respect for Irving. But, as far as I'm concerned, he'll never match the amazing career of another one of the guys who started out when we did, David Geffen.

One of the funniest things Irving ever said to me was during a phone call in 1973.

"Barry, I just left Geffen-Roberts. I took the Eagles with me. We're going to release a huge song, 'The Best of My Love'. I wonder what Geffen's going to do now!"

I retold that story at my roast in 1992 and added, "By the way Irving, David's fine."

One of the first times I met Irving was in Los Angeles. He had this little car, which I recall because fat guys don't fit well into small cars.

"What are you doing tonight, Barry?"

"Irving, I'm from Denver. I don't know many people here. I'm not doing anything."

So, he picked me up and we went to see a band he was representing called Jo Jo Gunne. They had a minor hit called "Run, Run, Run" in '72. We also went to have ribs—we both loved ribs and there was a place on Western Avenue in L.A. called Noonan's Ribs that supplied ribs to other restaurants. We found a place on Sunset that served Noonan's ribs and went there a few times. Once, maybe the last time we went, Irving got aggravated at the waiter and turned over the table.

I love Irving, but that was fucking embarrassing.

I'm apparently not one to talk. I'm reminded that I turned over a desk or two at Feyline. I'm sure I had good reasons, though.

Bruce Springsteen's Pink ~~Cadillac~~ Jeep

In the mid-1970s, Springsteen was getting huge on the East Coast and I thought he'd be perfect for Red Rocks. But, I wasn't able to convince him to play there. His agent was Frank Barsalona of Premier Talent, the legend with whom I'd booked a lot of acts over the years.

I said, "Frank, tell him that Red Rocks is indoors without a roof!"

It worked. He came to Red Rocks in 1979, but I couldn't sell it out. About 3,000 of the 9,000 seats were empty. The next year,

October of 1980, he played McNichols Arena. But, I got him back to Red Rocks in 1981. He sold out this time. Back-to-back nights under the stars; well, at least one night under the stars. The first night was perfect. The second night, it poured. Rained like hell. And there he was, soaking wet, telling the crowd, also soaking wet that if they want to call it off and go home, he'd come back the next night and play somewhere indoors for free. The crowd booed, loudly, or maybe they were yelling "Bruuuuuce". At any rate, the show continued in pouring rain until lightning started and that was the end of it. (A few years after that, I got the city to put a roof over the stage. Feyline had it built and received a rent credit for it.)

The next day, they had an off day and we had a party planned at my house for that night. That morning, I got a call from George Travis, his tour manager.

"Barry, Bruce wants to go four-wheeling."

"What the fuck does he know about four-wheeling?"

"I don't know, he wants to go."

We found a couple of Jeeps within the Feyline family for him and his band. They decided to go to the Garden of the Gods near Colorado Springs, which is made up of the same type of huge, gorgeous, red sandstone formations that created Red Rocks Amphitheater. That evening, the party's starting and nobody's heard from Bruce. An hour goes by and still, no Bruce. Since I knew the general area they were going, I called a guy at KILO Radio in Colorado Springs.

I said, "Bruce Springsteen went jeeping and may be lost. I think he's in the Garden of the Gods somewhere."

The radio guy said he had a small RV, big enough to hold all the jeepers, and he'd go out and look for them. He found them; both Jeeps had overheated and at least one of the band decided that ice cold Heineken beer would substitute as a coolant. When the beer was poured into the radiators, the blocks cracked on both Jeeps and that was that. The engines were dead. They left the Jeeps, piled into the RV and were driven about an hour north to my home. But, the adventure wasn't yet over. The alternator or something went bad on the RV and the headlights didn't work very well. So, Bruce and the guys held flashlights out the side windows to light the way.

At last, they get to the party and everybody's having a good time. Bruce and I are playing pinball and one of his sycophants is rooting him on, "Get him Boss! Get him Boss!"

I looked at him and said, "I beg your pardon. This is my house. I'm the fuckin' boss." I cleaned Springsteen's clock, but it wasn't really fair. I had home field advantage because I played a lot on that machine; a "Captain Fantastic" version given to me by Elton John.

Bruce got me back—whether he meant to or not—a few years later. He brought his "Born To Run" tour to McNichols Arena in November of 1984.

Bruce was always fair. He kept his ticket prices low and the splits were reasonable. But, when the "Born To Run" tour came, he wanted an 85-15 split of the net. That's more than I'd been paying and didn't want to do it. But look; he's a big act and there really aren't that many expenses for advertising and promotion. It's the mid '80s, the heyday of rock 'n roll concerts. Tickets were selling automatically.

Just before the tour, Bruce announces that he's going to be donating $10,000 from each of his concerts to local food banks. The next day I get a call from Barry Bell, a great guy who worked for Frank Barsalona and handled Springsteen.

"The deal has changed. It's gone from 85-15 to 90-10".

You've got to be kidding me. Springsteen changed the deal and uses MY money to give to the food banks?! Fuck.

But, Springsteen shows were huge and I made a lot of money from them. When we booked the outdoor portion of "Born in the U.S.A." in September of 1985, the first day sold out in minutes. The second sold out in minutes. 137,000 tickets at Mile High Stadium! (We could have sold more, but Springsteen insisted that every seat have a clear sightline to The Mighty Max's feet.) Springsteen was a monster, selling far better than many other acts who were getting more airplay and selling more records.

When Springsteen shows up for the first show, I present him with one of the Jeeps he wrecked—restored and painted pink. You know, "Pink Cadillac".

He was thrilled. "Oh, man...Jump in!" and we go for a ride. He loved it. So did I, for that matter, racing around the parking lot at Mile High with a giddy Boss.

Now, I've given a lot of gifts and mementos to acts and you never know what's going to happen with them; whether they keep them, use them, sell them, give them away or throw them away. A year or so later, I'm in New York at Castellano's Restaurant eating with Jack Craigo, who was the head of Columbia Records. And, as we're sitting there facing the windows, we see this pink Jeep pull up. It's Bruce and his wife at the time, Julianne Phillips, coming in for dinner and driving the pink Jeep I gave him. Bruce spotted me, came over and sat with us for a few minutes, reminiscing about his Jeeping adventure in Colorado. I should have bought him a Heineken.

One of his best off-stage moments, I think, happened when he found out that Ticketmaster was scalping his tickets on its own scalping site, TicketsNow. In 2009, when his "Working On A Dream" tour went on sale, the tickets showed up within minutes on TicketsNow. Reuters reported that he called out Ticketmaster on it and said, "Some artists or managers may not perceive there to be a conflict between having the distributor of their tickets in effect scalping those same tickets through a secondary company like TicketsNow. We do."

You can't see or hear me, but I'm standing and applauding. Bruce is one of the few stars who's still looking out for his audiences and doing the best to keep ticket prices somewhat affordable.

There's one more reason I love Bruce: before his August 16, 1981 show, my oldest son Alan was having a birthday party with some of his buddies backstage at Red Rocks. Bruce walked in and led the partiers in "Happy Birthday".

Bob Dylan's Hand Carved Chess Sets

Just to show you that it wasn't all about the money for me, I was hoping that Bob Dylan would never go on tour. He was a God. He was the prophet of our generation. He hadn't played in many years and I thought he should have remained in the shadows, remained that God-like figure in our minds.

Look, here was a guy who had nothing to prove. He could have lived like a king forever off the royalties from all the songs he wrote: "All Along the Watchtower", "Blowin' In The Wind", "Don't Think Twice, It's Alright", "Forever Young", "Hurricane", "It Ain't Me Babe", "Knocking On Heaven's Door", "Lay Lady Lay", "Like A Rolling Stone", "Rainy Day Women", "Subterranean Homesick Blues", "The Times They Are a Changin'" and on and on and on. He couldn't have needed the money. But, fucking Bill Graham talked him into touring in 1974 with The Band.

It was a great show. Come on! It was Bob Dylan and The Band. Great concert. But, touring made him human. And, then he kept touring, which made it worse. When people can see you every year or two, it's no longer that big of deal. The mystique is gone.

Listen to this: in Dylan's 1974 rider, he demanded a hand-carved chess set. We got him one, and every promoter got him one. He must have the biggest collection of hand-carved chess sets in the world, unless he threw or gave them away.

But, I had him several times and we got friendly—as friendly as I could be with a myth who I held in such high esteem. (A *Denver Post* writer in 2011 described me as "near mythical". I wonder if Bob knows that.)

One day I'm walking through the Burbank airport and I hear my name.

"Barry!"

It's Bob Dylan. He's there with his band. He waved me over, friendly as could be—very unusual for him. He wasn't normally that way. He always seemed quiet and a little shy. But, we sat and talked for a half hour. I had plenty of time before my flight, but I would have sat there as long as he wanted me to. It was Bob Dylan!

I don't get impressed easily. If it had been Rick James calling me over, I would have waved and said, "Sorry, Rick baby, gotta catch a plane." Don Henley? Nope. Besides, he probably would have wound up hating me after a few minutes. But, Bob Dylan—even after he disappointed me by going on tour—you bet your ass.

In 1976, I booked Bob Dylan's "Rolling Thunder Revue" which had been touring the country for a May 26th date outdoors at Hughes Stadium in Fort Collins. That was home to the Rolling Stones/Elton John debacle just a year earlier.

But, this was Dylan; what could possibly go wrong?

I was in Denver, getting ready to drive the 90 minutes to Fort Collins. I called backstage and spoke with my associate Chuck Morris.

"God, Barry, when are you getting here? It's pouring!"

I hung up, drove to Stapleton and caught a plane to New York. I had no interest in hanging around a Dylan concert during the rain. Plus, Chuck was already there. Let him deal with it.

It rained hard throughout the concert which Dylan opened with his famous "A Hard Rain's A-Gonna Fall". The concert was being recorded for an album and filmed for an NBC television special that would air in September when the album came out. The concert and the album got bad reviews and the TV special had poor ratings, all of which proved my ongoing argument about Dylan: He shouldn't have started touring. I never wanted to book him (although I obviously did) because I didn't want to be part of ruining the Dylan mystique.

One of my funniest Dylan moments was after he converted to Christianity in the late '70s. I had him at the Rainbow Music Hall in Denver and he was playing all Christian music. Can you imagine? Between songs, some frustrated kid yells out: "Hey, Bob. Jesus likes the hits, too!" I couldn't see Bob's face, but I'm sure he was smiling.

Speaking of religion, in the '80s, I had Little Richard booked for a Friday night concert somewhere. I got a call from his manager.

"Barry, we need to cancel that date."

"Why? What happened?"

"Richard has become an Orthodox Jew and can't play on Friday nights."

I didn't know what to say, so I just hung up the phone. I lost my chance to play Little Richard.

I later heard that he'd converted to Judaism after talking with a fellow musician and longtime fan who'd defected from Christianity a few years earlier: Bob Dylan.

Eric Clapton

There isn't much we don't know about Eric's career and personal life. His autobiography included everything he could remember, warts and all, and his ex-wife Patti Boyd's tell-all, "Wonderful Tonight" filled in a lot of the blanks, and then some. That he's still alive is pretty remarkable.

One story that didn't make his book was from 1975. I had him in Denver for a concert at the Coliseum on August 12th. Nearly 12,000 seats were sold for a show by the world's greatest rock guitarist. Everything was all set. Except one thing: Eric couldn't get his eyes open.

He'd been doing so much heroin and whatever, that he developed a severe case of conjunctivitis. His eyes were caked shut. I'm sure he could have done his concert with his eyes closed, but I thought it was better to get him to a doctor. I asked an ophthalmologist to meet me at Clapton's suite, but he said, "Barry, I can't go to his hotel, all of my equipment is at my office." So, we picked up Clapton, guided him to the car like a blind man, and took him to the office. The doctor got his eyes open and the show went on.

I played Clapton a lot over the years, probably as much or more than any promoter, but he was always in the bag; he binged on booze, coke and heroin for 30 years and there really wasn't much room in his life for meaningful conversations with me.

In 1998, I watched and listened to a much different Eric Clapton. A sober one. I had him at the MGM Grand in Las Vegas and, while his playing had always been effortless, that night the sound he was getting from his guitar was beyond anything I'd ever heard. That same night in another part of the MGM, there was a tribute concert honoring Frank Sinatra, who died on May 14, 1998. It was a black tie event with Gregory Peck, Jack Lemmon, Paul Anka, Wayne Newton and other luminaries performing and attending. When it ended, some of the audience moved over to the Clapton concert. During "Cocaine", we turned up the house lights and there were all these people in formal wear dancing and singing along to "Cocaine". It was a funny sight.

When I played Eric in 2000, I found out that he really liked old watches. I bought him an expensive, antique pocket watch and had engraved on the back the places that I'd played him in the '60s, '70s, '80s, '90s and 2000. I played him first at the Family Dog as Cream. I played him with Derek and the Dominoes. I played him with Blind Faith. And, several times as Eric Clapton.

Pink Floyd

Pink Floyd sold a lot of tickets for me. I had them several times, including at Mile High Stadium at least twice: in 1988 and again in 1994. One nearly turned into a disaster because the weather for several days leading up to the concert was awful. It was cold and rainy and ticket sales weren't going well. I think we had about 30,000 tickets sold, but in a place that holds twice that many, that wasn't going to turn out nearly as well as I wanted. The morning of the show, the skies are clear and the sun comes out and it's just a gorgeous Denver day. That evening, we had the biggest walk up in history: Over 19,000 fans lined up and bought tickets at the gate. It was just about time for the show to begin and people were still streaming in. I walked outside to see what the holdup was and saw lines blocks long. At the gates, security was checking bags and backpacks, confiscating bottles and anything dangerous. That was slowing things down so much that I told the guy in charge, "I don't care if they have a hand grenade. I don't care if they carrying a fucking bazooka. Stop checking them and just let 'em in."

Pink Floyd always did well for me, and they played great songs at their shows, like "Shine On You Crazy Diamond", "Time", "Money", "Another Brick In The Wall", "Hey You", and "Comfortably Numb". But, to me, they were just a faceless product. I doubt if very many fans could name any of the band members. Roger Waters didn't get well known until after he left Pink Floyd.

Diana Ross

On the night I flew from Denver to New York to attend Woodstock, I had Diana Ross and the Supremes at Red Rocks. This was August 14, 1969, just months before she shed the Supremes and went on her own.

From the beginning, she made it clear that I was very lucky to be booking her. One of the things she insisted on backstage was that the crew not be able to see her as she walked from her dressing room to the stage. So, we had to put up pipe and drape, curtains, and create a passageway where only the people she approved of could see her. Whatever, honey, I didn't care. Just put on a good show. She allowed me to see her and be around her, but I wasn't allowed to speak to her. It wasn't like we had a lot in common and much to talk about anyway.

But, I was always very polite to her and gave her utmost courtesy at all times. After a show in San Diego I was walking with her, silently of course, to her limo. She turned abruptly before getting in.

"Mr. Fey, you're quite good. In the future, you may call me Ms. Ross."

Wonderful.

That intense friendship continued a year or two later when I was invited to attend a birthday party at her home in California. I think it was for Michael Jackson's birthday.

Anyway, Diana—I mean Ms. Ross—held herself in high esteem.

Elton John

My phone rang at about two o'clock in the morning on August 31, 1970. It was Jerry Heller, a friend of mine in Los Angeles who was a booker for a bunch of acts, from War to Creedence to Otis Redding and Van Morrison.

"Barry, I just came from The Troubadour and I saw the greatest act. You've got to get this one. He's fantastic. Don't ask me nothing, just book it."

It was Elton John. I'd never heard of him. He was being managed by Nat Weiss, who also ran Tommy Bolin's record label. I called Nat and set up shows on May 16th and 17th of 1971. One show at the Auditorium Arena and the next night in Boulder at the University of Colorado.

He was terrific. I watched that show and remember saying to myself, "He's amazing, but he's another strange man in a land of strange men." You've got to remember that I'd already had some of the strangest of the strange, like Janis, Jim, Jimi, Moon and Zeppelin. And, when I saw him the first time, Elton hadn't started dressing flamboyantly yet and stepping on his piano all that shit. But he was unbelievable. The shows sold out. Word got around real quickly. Elton was on his way.

There were a couple of low points. One was in 1975 when Elton was recording at Caribou Ranch west of Boulder. On July 20, the Stones were going to play at Hughes Stadium, the football field at Colorado State University. It turned out to be one of the worst, if not the worst, dates I did with the Stones. Part of the reason was they had some new musicians, like Billy Preston on keyboards, and weren't quite in sync yet, but Elton sure didn't help things. He went to Fort

Collins for the show, watching from off stage. But, what was most important to me was that after the show, back at Caribou, Elton had promised to throw a huge barbecue for everyone: The Stones, the crew, me, everyone. I could just visualize, after a long, difficult day of promoting, that I was going to eat like a pig.

After the Stones did a few numbers, Mick said, "There's a friend of ours who's going to sit in on piano. His name is Reg Dwight." There was a smattering of polite applause. Few people knew his real name. He comes out in a blue Dodgers jacket and a cowboy hat so he wouldn't be recognized. Elton was supposed to play two or three numbers, but he plays and plays and doesn't get off the stage for over an hour. Mick and the boys are getting so pissed off and after the show, told Elton, "Fuck you and your barbecue, we aren't going." I was crushed because I missed out on a meal. But, Elton was more crushed. He was devastated that the Stones felt that way about him. I was told by people who were at the ranch that Elton was so despondent that night he tried to commit suicide.

There was a "Drama Queen" moment in 1988 when I had Elton at Fiddler's Green near Denver. All the pre-show prep was going well when I got a call. Elton was refusing to get off the plane because he'd had a fight with his lover, who was also the pilot. We had to beg and cajole him into coming off the plane to play. You know the reputation. Elton did crazy things, and did wildly crazy things for years. What a handful! But, what a talent. Some of those songs are amazing. We got to be fairly friendly. He had an apartment in Atlanta where he had a glass staircase. He showed me a photo of it and I decided that my house needed one, too. So I had one installed.

On March 24th and 25th of 1995, I put on the Las Vegas shows of the Elton John-Billy Joel "Face-to-Face" tour. It started in the summer of '94, covered about a dozen shows across the country and Vegas was the final stop. Those were great shows; about four hours long. They both came out at the beginning, then Billy left and Elton played; then Elton left and Billy played and then they both played together again. They played each other's songs. Great stuff. "Levon", "Bennie and the Jets", on and on. March 25th was Elton's birthday, so Billy started singing the birthday song and the whole crowd joined in.

Elton wasn't always a pain in the ass. It just depended on his mood. Anything could happen at anytime. High maintenance, but not the highest maintenance guy I booked. That title would probably go to The Who, or—for much different reasons—to Cat Stevens. More about him in another chapter.

Elton and Billy signed a baby grand piano that I have in my memorabilia collection.

Lynyrd Skynyrd and Ronnie Van Zant

I had nothing in common with the groups. Nothing. It wasn't like we were going to hang out and get loaded after their shows, mainly because I didn't drink and didn't do drugs. (There was a Mick and Keith inspired exception to that, but that's in another chapter.) With all these groups, when I first met them, it was pure business. I put asses in seats and made sure the bands got paid. They grew to trust me and in some cases that led to life-long friendships, but I never started out with any group by trying to be their buddy, or wanting to promote them solely because I was a fan.

Ronnie Van Zant, the lead singer of Lynyrd Skynyrd turned out to be, probably, my best friend in the business. He was the nicest super-star I'd ever met. He'd call, out of the blue, every week or so, just to say "hi" and see how I was doing, just shoot the shit. We both loved baseball. He loved the Dodgers and we'd talk for hours about baseball. Ronnie, with all the hyped up bullshit surrounding the band and the business, all he wanted to do was sit at his home near Jacksonville, where he had a lake. All he wanted to do was fish, drink beer and talk baseball. We talked about "Super Jew", Dodgers' pitcher Sandy Koufax. One time I went to his house and Ronnie was out back, sitting on a lawn chair, fishing, drinking a beer and watching baseball on TV.

The band would stay at my house whenever they were in town. The photos for one of their album covers were shot in my yard, including one of us playing football. They were all good guys, but later on, I didn't have much use for the rest of the group because they were so into drugs, a bunch of drug addicts. They loved Dilaudid, which I was told is a synthetic heroin. I remember seeing them at the Rainbow Music Hall after Ronnie died in the plane crash. They were playing as The Rossington-Collins Band. They were so fucked up, I took them aside and said, "Didn't you guys get the message from God? What the fuck is the matter with you?" I think they're all dead now, except for Gary Rossington.

On October 22, 1977, the band finished a show in Greenville, South Carolina and was flying to Baton Rouge for a show at Louisiana

State University. Over southern Mississippi, reports say the plane ran out of fuel and crashed while making an emergency landing at a small air strip. How the fuck does that happen? Running out of fuel? Who fucked that up? Somebody had to have made the decision not to top off the tanks.

Here's what kind of friend Ronnie was, and this also tells what kind of guy Peter Rudge turned out to be. When I first saw Lynyrd Skynyrd at Ebbets Field in 1973, I was so impressed with them that I put myself out on a limb and told Peter that he should put them on the Who's tour that year. He did and it wasn't long before he swooped in and convinced them to fire their manager and hire him. So, Rudge, who I'd worked with on the Stones tours, too and who I got along with fine, called me.

"Barry, we've decided to let someone else promote Skynyrd in Kansas City. We're taking it away from you and giving it to Stan Plesser."

"What the fuck are you talking about? I've always done them there."

"Well, not this time."

"We'll see, Peter. We'll see."

I called Ronnie and told him what was going on.

This guy! He said, "Barry, let me tell you something. I will never play Kansas City for anybody but you."

So, the tour dates are announced and Kansas City is on it.

I called Ronnie. "What happened?"

Ronnie said, "Don't worry, Barry. I told you I'd never play there without you."

Two days before Skynyrd was supposed to play Kansas City, Ronnie says he's sick. So, the date is cancelled. It was rescheduled for a couple of months later. A day before that one, he gets sick again. He never played Kansas City for anyone else! That tells you what kind of guy Ronnie was. Nobody else would have done that. Great guy. So loyal. We had many great times together, Ronnie and the band. I spent as much time with them as I could.

What a sad, sad funeral. Charlie Daniels and 38 Special played "Amazing Grace" for Ronnie. I think Charlie read a poem, maybe did another song that he wrote for Ronnie. Really sad. And, of all the rock and roll funerals I'd been to, this was the only one where the guy had absolutely no hand in his own death. He was not a self-destructive guy. If you'd ever met a guy who wanted to live, it was Ronnie Van Zant. He loved life. And baseball. And fishing. He was buried with one of his fishing poles. A sweetheart. That's what he was. He was 29.

And, "Free Bird." What a great song. I don't know if it started out that way but it turned into a tribute to Duane Allman, who was killed in a motorcycle crash. Man, when those three guitars came out front, my God! That's one of the most powerful moments in rock music history.

There's a funny story—funny to me because of how much I hated Bill Graham—from when The Who Tour was in San Francisco in 1973. On the first night at the Cow Palace, The Who was on stage and Billy Powell of Skynyrd tried to get up close off stage to see the show. He wasn't wearing his pass, Graham saw him, figured he was somebody up to no good and punched him in the mouth. Ronnie, who was never afraid to mix it up, Gary and another band member or two all went to Billy's rescue and they wound up giving the promoter of their first night on tour a nice bloody taste of Southern charm.

As I'm sure everyone else did, I asked Ronnie about the band's name. It came from a gym teacher at their high school named Leonard Skinner who repeatedly sent boys to the principal's office because of long hair. Anything below the collar violated the school's dress code. What a blast to name your band after your gym teacher who tells you to cut your hair, just to piss him off! It was revenge, in a weird kind of way, but it wound up making Skinner a cult legend. He apparently went into real estate at some point and the band used a photo of a Skinner Real Estate yard sign in its *"Nuthin' Fancy"* album.

I still miss Ronnie.

Crosby, Stills, Nash and Young

When I was at Woodstock, Jerry Heller, the agent for Creedence Clearwater Revival was there, too. He and I booked them into the Denver Coliseum. October 4, 1969 with CCR and Lee Michaels. That was my first show at the Coliseum and we sold it out! 11,180 seats. The day of the show, Denver got 11 inches of snow, but the show went on. That was my first big show—other than the Denver Pop Festival—and I celebrated by using some of the ticket money to buy a Rolex.

As a rock venue, the Coliseum was a dump. The sound was terrible. It smelled like the stockyard and slaughterhouses across the street. Fans hated it. Bands hated it. But, we had no choice, it was the only venue of that size in Denver. My next show there was Thanksgiving weekend, 1969. What a great show: Crosby, Stills, Nash and Young with Santana opening. I'd never seen Santana until Woodstock, and their brilliance there made me regret even more my decision to take Aum instead of Santana for the Denver Pop Festival. Anyway, I booked CSNY and Santana for Denver on Wednesday night and Salt Lake City the next night, Thanksgiving night.

Everybody told me I was nuts and would lose my shirt with the Thanksgiving show. "This is Salt Lake. Kids will be with their families. You can't do a show on Thanksgiving."

We sold it out. Kids didn't care; they'd been sitting around all day and wanted to get out.

Another promoter booked CSNY and Santana for Friday in Dallas. I had them again on Saturday in Phoenix. We're at the Arizona Coliseum. CSNY made it, but their equipment was sitting at the Dallas airport. American Airlines forgot to load it. The production guy for CSNY was Leo Makota; he was their road manager for a long, long time. In fact, Neil Young and David Crosby were at his house in California just after the Kent State shootings and that's where Young wrote "Ohio". Anyway, I don't know how he did it, but Leo got through on the phone to the president of American Airlines at a golf course early that Saturday morning. He told him, "If you don't get that equipment here, we're going to have a riot and people are going to die and it's going to be American Airlines' fault!"

American chartered a plane and delivered the equipment. It arrived at the Arizona Coliseum at nine p.m. The show started at ten.

The first time I met David Crosby was in Rockford, Illinois, when I booked The Byrds into the Rockford College gymnasium. He was a prick to me and must not have been much better to the rest of the band, because they eventually threw him out. But, in 1968, when I booked the Byrds again, this time in Denver, he was a pretty mellow guy. We got along well and I enjoyed being with him. And we continued the friendship when I booked CSNY.

In 1973, when I was with the Stones in Hawaii, David invited us for a cruise on his sailboat. Now, I don't get really impressed by much, especially the fancy toys of the rich, but this sailboat, a huge thing, must have been 70 feet long, was called the Mayan and was absolutely gorgeous. It was a classic wooden sailboat that was meticulously cared for. Probably the most beautiful boat I'd ever seen, much less been on. David said he wrote some of his songs on the Mayan, including "Wooden Ships" and "Carry Me". Keith and Mick and the boys and Leslie from my office and me were taken on a cruise around Oahu. It was a perfect day, as most of them are in Hawaii. God was having a good day when he made Hawaii, no doubt in my mind.

But, David lost everything to the drugs he was doing, most notably cocaine that he was freebasing. He may have held on to the boat, but he lost pretty much everything else, including his career. He wound up in a Texas jail in 1982 for several months admitted later that he spent millions on drugs until 1985 when he was sent to prison for a year and a half on drug charges.

Most people don't realize the depths that he'd sunk to because of drugs. He was so fucked up when he came to Denver with "The David Crosby Band". Where he had played for full houses of thousands—tens of thousands—he was playing for 1400 people at the Rainbow Music Hall. The next day, they're leaving town to play another show. Around one or two the next afternoon, my office got a call from his band, which had already gone down the road a ways in their bus before they noticed something.

"David's missing."

"What do you mean, he's missing?"

"We can't find him."

They didn't look very hard. I sent someone over to the Holiday Inn where they'd been staying and he found David, still sleeping off whatever his drug of choice was the night before. Luckily, he woke up.

What a talented guy, but the drugs landed him in prison, twice, and nearly killed him. He picked up hepatitis along the way and received a well publicized, and controversial, liver transplant in 1995.

His story had a happier ending that Jimi's or Jim's or Janis's, but it's still sad.

There's no question that Neil Young is a musical genius. Just look at the songs he's written: "Heart of Gold", "Cinnamon Girl", "Only Love Can Break Your Heart", "Old Man", "Ohio". But, I was never quite sure what to make of him. He was a quiet guy, kind of moody. I didn't know how much of his other shit was put on, and how much was real.

Like one time when I had CSNY and I wanted all four of them to sign a guitar, David signed it, Stephen signed it, Graham signed it, but Neil wouldn't.

He said, "Wait a minute," and went back to his dressing room, brought out another guitar, signed it and gave it to me. He didn't want to be on the same one as the other three. The four of them made some great, great music together, some of the most memorable in rock history. But, for whatever reasons, they couldn't get along. Young always had his own thing going on the side with Crazy Horse.

Another time, I had Neil by himself, maybe with Crazy Horse. I was back stage, doing my thing, making sure everything was smooth.

He told me, "You look like a slob. How dare you come to one of my shows dressed like that."

Like "that", was in my typical attire: shorts and tennis shoes with a t-shirt and sport jacket. That's what I wore 90% of the time, not to be disrespectful or for any reason other than it was comfortable. I'd even gone to the White House dressed in shorts and tennis shoes.

President Clinton told me, "Barry, you look pretty comfortable."

"I am, Mr. President, you should try it sometime."

The next time I saw Neil Young, I figured I'd show him. I dressed up in a nice black suit and dress shoes, even wore a tie.

He came up to me and said, "Aren't you the fucking narc who busted me in '69?"

He had a weird sense of humor, to say the least, which was demonstrated again at a show in Portland, Oregon. My former employee Jeff Krump was working on Neil's tour. Thank God this wasn't one of my shows, because Neil decided he wasn't going to perform anything that he'd ever recorded. Now, people who buy tickets to see Neil Young want to hear the hits. He told the audience that he was going to play songs he'd never played in front of an audience before. They were a nice audience; they applauded warmly after each unfamiliar number.

When he finished, they brought him back for an encore. He said, "Okay, I'm going to play something you've all heard before." The place goes crazy! Which of his greatest hits would it be? Neil played the song that he started the show with! He thought it was funny.

He was a talented guy, though. Probably the most talented of the group.

The Ozzy Osbourne Blood Drive

June 24, 1997, I brought Ozzfest to Mile High Stadium in Denver. I think it's safe to say that never, in all of that stadium's years of events, had it hosted such a collection of freaky fans. Just consider some of the acts:

- Ozzy Osbourne
- Black Sabbath
- Marilyn Manson
- Pantera
- Type O Negative
- Fear Factory
- Neurosis
- Vision of Disorder

Those bands drew the types of fans you'd expect them to draw. Lots of black clothing.

Peter Boyles, a well known Denver radio personality, was with me as we walked through "the village" where fans could hang out and a smaller, second stage was located. A young woman, probably 20 or so, walked toward us. At first, I thought she was wearing a tight, flower print top, but as she got closer, I could see that she had no top on, just body paint.

"Are you Barry Fey?"

"Yes, I am," trying to look her in the eyes.

"Can I go see Ozzy?"

"No, I'm sorry, he's backstage getting ready to play."

"Would you give him this?" And she handed me a quart jar about half full with a dark colored liquid.

"What is it?"

"My blood. I want him to have my blood."

"Oh, I'm sure he'll be thrilled."

The whole Ozzfest deal, which wound up becoming a yearly event, was started because the people who came up with Lollapalooza wouldn't let Ozzy join the tour. So, Sharon, his wife and manager, created Ozzfest.

Ozzfest was getting a lot more attention than it normally would have because of Marilyn Manson. At each city, including Denver, there were protestors outside the stadium, mostly from religious groups or so-called "pro-family" and "pro-America" groups who were appalled by Marilyn Manson's "Satan worshipping" songs and I doubt they were too fond of his cross dressing, either.

But, the shows went on and Ozzfest was a success.

As for the jar of blood, I showed it to Ozzy, who poured shots for Peter and me and we toasted Satan. Of course we didn't. What really happened is when we went backstage, Ozzy was on the Stairmaster. He got a good laugh out of the blood story and I threw the jar into the trash.

That's the thing about Ozzy. He's a showman. One of original heavy metal showmen and one of the best ever. From the moment he walked on stage after I introduced him and yelled, "WHADDYA DOIN' MOTHERFUCKERS!" it was all show. He used to scare a lot of people: venue operators, police departments, parents; anybody who believed that he was really like he was on stage. The bat, dove, the Alamo and other stuff you hear and read about, that isn't who he is off stage. He's a good, gracious guy and we sold a lot of tickets together. That isn't to say that he didn't spend decades abusing drugs and alcohol, but that doesn't make him the bad guy so many people thought he was.

Here's how Ozzy and I met. In 1971, Frank Barsalona offered me a tour of Mountain, which was big in several places with its song, "Mississippi Queen". He had a new band he also wanted to tour called Black Sabbath. We booked them to smaller shows all over the Midwest and West to start and it became clear real quickly that Black Sabbath was selling over half the tickets and they were only getting $1,250 a show. I had to do something. Believe it or not, promoters can feel guilt.

In downtown Denver, I went to Kortz Jewelers and bought five beautiful watches that cost over $1,000 a piece. I had them engraved and gave it to the band. Ozzy says he still has his. He's been a good friend and a great guy. He gave me a guitar once and wrote on it, "To the greatest promoter that ever lived."

Arguably the greatest New Year's Eve party in the history of Denver included Ozzy. I'd developed a blood clot in my leg, Lisa and I were separated and I was feeling down, so naturally, I decided to throw a party. On December 31, 1996, Ozzy played McNichols Arena in Denver with his "Retirement Sucks" tour and had Korn as his

OZZY OSBOURNE

July 16, 1996

Dear Barry,

You were the first promoter in America to ever believe in me. That was 25 years ago. Now you're not only my favorite promoter in America, but also through the years you've become my good friend who I love and respect.

Happy Birthday!

God bless you.

Your friend always,

OZZY

opener. After the show, Ozzy, Sharon the rest of the band and Korn came to my house and so did strippers, hookers, bikers, lawyers, TV newscasters, the famous rock artist Denny Dent, Big Head Todd and the Monsters, Ugly Americans, Zoo People and a variety of uninvited but welcome drop-ins as word of the party spread. My juke box was blasting and I cooked about 40 pounds of my Cajun shrimp. We partied 'til 5:30 a.m. when the sound of the bikers leaving must have rattled the neighbors out of their beds, if they'd even been able to get to sleep with all the noise.

On the wagon now, Ozzy often mentions what a mystery it is to him that he was able to survive all the years of hard partying with drugs and booze. Sharon added recently "I've always said that at the end of the world there will be roaches, Ozzy and Keith Richards. He's going to outlive us all. That fascinated me—how his body can endure so much." She said that at a news conference in 2010 where a genetics company had discovered that Ozzy is a genetic mutant! He actually has a variant in his genes that impacts how his body absorbs booze, methamphetamines and other recreational drugs.

Backstage with Roger Daltrey

Mick and I at one of the famous Fey house parties

That's me, warming up the audience for Fleetwood Mac.

John doing a live concert on KFML Radio in Denver

Mick tuning up backstage at the Denver Coliseum

Even backstage at stadium shows, it's important for the promoter to be comfortable.

A denim-clad Elton in his pre-glitz era, backstage with Doobies' drummer Keith Knudsen

Arlo Guthrie and his band during a sound check at Red Rocks

22-year-old Stevie Wonder getting primped before opening for the Stones

A wild-eyed Chuck "give-me-the-cash-up-front" Berry

Pete Townshend cut his finger on a champagne bottle. Luckily, it was after the show.

Keith Moon and John Entwistle at the dinner I hosted where Moon ate the floral centerpiece

Shots from the Rolling Stones Luau in my backyard

"The Rocks of God". There's no better place to be on a cool, summer night than Red Rocks!

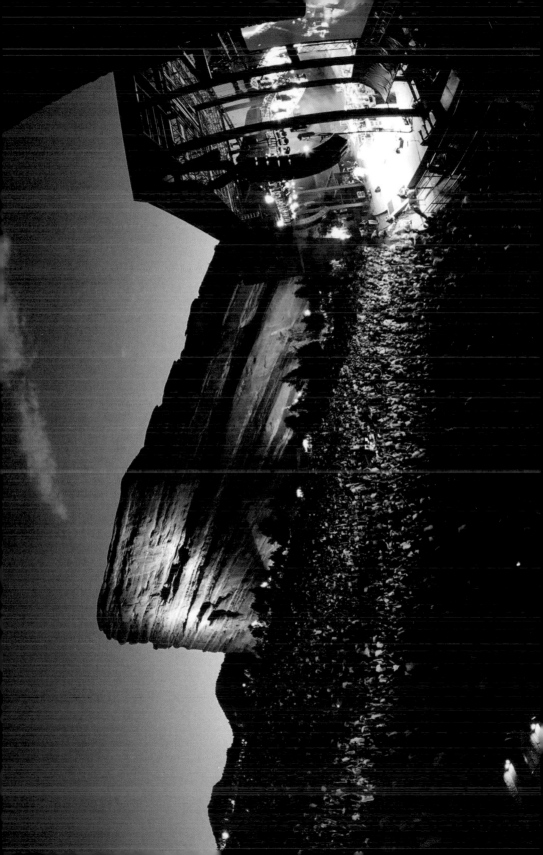

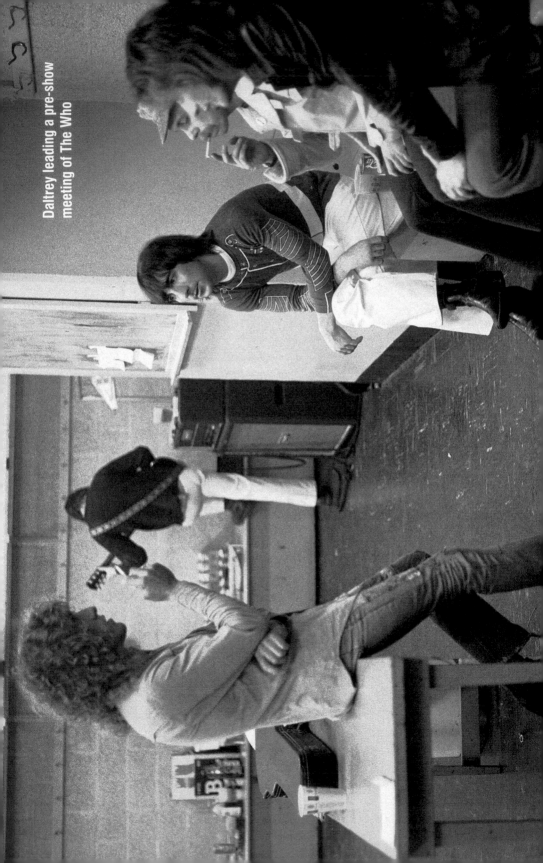

Daltrey leading a pre-show meeting of The Who

Essentially, his body is resistant to the drugs. The other thing that saved his life is Sharon. You've got to admire her for all of her business sense and for not only saving Ozzy and his career, but keeping their family together, too. And now she's got a huge career with the TV shows she's on. I teased Ozzy recently that he'd better watch out; Sharon was getting bigger than him. He said, "She already is!"

They're both entertainment icons, but one thing's for sure: in the history of heavy metal, there's never been, and never will be, a showman like Ozzy Osbourne.

Neil Diamond

He was so underrated. It became cool at one point to not like Neil Diamond. I guess that happens to some artists who are around for a long time. It happened to John Denver, too. But with Neil, you can't count on one finger anyone who was a better song writer. I mean, you had Lennon and McCartney and Jagger and Richards, but Neil wrote the lyrics and the music by himself.

And what great fucking songs! "Solitary Man", "Cherry Cherry", "Girl, You'll be a Woman Soon", "Thank the Lord for the Nighttime", "Kentucky Woman", "Red, Red, Wine", "I Am, I Said", "Holly Holy", "Song Sung Blue", "Cracklin' Rosie", and of course the one that's turned into a cult sing along song at sports events, "Sweet Caroline".

My favorite? That's a tough one, but I'm going with "Holly Holy". Neil didn't like to play it during concerts for some reason. When I'd greet him backstage, nearly the first thing out of his mouth was, "I'm not playing Holly Holy, Barry." The nudge that I am, I'd beg him, knowing that he probably never would. But, one night, he surprised me. Great song.

Just before taking the stage, Neil would gather his musicians and crew around in a huddle, like football teams do along the sidelines before they run onto the field for the kick off. As I watched the dozen or so people gather around Neil, he shouted, "Barry, get in here!" I don't recall what he or anyone said, but that was kinda cool.

Jerry Weintraub, who managed Neil, told me once that Neil was a handful. "This fucking guy is the biggest pain in the ass. He's so fucking miserable. He comes up to the office everyday and moans and groans. The cocksucker's got more talent and more money and is miserable." Jerry used to talk about people like that.

Years later, I had Brian Wilson opening for Paul Simon at Fiddler's Green in Denver. Neil was vacationing in Aspen and called me.

"Barry, you know how much I like Brian and Paul. Can I come down to the show?"

"Neil, of course you can. I'll take care of it."

Backstage before the show where everybody's eating and whatever, standing off to one side talking are Brian Wilson, Paul Simon and Neil Diamond. Three of the greatest writers in music history standing and talking. I remember bringing a photographer over and having him take that picture. What a trio of talent.

The people who run the Rock 'n Roll Hall of Fame just now, in 2011, got around to inducting him. Before Neil, they saw fit to induct Abba, Jeff Beck, The Hollies, The Stooges, Run DMC, John Mellencamp, Madonna, Blondie, Elvis Costello, The Clash plus dozens of people you've never heard of. Give me a fuckin' break. None of those people should have gone in before Neil Diamond. If it was me, I'd tell the H.O.F. to go get fucked. That's ridiculous.

Van Halen and the Brown M&Ms

Feyline, KDZA & USC's Concert Crew
presents
VAN HALEN
Sunday, March 30, 1980 — 7:00 p.m.
MASSARI GYM — Pueblo
USC Student $7.50
NO REFUNDS OR EXCHANGES

Nº 0572

munchies

- Potato chips with assorted dips
- Nuts
- Pretzels
- M & M's (WARNING: ABSOLUTELY NO BROWN ONES)
- Twelve (12) Reese's peanut butter cups
- Twelve (12) assorted Dannon yogurt (on ice)

supplies

- Forty-eight (48) large, bath-size cloth towels
- One hundred (100) cups for cold drinks (16 oz., waxed paper)
- Fifty (50) styrofoam cups (minimum 10 oz.) for hot drinks
- Forks, knives and spoons (metal, not plastic)
- Serving utensils, corkscrew, bottle and can openers

- Salt and pepper (in shakers)
- Tablecloths
- Napkins (paper)
- Two (2) large bars Ivory soap
- One (1) large tube KY Jelly

Part of Van Halen's contract rider, 1980

I did several shows with Van Halen over the years and in 1980, I had three shows in Colorado. The first one was at the University of Southern Colorado in Pueblo on March 30th which was a warm-up for the summer World Invasion Tour of Europe and North America. I brought them back in September for two shows at McNichols Arena on the 12th and 13th.

The Pueblo show was the first time I'd heard about the brown M&Ms. There are different stories about it, but one I was told is that the band wanted to make sure its contract rider, which detailed every little thing from trash bags to what kind of foods would be served to the roadies and at what time; virtually nothing was left to chance. So, someone suggested they put in "no brown M&Ms" as a gotcha; if there were brown M&Ms, then whoever was supposed to read the rider didn't and other important details, like the tube of K-Y Jelly, might have been overlooked.

In their Pueblo dressing room, the band found brown M&Ms and the boys, who had proven that they didn't need much of an excuse to damage hotel rooms and the like, tore up the college's dressing room. Tore it up so badly that the University banned not only Van Halen, but all rock concerts at the school.

Just because I enjoyed being a smart ass, I guess, four years later when I booked Van Halen to headline The US Festival (more on that in another chapter), I bought a big, silver chalice, had it filled with ONLY brown M&Ms, walked into Van Halen's dressing room and put it down on the table. The guys—Eddie and Alex Van Halen and David Lee Roth—laughed their asses off.

Van Halen's first manager was the guy who really discovered them and was getting them gigs around Los Angeles. But the band got rid of him at the insistence of Warner Brothers, their new record company. An A & R (Artists and Repertoire) manager at Warner Brothers became their manager. Then, they got rid of him in favor of

Ed Leffler, who had managed The Carpenters and a few other acts, including Sammy Hagar.

Ed and I had gotten along real well when I booked with him, but, for some reason—greed is my guess—when he took over Van Halen, Ed tried to screw me on a 1986 tour. He was trying to go around me. When I found out he was booking them into Folsom Field at the University of Colorado, I booked another show for the same day, July 12, 1986 and I was going to put on my own heavy metal stadium show. It was a standoff. They had the big name band, which would have buried mine if they had changed their date by a day or two; but, they would have had to re-route their tour at great expense. So, we made a deal to split it, 50-50. We co-promoted the show. I remember him coming up to me backstage.

He said, "It's a beautiful day, Barry."

"It was until you showed up."

Apparently, I wasn't the only one with hard feelings about him. A week later in Dallas where Van Halen played the Cotton Bowl, Ed got into a hotel elevator and barely made it out alive. Someone beat the shit out of him; knocked out some teeth and broke some ribs. He was in the hospital for a couple of weeks. One day when he was recovering, he called me:

"It was you, wasn't it!"

I said, "What the fuck are you talking about?"

"You had me beaten up."

"Ed, I wish! I wish it had been me."

I never knew the name of the hero who beat him up, but in Sammy Hagar's book, "Red, My Uncensored Life In Rock", he wrote that things didn't go well during the opening band's set. Butch Stone (who I knew from when he managed Black Oak Arkansas) had a band called Crocus. Sammy wrote that Crocus's set was supposed to be broadcast live on a radio station, but Leffler pulled the plug. There was a screaming match. Butch was upset and later at the hotel someone, Sammy doesn't suggest who, nearly killed Leffler.

Thyroid cancer finally did. He died in 1993 at the age of 57.

When David Lee Roth quit, Ed's other client, Sammy Hagar, became the lead singer. Nothing against Sammy, but I didn't think he was as good as David and, to me, Van Halen was more important when David was with them.

I had them back often including their Balance tour in 1995. It was September 20th at Fiddler's Green Amphitheater, which holds 18,000. As anyone who's spent time in Denver knows, the weather can do weird things and on that day, it snowed 11 inches. But, the band played on.

After that tour is when Sammy lost his job with Van Halen. Ed was gone and had been replaced by Alex's brother-in-law, Ray Danniels.

Several years later, I thought I'd had a stroke of genius. A can't miss: David Lee Roth and Sammy Hagar together. I thought people would just love it. It cost me $150,000 and I barely broke even.

Once again, I learned that it's much better when Barry Fey learns what the kids want and brings it to them, instead of trying to tell them what they should like.

The Beach Boys

There was probably no harder act to follow than the Beach Boys. Only two bands that I can think of stood a chance of maintaining the audience's energy: The Stones and The Who.

I wasn't in the business when they were in their surfing music heyday before they got blown out of the water by the Beatles and psychedelic music. But, in 1973, when they started to get a buzz going again, I played them several times. In 1974, Bill Graham was going to do a stadium tour of Crosby, Stills, Nash and Young with Santana as their opener.

"That's a pretty fucking boring show, Bill."

"You got a better idea?"

"Yeah. Put the Beach Boys on instead of Santana."

He did and we did several stadium shows together. It was great for the Beach Boys, but had to be a nightmare for CSNY. Live audiences loved the Beach Boys. They had all of those short songs that everybody knew the words to: "I Get Around", "California Girls", "Fun, Fun, Fun", "Little Deuce Coupe" , "Help Me, Rhonda", "Surfin USA" and on and on. Everybody was dancing and singing at the top of their lungs. By the time they were done, the crowd was in a frenzy. Then came CSNY, doing an acoustic set to open their act! The audience was all worked up with no place to go. CSNY got their higher energy stuff going later, but by then, they'd mostly lost the audience.

At the 1974 stop in Denver, Dennis Wilson came to me and said, "Barry, I've heard that there's some new kind of drug going around, called cocaine. Have you heard about it? Can you get me some to try?" Hah! Fucking Dennis. I knew that he was already well aware of cocaine. I told him, "No, man, haven't heard of it."

The year after the CSNY tour, I headlined the Beach Boys at Mile High Stadium in Denver. That was the first stadium headliner they'd done since the old days. We had Fleetwood Mac as their opener. 70,000 people showed up and went crazy. It was on my 37th birthday and, as I'd done before and did several times after, when the Beach Boys did "Barbara Ann" for their encore, they called me on stage and I sang the chorus with them. Of course, I assumed my microphone was off. Not until 2011, when I went on stage again with Al Jardine's Beach Boys and sang, did I find out that my microphone had been turned on all those years. But, at the '75 show, after the encore and as the boys were taking their bows, I started walking down the stage stairs and, Boom! Boom! Boom!—it was like Omaha Beach. I was hit with pie after pie. Front and back. They hit me in the head and on my body. The first one I saw throw a pie was Tom Ross, Fleetwood Mac's agent. After that, I don't know who all was bombarding me. I was so pissed off; obviously I didn't feel the love that I'm sure they all intended. Happy fucking birthday, Barry!

Brian wasn't touring with the band then. He was still locked in his room or whatever. Carl was alright, but he was pretty quiet. Dennis was just crazy and his friendship with Charles Manson tells you something. Mike Love thought he was better than everybody. Al Jardine was really a good guy. I liked him.

The Beach Boys were amazing. They still are. There are two "Beach Boys" touring: Al Jardine's band and Mike Love's band. They're both great. They still get the audiences worked up.

Bette Midler

The Divine Miss M! I love her. She was so much fun. Bette was the modern day Sophie Tucker; bawdy and just such a great performer.

I did a lot of dates with her when Barry Manilow was her piano player. She was so mean to him. He was good, but there was no question who the star was. I had Bette in Texas once and finally, she let

Barry do his own song right after intermission at the beginning of the second act. He played "Mandy", which Clive Davis got for him and we all know how Barry's story worked out.

Bette purposely avoided Las Vegas for years because she knew the crowds wouldn't respond the way she wanted. Here's the problem with many Vegas crowds: half the men are there because their wives dragged them away from the casinos. The guys can't wait for the show to be over so they can get back to the tables. But, the offers kept coming and the money got too big for Bette to turn down.

When she played Caesars Palace, she invited me to the show. Bette was great, as always. She played three hours and worked so hard to get the people off, but, the audience was dead. When I went backstage to the dressing room, she was crying, because she couldn't get those people to respond. They just politely applauded.

I can't say enough good things about Bette. Wherever she played for me, she killed. Take any of the current crop of female acts: Lady Gaga, Madonna, Britney, Katy Perry—Bette has more talent than any of them.

And what a personality! She's the same off stage as she is on.

If Bonnie Raitt had accepted my marriage proposal in the late '70s, I probably would have had to dump her for Bette.

Part Nine

ROCK 'N ROLL

○ **From A to Z**

Alice Cooper

As far as heavy metal goes, no one put on a show like Alice Cooper. The combination of great music and all of the tributes to horror-flicks—the fake blood, face makeup, the electric chairs, the snakes and guillotines—had never been seen before. It was more show than concert, but like I said, the music was great. "I'm Eighteen" hadn't become a big hit yet when I booked them to play in 1970 at the University of Denver football stadium, which was torn down shortly after that.

A couple of numbers into their set, the lead singer jumped off the stage and ran a couple of laps around the track. Along with most of the audience, I was wondering "What the fuck?!"

I found out later that his name was Vince Fournier, who was a track star growing up in Phoenix. His band and crew were full of good athletes. I hosted several basketball and softball games at my house and elsewhere where Feyline teams would take on the bands. The basketball champion was probably Alice Cooper, because they had a roadie who was nearly seven feet tall. They had a good softball team, too.

Just the opposite of the on-stage persona, Vince is one of the friendliest, most outgoing, wittiest people I've ever met.

Aretha Franklin

Undoubtedly, the Queen of Rock 'n Roll. Among her fans, and among others in the industry, she's a goddess. That's why I was shocked that we were able to get her for the Jamaican World Music Festival. She didn't like to fly much, but we had chartered some planes to ferry the bands down there, so at least she didn't have to fly commercial.

She was a trouper, though, and as she always did, put on a hell of a show.

Billy Joel

People tend to devalue Billy because of the alcohol problems he's had over the last several years. Three crashes in two years; his marriage to Christie Brinkley fell apart. He's fallen on hard times, image wise. But, where is today's "Piano Man"? There isn't one. That's one of the greatest songs ever written.

We had a show with him at McNichols, a big show. My son Alan wanted backstage passes for himself and a couple of his buddies, all teenagers.

"Really, *you* want backstage for Billy Joel?"

"Oh yeah, Dad. We've got to see Billy."

They didn't give a shit about Billy. All they wanted to see was Christie. Wherever she was backstage, they were close by. She'd move. They'd move. Can't blame them, she was a pretty lady. How do you divorce Christie Brinkley? But then a lot of people were wondering why she married him. Love is strange.

It wasn't long after that I had Crosby, Stills, Nash and Young at Red Rocks. Christie showed up with another guy. How did I miss out on that?

Bob Seger

The first time I had Bob Seger was in July of 1974 at Ebbets Field in Denver and then many, many times elsewhere. Seger put on a great concert. That album, "Strangers In Town" in 1978 was my favorite. Seger was a poor man's Springsteen, which isn't a knock on him at all. His songs are great. He's great. He always played "Get Out of Denver" when he played in Colorado.

There was a period when I couldn't book him. Nobody could. Turns out it was because he was self-conscious about his weight.

The longest night I ever had at a boxing match was because of Seger. It was the first Tommy Hearns and Sugar Ray Leonard fight at the outdoor arena at Caesars. A bunch of us went to the fight. I thought Leonard would kill him and I bet that way. But, Seger is sitting right behind me during the fight and he's from Detroit and his money was on his homie Hearns. Every time Hearns would land a good punch, Seger would pop me in the back of the head, the neck or the shoulder. Not to hurt me, he was just into the fight, excited for Hearns. He was very effusive in his support.

Fourteen rounds of that! I wanted to root for Leonard and my money; "Go Sugar, get 'em Sugar!", but each time I thought about it, I envisioned not having any more Bob Seger dates.

So, I just shut up and took the punishment. But, I got paid; Leonard won.

A bit of irony: Seger's manager's name was "Punch" Andrews.

Bon Jovi

It was common to have basketball and softball games between roadies for the bands and my Feyline crew. We won a good share of the games because of my security guys, who were not only huge, they were mean.

One of the times I had Bon Jovi at McNichols Arena, his roadies challenged my crew to a basketball game. I arranged for the Denver Athletic Club to be open for a midnight game after the concert.

When I went over a little early to make sure everything was all set, I found Jon Bon Jovi engaged in a pregame workout: having sex on the basketball floor.

Bonnie Raitt

There weren't many female singers more appealing to me than Bonnie Raitt. Not only was she talented beyond measure with her white R&B songs, she was smart with a fabulous personality, had a social conscience, stood up for what she believed in politically and, last but not least, was gorgeous.

In the mid to late '70s, I booked her on the same bill with ZZ Top in Honolulu. We were staying on Maui in Lahaina and I can't remember what the occasion was, but we were both at some event.

Hawaii is such an incredibly beautiful place where romance comes easy and I was caught up in the moment.

She's talking and I'm hanging on every word.

Her beautiful red hair was blowing gently in the tropical breeze.

I'm lost in her big brown eyes.

The moment was perfect.

"Bonnie?"

"Yes, Barry."

"Will you marry me?"

"Nooooo!" in a tone of voice that to me said, "Where in the fuck did that come from?"

Clearly, she wasn't interested in giving anyone something to talk about.

Carly Simon

Who didn't love Carly Simon's album covers? The "No Secrets" album with her very large nipples protruding through her sweater, and the "Playing Possum" album where she's kneeling and wearing a black negligee and black boots? My God.

Before I had a chance to play her, I saw her in London at Mr. Chow's restaurant. I was going to introduce myself and see if I could get her to tell me who she was singing about in "You're So Vain". But, as I watched her in the restaurant, I couldn't believe what a shit she was to the wait staff. She was horrible to them. I decided not to talk to her.

She ended up doing several concerts for me, but after the display I saw in London, I had no interest in getting to know her.

Cat Stevens

One of the most truly auspicious debuts in Denver music history took place in the early '70s. There was a guy out there named Cat Stevens who had captured the attention of the whole country. I don't think there was a radio format that wasn't playing his songs: "Moon Shadow", "Peace Train", "Wild World", "Morning Has Broken" and on and on. Great songs that appealed to a wide range of people.

Cat was probably my highest maintenance act, not because of any stupid demands for the correct color of candy or anything like that. He'd had tuberculosis in 1969 and wanted the temperature to be exactly 78 degrees. And we had to be able to prove it. So, there I am, walking around the arenas with a thermometer before and during the concerts.

His sound checks were unbelievably thorough and precise. In 1972 at the Denver Auditorium Arena—where I introduced relatively unknown congressional candidate Patricia Schroeder to Cat's audience—Cat had his sound guy take a meter to every corner. Later, at 20,000+ seat McNichols Arena in Denver, they followed the same routine: they checked every corner with the sound meter to make sure the sound was as good as it could be. He was a perfectionist. He said Big Mac, may it rest in peace, was the best sounding big building he'd ever been in.

Cat's tuberculosis may have been the best thing that could have happened to him in terms of his career. While he was recuperating—and it took several months—he wrote a bunch of songs and I defy you to find back-to-back albums that were better than *"Teaser and the Firecat"* with "Moon Shadow", "Morning Has Broken", "Peace Train" and the rest. *"Tea For the Tillerman"* with "Wild World", "Father and Son" and "Where Do The Children Play?" was a year earlier. Great, great songs.

And talk about captivating, when Cat was singing, everything froze. People stopped talking, vendors stopped vending and I can say for sure that promoters stopped promoting and measuring the temperature. We were in awe. It was like everyone was in their own living room with Cat sitting there. He could have played as long as he wanted to. We brought him back to Denver many times and it was always 78 degrees.

Before I booked Cat's first show in Denver I received a letter from his New York-based manager, Nat Weiss. Nat was one of the best in the business and we had a long, wonderful relationship. But, it didn't start out on the best foot.

In his letter, Nat wrote that he and I would be partners for this show. We would be co-promoters. 50-50. I had never seen anything like that and I wasn't going to agree to it. So, I called him.

"Mr. Weiss, this is Barry Fey."

"Oh, yes Barry, how are you?"

"I'm fine. I received your letter.

"Wonderful. I'm looking forward to doing business with you."

I said, "Yes, well, there are only a couple of things. First, when are you going to arrive?"

"What are you talking about?"

"Well, if you're going to be my partner on the date, I assume you're going to come out here and put up posters and hand out handbills and do the things we do to make the date a success."

"No, I don't do that. I'm not going to do that."

"Well, then you're not getting half the fucking date."

He was quiet for a moment.

"I can see that this is going nowhere, so I won't be insisting on doing the partnership with you, but everybody else is doing it, so please don't say anything and we'll just forget about it."

Apparently the other chicken shit promoters would just take that kind of crap. For a couple of years, until he stopped that practice, I was apparently the only one who wasn't splitting the dates, although I can't believe Bill Graham would have agreed to that. He just wouldn't have been as clever as I was. He would have just said, "Fuck you."

Celine Dion

Celine Dion and I are a lot alike. Just like me, she made it really big with very little talent. I know how great her fans think she is, but I think her performances were unremarkable.

The first time I booked Celine was at Fiddler's Green, an outdoor amphitheater in the Denver area, when she opened for Michael Bolton. The next year, when I wanted to book her again as a headliner, I was told that she didn't want to do Fiddler's, she insisted on Red Rocks. I said, "No, no offer."

Her manager asked, "What do you mean, 'no offer'? It's Celine Dion!"

"The reason I won't give you an offer is because the people who like her and want to see her aren't Red Rocks people. They don't want to climb the mountain and the stairs and sit on the benches at Red Rocks. They want to go to more comfortable Fiddler's Green where there are sidewalks and ramps and seats with backs and arms and it's easy."

Well, the order came from her husband, Rene Angelil, who once cost me a date and a lot of money in Vegas. In the late '90s, Rene was famous for his high stakes gambling and "high stakes" doesn't do it justice. He's known as the highest of the high rollers, throwing down millions and, of course, not always winning. I was informed that my 1998 date for Celine at the MGM Grand was cancelled because Rene had agreed to some kind of arrangement with Caesars and made a deal to put Celine in the Thomas and Mack Arena as "Caesars Presents Celine Dion". On October 16, 1998 over 17,000 people showed up. Those should have been my tickets.

Anyway, as for the Red Rocks show, I was having dinner at Charlie Lyons' house. Charlie started and ran Ascent Entertainment, which owned the Colorado Avalanche of the National Hockey League. Also at the dinner was Pierre Lacroix, the general manager of the Avalanche. Pierre was a good guy and when I told him my story and why I thought Red Rocks wouldn't work for Celine, he called his close friend Rene right there from Charlie's house.

"I think you should listen to Barry," he told him. Rene refused and insisted on Red Rocks.

Tickets weren't selling very well and I tried again to move it to Fiddlers, but Rene refused again and Celine did Red Rocks. Only 6,000 people showed up.

Guess who she and Rene blamed.

Charlie Sheen

Long before Sheen's 2010 meltdown that led to him being fired from "Two and a Half Men" and resulted in that ridiculous tour where he demonstrated to anyone stupid enough to buy a ticket that he was a train wreck, Charlie showed me what a mess he was.

As I mentioned in the chapter about U2, during 1987's "Joshua Tree Tour" and after our success with the "Under a Blood Red Sky" documentary, Bono asked me to help with the "Rattle and Hum" documentary. I arranged for most of it to be shot in Denver. The rest was going to be shot in Rio, but something went wrong and Bono asked me to come up with another site. I booked them for two nights into Sun Devil Stadium at Arizona State University, where "Joshua Tree" had started in April.

On the second night, I was backstage in the hospitality area when Charlie Sheen walked in with a pretty young female companion. I recognized him from "Platoon". Charlie said some quick hellos and went straight to the refreshment table, grabbed a fifth of something and started drinking, right out of the bottle. The show had started, so I went up to watch, stage right. About a half hour later, Sheen and his girlfriend walked up beside me. He's obviously drunk and within a couple of minutes, he pukes all over the floor. I got some security guys to get him out of there and I thought that was the end of that.

This was the 21st of December. The boys had been touring since April. They were going to fly home the next day for Christmas. After the show, I joined them at the Biltmore Hotel for an after-party. It was a small, quiet, invitation-only affair. It was about one o'clock in the morning and the band was flying home at ten. People were sitting around reminiscing about the tour and feeling excited about being able to go home for the holidays. It was a real nice moment. All of a sudden we were interrupted by the sounds of someone retching. It was Charlie, drunk and puking in Bono's bathroom.

What a pig.

Cher and Gregg Allman

The Allman Brothers had some stupid shit in their contract addendum, better known as the rider. When they showed up, you had to give their roadie, Red Dog, a corkscrew. And, they demanded 16 ounce cans of beer, not 12 ounce cans. But, they really could play.

I had them in Kansas City once when they were big as could be. It was at the Royals' baseball stadium. Less than an hour before they're supposed to take the stage, everybody's there except Gregg. Someone went back to the hotel and found him passed out on the floor. He'd overdosed on drugs; not enough to kill him, just enough to make him late for the show. They woke him up and he made it to the show. But, I never forgave him for that. The fans pay good money for tickets and for some asshole to not care enough about them like that, is unforgiveable.

Years later, I had Bette Midler playing at the Kansas City Music Hall. I'm backstage before the show and someone tells me that Cher is at the back door and wants to come in to say hello to Bette. I go to the door and she's there with Gregg Allman.

"Cher, you're welcome to come in, but he can't come in."

"But, he's my date."

"I'm sorry, Cher, but he can't come in."

The look on her face was precious. She left unhappy.

Chuck Berry, Sha Na Na and Steely Dan

Donald Fagen remembers the 1973 show at the Denver Coliseum as one of the worst ever for him and Walter Becker: Steely Dan. The band was only a year or so old and they were touring to support their first album that had "Do It Again" and "Reelin' In The Years" on it. Somehow, they wound up on my bill with Sha Na Na and Chuck Berry.

Steely Dan opened, and as good as they were, the crowd just wasn't into their music. They were there for the '50s bee-bop stuff from Chuck and Sha Na Na.

Just as Becker and Fagen were finishing, Chuck showed up. We chatted for a while—I'd played him several times before. He wanted to be paid up front, which was standard for him and, frankly, for a lot of the older black acts. There was no question he was taken advantage of in the old days, but not during my time. But, he took it out on everybody. In his rider, if you didn't have a certain amplifier, you'd be fined $2000. He never traveled with a band; we'd use a local group as his back up. Once, when he didn't like the job the bass player was doing, he kicked him off the stage, in front of 15,000 people. He was difficult.

After I paid him, he said, "I want to go on now."

"Chuck, you can't. Sha Na Na is setting up and when they're done, it'll be your turn."

"Put me on now, or I'm gone."

Well, he had my money, so what could I do? I told the crew to get Sha Na Na's stuff off stage and set up for Chuck. Sha Na Na was pissed. One of them went off on me yelling, "Bill Graham would never let any shit like this happen." And the guy—Vinnie Taylor was his name—came at me, so I popped him in the jaw. Knocked him on his ass. I was a tough guy back then. I didn't go looking for fights, but I sure wouldn't back down if somebody came after me or was screwing with my business. Chuck played, the crowd loved him. Then, Sha Na Na had to try to keep them. By the way, Taylor died a couple of years later from a heroin overdose.

Another time, I got pissed off at one of Cheap Trick's crew. I took a swing at him, but he was really tall, near seven feet, and I whiffed. I jumped and tried again, and whiffed again.

Cream

Jimi Hendrix played for me at Red Rocks on September 1, 1968. He was supposed to play on the second and I'd promoted it that way and had already sold tickets for the show when Hendrix moved it to the first. We had enough lead time, I thought, and everything seemed to work out okay.

Three days after the concert, my office phone rings. On the phone was a kid from Wichita, his father and his father's attorney.

The kid had bought tickets for the September 2nd show. He flew into Stapleton, took a cab to Red Rocks, a twenty-mile cab ride, and there's nobody there. He goes back to Denver, stays in a hotel and flies back the next day. The kid's disappointed, the father is furious and the attorney says he's going to sue.

I said, "I'm really sorry about what happened. I wish you wouldn't sue me...I'm kind of new at this...I had no idea that I needed to let someone in Wichita know that the date had been changed. In a couple of months, I have Cream coming."

The kid says, "You what?"

"I have Cream coming."

"You get me two tickets to Cream and we'll forget the whole thing."

"No we won't!" said his dad.

"Oh, yes we will, Dad."

And that was the end of that. Well, almost the end of that. The kid probably got much more of a show than he expected. I couldn't find an opening act for Cream, so I booked Dr. Dante, a hypnotist. He got on stage and starts his thing; I don't know if it's real or not, but he invites an audience member to come on the stage. A young woman volunteers. And before long, she's under Dr. Dante's spell and starts taking off her clothes! Her brother runs out of the audience and jumps on stage, covering her up with his coat.

Booking Cream wasn't as easy as I thought it was going to be. I wanted to book them in the Auditorium Arena on October such and such. You had to go through the city to book the arena. Sam Feiner ran the arena.

"You can't have that date. There's basketball practice."

"Basketball practice?" The Denver Rockets of the American Basketball Association were a year or two old at that time. "I can understand it if there's a game, but practice?"

"You can't have the arena on that date."

Well, back when we opened The Family Dog in September of 1967, an older Jewish man came up to me accompanied by a young woman.

"My name is Nate Feld and this is my daughter Shayna and she really wants to go to this show, but I'm really scared to let her go. You're the boss here, right?"

"Well, I work here."

"Will you keep an eye on her and make sure she's okay? I'm very well connected. Tom Currigan (the mayor of Denver) and I are very good friends. Anytime you need anything, just call."

Okay. I made sure Shayna had a good time and that was it.

Fast forward to the Sam Feiner conversation about the basketball practice. I called Nate Feld and said, "If you can get me the arena, I'll give you ten percent of whatever I make."

Nate, who became a good friend and partner we called Uncle Nate, called the mayor. The mayor called Sam Feiner. I get the arena. That was October, 1968 and was the first of a string of shows I put on at the arena. Janis and Big Brother are in November. On December 26th, I booked a Christmas show for Vanilla Fudge with Spirit as the opener. I decided to go on the radio to SING my commercial.

"You'd better not shout, You'd better not cry,
You'd better not pout, I'm telling you why;
Vanilla Fudge is coming to town!"

We sold out. 7500 seats. But, the biggest story of that concert wasn't my singing commercial, nor Vanilla Fudge or Spirit. That was the show where Led Zeppelin made its North American debut.

Dan Fogelberg

Dan was just like his music. Gentle. There was nothing pretentious about him, just a quiet guy who made a lot of people happy with his songs.

He died way too young at 56. He'd been diagnosed three years earlier with prostate cancer.

When he married Jean in 2002, I went to their wedding in Pagosa Springs and, just as anyone who knew him would expect, it wasn't a glitzy pop star wedding. What you saw is what you got with Dan.

Dan's beginnings go back to my old buddy Irving Azoff. Dan had dropped out of the University of Illinois which is where Irving got his start in the music business. They had plans to head for Los Angeles and the "big time" together. Irving gave Dan a couple of hundred bucks for the trip, but he ran out of money in Estes Park, Colorado, which was probably the best thing that ever happened to his career. He fell in love with and settled in Colorado and wrote many of his big hits there. He bought a place in Nederland, near the Caribou Ranch studios, and later bought a ranch in southern Colorado.

The first time we played him was at Ebbets Field in downtown Denver. Irving traveled with him and my Ebbets partner Chuck Morris remembers Irving saying that this guy would be selling out arenas in a couple of years. He was right. Dan put on some magnificent shows, but I have to believe that given his love for Colorado, the shows at Red Rocks were his favorites.

Deep Purple

Deep Purple was on the next wave out of Britain just after Vanilla Fudge. They were heavy metal before that category existed. And loud? Wow. But, they sold a lot of tickets.

Every now and then, some asshole roadie or band would threaten to call off the show if they didn't get such and such. Deep Purple came to Denver for two shows at the Denver Coliseum through some other promoter. But, they cancelled because one of the singers lost his voice. About a year later, I brought Deep Purple back and kids had held on to their tickets from the first show, so I honored them, even though I hadn't sold them. What could I do? We sold out two shows at the Coliseum, 23,000 tickets. Deep Purple was huge. One of the Super Trouper spotlights wasn't working. The road manager and one of the roadies came out and said, "If that light doesn't work by show time, we're not going on."

I said, "You motherfucker, these kids have held on to their tickets for a whole year and you're not going to go on? Let me show you something." I grabbed all the security guys I had on the floor and put them at the back door, the stage door. "If you think you're going to leave, you're going out the front door. I'm going to get on stage and tell the crowd that, 'I'm sorry, Deep Purple doesn't want to play, they don't care that you've held onto your tickets for a year, they're going to leave and they'll be walking through the audience on their way out.'" That straightened that out. You ain't gonna play! Hah! Don't tell me that shit.

Fleetwood Mac

In 1969, I brought Fleetwood Mac to the Denver Coliseum for my Christmas show. I decided it was time for another singing radio commercial:

"On the fifth day of Christmas, Feyline brings to you,

Johnny Winter, Fleetwood Mac, Zephyr and the Flock,
And all for three-fifty."

$3.50! We sold it out, of course.

It must have been 1973 or '74 that I had Fleetwood Mac back at the Denver Coliseum. When I showed up for the sound check, there was a band on stage. I went up to my stage manager and asked, "Who's that on the stage?"

He said, "That's Fleetwood Mac."

"What the fuck are you talking about?" Fleetwood Mac is instantly recognizable, if for no other reason, because Mick is 6'8" tall. There were no tall people on the stage.

I climbed on stage and said, "Who are you people?"

One guy said, "We're Fleetwood Mac," and he tried to run some bullshit by me that John McVie and Bob Welch had quit the band and Mick and Christine were taking a break and would catch up to the band at a later date.

I told him to get off the stage. He said, "Listen, fella, we're the only Fleetwood Mac you're getting tonight."

I said, "The only way you're getting into this building tonight is with a ticket. Now, get the fuck out of here." I had my security guys encourage them to pack up and leave. I went into Uriah Heep's dressing room—they were the opening act—and told them the situation. They said they'd play the whole show, not to worry about it.

As the show was ready to begin, I went on stage and made an announcement. "Ladies and gentlemen, a band impersonating Fleetwood Mac showed up here tonight to try to steal your money. I refused to let them insult you and tarnish Fleetwood Mac's name. Uriah Heep has agreed to play the whole show. We'll wait 15 minutes and if anybody wants a refund, please go to the box office now." A few people did, but most of them stayed and Uriah Heep put on a good show.

Mick Fleetwood thanked me later for doing that and never forgot it.

When Lindsey Buckingham and his girlfriend Stevie Nicks joined Fleetwood Mac in 1975, the band really took off. Their big break was on July 16th, 1975, my birthday, where I had them open for the Beach Boys in front of 70,000 fans at Mile High Stadium. That was their first big stadium show and proved that they could do it.

When they went on their Tusk tour in 1979 and 1980, they sold out in every city. 122 shows in the United States, Europe, Australia,

New Zealand and Japan, but it wasn't possible for them to sell enough to meet their expenses. First of all, they had such a big entourage that after the band leased a big private plane, a 737, it was so full, that they leased another plane just for the band. Backstage was a bacchanal. Their rider required a catering service the likes of which we'd never seen. Fine wines—$400 to $500 per bottle, china plates, crystal glassware, Sterling silver and on and on. They demanded so many liquor stations backstage that you couldn't walk in any direction without bumping into one. They had them on the way to the stage, all over the place; more than you'd see at a large hotel convention. John Courage, J.C., was their tour manager and he'd go ballistic if things weren't just right. Fleetwood Mac was a band of extreme excess.

One of Stevie Nicks' most embarrassing moments had to be at Red Rocks in Denver. She was so coked up that she stumbled and had to be helped up the ramp to the stage.

After Mac broke up, we took Stevie on tour in 1981. Actually, we took Stevie and her dad on tour. This was after the decadence of the Fleetwood Mac years. Stevie was clean and hired her dad, Jess, as her promoter. Jess hired Feyline, which meant that Jess was our partner.

Jess was a good guy, a very smart man. Before he retired from his corporate life in 1974, he was President of Armour/Dial and Executive Vice President of Greyhound Bus and brought both corporate headquarters to the Phoenix area where he lived with his family. After he retired, he got into the concert business. He opened a music shed called Compton Terrace in Chandler, which, not coincidentally, hosted many Fleetwood Mac and Stevie Nicks concerts.

We started the tour on November 28th, 1981 in Houston. Jess and, often, his brother Gene, would go on tour with us. Like I said, he was smart and shrewd and like most smart, successful people, he knew what he didn't know and he knew he needed us to run the tour. That pissed off a lot of the local promoters because they had to split the revenue with two promoters. Jess and Gene were also pretty enthusiastic drinkers and my national tour guy at the time, Jeff Krump, had to include "Jess and Gene watching" on his list of duties.

Jess had heart disease and had been through a few heart surgeries. He was on the board of directors for the Arizona Heart Foundation for many years and, again, no coincidence, Fleetwood

Mac and Stevie Nicks did some benefit concerts for the foundation. Jess died in 2005.

The Four Tops

I loved these guys! "Can't Help Myself"...what a song! Whenever I booked an oldies show, I put them on it. The biggest was the KOOL concert at Mile High Stadium in Denver. Over 81,000 people showed up.

Frank Zappa

It was often difficult for me to tell whether the groups I put on stage were having fun. That was never a question when it came to Frank Zappa. He had such a playful, mischievous, boyish way of engaging the audience. I played him in May of 1968 at the Dog in Denver and again in June of 1969 at The Denver Pop Festival at Mile High Stadium. When he got on stage at Mile High, he had about 20,000 people in front of him. He pointed at sections of the audience and told them that when he gave the cue, to stand up, make certain noises and sit down right away. You know, a sing around, kind of like when a bunch of people sing "Row, Row, Row Your Boat"? That kind of thing. He made up a song using the audience as his living, breathing, moving instrument. Some say it was the invention of "The Wave". Zappa was brilliant. He didn't just stand up there and play, he was really into the audience, I guess "interactive" is how we'd describe it today. He was a great musician, just fucking brilliant.

George Clinton, P Funk, The Mothership and Bootsy's Rubber Band

The first day that tickets went on sale in Chicago for George Clinton and his assortment of Parliament-Funkadelic All-Stars and the rest of the acts that would show up to be part of his Mothership, we sold four tickets. FOUR fucking tickets. When you put on a rock show, you'll sell 25,000 or 30,000 tickets the first day. Four tickets! It ended up selling out at Soldier Field with over 80,000 people. $12.50 each. It was our first $1 million grossing show, but was instructive in how urban audiences tend to buy tickets. They'll wait, expecting that the shows won't sell out and tickets will be cheaper later. We had huge walkups on the days of the shows. More times than not, over 50% of the tickets were sold to walkups. We learned to put tickets on sale the day welfare checks came out. We learned that you didn't buy advertising the traditional way; you paid radio station DJs to promote the shows for you.

Settlements on some of those P-Funk shows were really interesting because the local promoter might sell 25% partnerships to six different people, hoping the show would tank and he'd make money. But, when the shows made money, there were some really tense moments at the settlement table. Most of the guys would pull out their guns and set them on the table. Nearly everybody in the room was armed except for me and my advance man and settlement guy, Jeff Krump, a skinny little white guy who had all the money. At the Chicago show, I gave Jeff a t-shirt and said, "I dare you to wear this". On the front it said, "I'm the one who got your 12 bucks". On the back it read, "This shirt is bullet-proof".

Before the Soldier Field show, someone backstage said, "Barry, there's a problem out front", which meant with the crowd. So, as I did at all my shows, I walked out in front of the stage to see what was going on and fix it. There were over 80,000 black faces looking at me: a middle-aged, fat, balding white guy who's going to tell them what's what. I didn't even slow down, I just turned around and went backstage. I don't even remember what the problem was, I just knew that at that particular place and time, I wasn't the one to fix it.

We did over 50 shows between 1977 and 1978. There was always something going on at those shows. They were pretty wild with pretty much every performer constantly high on one thing or another. Joel Brandes, who was my national tour guy before Krump, took the tour to Atlanta where race became an issue. The black promoters didn't like white promoters running shows in the South and, for some reason, they went to the Communist Party and got it involved. To get the show on, we had to give part of the action to a group of black promoters, who lived really large. They chartered planes to fly to dates and spent money, their cut of the concerts, like crazy. After the southern shows ended, they vanished.

At the L.A. Coliseum in June of '77, when the crowd thought it was taking too long to change sets between bands, they'd indicate their displeasure by throwing open pocket knives and bullets onto the stage. The crew would be slipping on bullets, knowing that the people who threw them had faster ways of getting those bullets onto the stage. Rick James was on the show and wasn't coming out of his dressing room. He was in there primping or whatever and we were getting nervous because he was supposed to be on stage. Out front in the restless audience, there was a gunshot. People scattered, many of them running around to the backstage area to try to get away from the apparent danger. It took a while to get things calmed down and get James on stage. That was my cue to get out of there. Too much tension for me.

But, as out of my element as I was, that was probably my best deal ever as a promoter. A two-year plus tour and I collected 15% of the gross. Thank you, George Clinton, who's still friendly with me. Brilliant guy. He was the brains behind Parliament and Funkadelic and was one of the creators of funk.

Gwen Stefani

I'll take some credit for Gwen's marriage.

There was a party at my house after a Bush concert. It's important to note that I would never host a party for Bush, but I often let the company use my house for parties. It was a big place, so it wasn't unusual for me to be at home, minding my own business in one section of the house while a party was going on elsewhere. On that night, I walked into one of my several bathrooms and there was Gwen, making out with Gavin Rossdale of Bush. And, he was shootin' up. He had his works out on the vanity in *my* bathroom.

But, at least it seems to have worked out. They've got a couple of kids and I hope they're living happily ever after. I'm sure my house helped out. No doubt.

Jeff Beck

What a spectacular guitar player! He's way up near the top. Just as Beck gives credit to Les Paul as a major influence, the heavy metal guitarists of the '80s and '90s should give credit to Beck. He took what Paul created and took it to a higher level. Beck has played with everyone over the years, from The Yardbirds to Kelly Clarkson. But, in the '70s, he often wouldn't show up. I have no idea why, but there's no acceptable excuse. He became so unpredictable that we—other promoters and I—wouldn't risk the brain damage of booking him because we couldn't count on him showing up. Sometimes, we'd get a courtesy call a day before the show, but just as often, he just wouldn't show and we'd be left with a venue full of unhappy fans. There's nothing that pisses me off more than an act, superstar guitar player or not, who causes my audiences to have a bad experience.

Jerry Weintraub

As I've mentioned in other chapters, I worked with Jerry a number of times over the years and against him a few times, too. There's no question that he's one of the most successful men in the entertainment business with his Karate Kid and Oceans movies and is in a league of his own as a *self*-promoter, too.

At the Beverly Hilton Hotel in 1978, Jerry was the subject of a panel at the Billboard Magazine convention. Those Billboard conventions were the big thing in the industry in those days. This was the first of three years that I won "Promoter of the Year". I attended a panel discussion and on the dais was Frank Barsalona, Dee Anthony, who was Peter Frampton's manager and Bill Graham. The topic was how dangerous Jerry Weintraub was. Jerry was getting a cut of some of the acts that Concerts West managed and promoted. Pat O'Day started Concerts West in Seattle and later partnered with Danny Kaye, Lester Smith, Tom Hulett and Terry Bassett

After listening to all the bitching and moaning about Jerry and his national tours, I stood up in the audience. I said, "You know, I don't understand you guys. You don't know how to battle Weintraub. If one or two of us tries to fight him, it won't work." This was about two years after Concerts West brought Paul McCartney and Wings to Denver but went around me and dealt directly with the venue. I described to the audience and panel how mysterious things happened at that Denver show. The lights went on in the middle of sets. The tour trucks' tires were slashed. Odd things like that. I said, "If they run into that in one or two cities, it won't make a difference. If they run into it in 50 cities, there will be no more Jerry Weintraub or Concerts West problems. It won't be worth it." I got a huge round of applause, but when it came down to it, most of the other promoters were too afraid to do it. There was nothing I wouldn't do to defend my turf. I didn't slash his tires or turn on the lights, but I could understand how people who liked me and the job I did as a promoter might take it upon themselves to demonstrate their appreciation for me and dismay that I wasn't being allowed to do my job.

Joe Cocker

My first encounter with Joe was a month before Woodstock at the Denver Pop Festival. He was supposed to be going on stage, but the cops' teargas had sent the crowd running all over the field and it was pure chaos for a while. I found him in a restroom under the north stands at Mile High Stadium, not too sure about going out. He said, "So, this is America?"

He went on and had a great show. The next year was the "Mad Dogs and Englishmen" tour he was on with Leon Russell. I had them at Mammoth Gardens in Denver in 1970. That was one of the greatest shows I've ever seen. There was a choir, several drummers, horns... just a great show. And, their touring party was quite a sight with all the musicians and their entourage of wives, girlfriends, kids, roadies and the groupies who managed to sneak by me—it was pretty cool.

I thought he was terrific, and off stage he wasn't anything like he was on, where he had those weird, spastic moves. That Beatles' song he did, "With A Little Help From My Friends" was huge. Most of what he sang were covers, like "The Letter", "Feelin' Alright" and "You Are So Beautiful", but who cares? What a great, one of a kind performer.

John Denver

Peter Paul and Mary's version of "Leaving on a Jet Plane" hit number one on the *Billboard* charts in 1969. It was a huge, huge, hit written a few years earlier by John Denver. That song's popularity gave John the confidence to start performing his own songs solo. He'd been with the New Christy Minstrels and the Chad Mitchell Trio, but rarely did shows on his own. He started playing small shows in coffee houses and on college campuses and as word got around, the crowds got bigger. And when he outgrew the campus venues, the first big, non-college show was at Denver's Auditorium Arena in 1971.

A very nervous John and his manager, Jerry Weintraub, arrived in Denver for the show, which I'd gotten permission to book at the Arena in the post-Iron Butterfly riot haze pretty easily because even the city officials didn't consider John a rock 'n roll act. John really was worried about being on such a big stage, especially in front of his "hometown crowd"; in the city whose name he borrowed. But once he started that first song, the butterflies vanished and he was on his way.

That audience—and pretty much every one after that—ate it up. I hate to use a cliché, but when he was performing, you could hear the proverbial pin drop. He had them in the palm of his hand, and he hadn't even played his soon-to-be anthem: "Rocky Mountain High". I know I'm not the only one who relates to that song, especially this verse:

"He was born in the summer of his 27ᵗʰ year
Comin' home to a place he'd never been before"

That's how I felt when I came to Colorado.

That show was not only important to John, it was huge to me, too. He got Feyline back into the Auditorium Arena after the Iron Butterfly violence. I did a lot of shows with John, but none were as special as the ones at Red Rocks. Not only is it the best venue anywhere, what better surroundings for a guy so closely identified with Colorado's mountains? On the strength of his "Rocky Mountain High" album, we sold out three shows, back to back to back, at Red Rocks. You can count on one hand the number of acts that could do that, and still have a few fingers left over.

John and I talked often about all sorts of stuff, most of it unrelated to music. As you probably have heard or guessed, I've got an opinion about pretty much everything and John had plenty of his own, too, on politics, the environment, AIDs and famine in Africa and other social issues where he thought he could make a difference. And, he did more than just talk about things he was passionate about, he walked the walk.

One reason he may have liked me is because when it became "uncool" to like John Denver, to even admit that you listened to his kind of folk/soft rock/country got you ridiculed, I never snubbed him. He was such an honest, openly enthusiastic guy with that "Far out!" thing he did. I think it was mostly the so-called music critics who gave him a bad time because he sure sold a lotta fuckin' tickets and records.

I had my own "Far out!" John Denver moment that only indirectly involved John. He had a new book out and there was some sort of book fair in Denver. He called me on a Friday and asked if I'd go by the convention center the next afternoon and introduce him at his event. "Sure, John. Of course I will. It'll be an honor." The next morning a friend of mine dropped by and said he'd brought me a present.

"What is it?"

"A pot brownie."

"Is it good?"

"Yeah, it's great. But be careful, Barry. Just eat a corner of it."

Well, it tasted really good and telling a chronic overeater not to eat is a waste of breath. I ate way more of it than I should have. About an hour later, I was watching TV and got up to go downstairs to get something and I could barely stand. I had to hold on to the bannister. Then I started giggling. I decided I was in no shape to drive downtown to introduce John. I felt very bad about that, but I called the book fair people and asked them to pass along my apologies to John, that I was ill and had to cancel. I left the phone off the hook because I couldn't stop giggling. That was the first time I'd been stoned. "Rocky Mountain High, Colorado...."

One of my favorite performances of "Rocky Mountain High" happened in a Coors commercial. It was set in a dingy bar in some Pennsylvania steel town. All the tough guys in the bar are drinking Bud. Another guy sits down, orders a Coors and starts whistling "Rocky Mountain High". A couple of black girls at the end of the bar start singing the chorus and within seconds, the whole bar's singing it.

In 1976, I had a cough that wouldn't go away. Nearly every breath I took, I coughed. My doctor put me in a hospital where I found out that, at the age of 41, I had developed asthma. Late one night, around 11:30, a nurse came into my room.

"Mr. Fey, you have a telephone call. We don't normally allow calls this late, but he says he's John Denver."

John had heard I was in the hospital and was checking up on me. Just a friendly call.

To me, it wasn't unusual, we talked quite often. But, the whole floor was a twitter because *John Denver* was on the phone! I'd like to say that the nurses treated me much nicer after that, but they were pretty good to me before he called.

◇◇◇

In 1985, I'd heard that John was hurt when he wanted to be on "We Are The World", but the geniuses who were putting it together were worried that John's involvement would hurt the song's credibility. Give me a fuckin' break.

John would have been very pleased, I think when, in 2007, the Colorado State Legislature made "Rocky Mountain High" an official state song.

There haven't been many entertainers on John's level. He had a rapport with his audiences that few performers can pull off.

John was a good friend. I miss him.

Lars Ulrich and Metallica

While the coolest guy in rock 'n roll is Keith Richards, Lars Ulrich isn't far behind.

He's got that confident air about him, does what he wants, when he wants and isn't afraid to say what he wants or make a stand for what he thinks is right. He testified before a U.S. Senate committee against the people who were ripping off Metallica and other bands through Napster and other Internet file sharing sites.

After I retired, Metallica was in Denver and Lars invited my son Tyler and me to sit behind his drum kit on stage during a concert at Mile High Stadium. James Hetfield married one of my former security girls and Lars has become like family.

Lars would always call with impossible shit. In January of 1997, they were playing Denver and Lars decided to get married to a woman named Skylar. He knew I had connections in Las Vegas.

"Barry, can you set the wedding up for me in Vegas?"

"I can try. When?"

"This weekend."

"Lars, it's Super Bowl weekend. That's going to be nearly impossible."

"Come on, Barry, I know you know people."

Once again, my pal Richard Sturm, the president and chief operating officer of MGM Mirage Entertainment and Sports came to my rescue and helped me get the wedding and the hotel rooms set up. They played Friday and Saturday nights in Denver and after the last show, hopped on a private plane for Vegas and a late night/early morning wedding. Lars invited me to go with them, but, I passed. He and Skylar didn't quite make it to "happily ever after", but he had two sons with her.

Another time, when the Rangers were in the Stanley Cup playoffs, Lars had his co-manager Tony Ciaccio call me.

"Barry, Lars wants to get some Rangers tickets. Can you fix him up?"

Of course, I said, "Let me see what I can do."

I found tickets, but they were $7500 each. I called Tony back.

"Tony, how many shows do you sell out each year at the Garden? And you can't call somebody there and get two tickets?"

He called and got them.

As I mentioned elsewhere in this book, Lars' standard greeting to me since a Metallica-Guns 'n Roses stadium show has been, "Barry, you packin' today?"

The Mamas and Papas

The Mamas and Papas had the best harmonies of any group I heard. Sure, you've got CSNY and the Beach Boys, but they're not as good as the Mamas and Papas. That was the most unique assemblage of voices. Their "30 Golden Hits" was one of the greatest albums I'd ever heard. They hit their peak before I started promoting concerts, so I never had the chance to play them. But, I tried.

In Chicago, probably around 1972, a couple of years before Cass Elliot died, I walked by Mister Kelly's on Rush Street, a small club where big names played: Sinatra, Streisand, Darin and many more. That night, Mama Cass was on the marquee. So, I introduced myself to the club manager who took my message to Cass that I'd like to speak with her.

She knew my name from the business and agreed to see me.

"Cass, I'm a promoter and I like money as much as anybody. But, if you guys would get back together, I would play all your dates and I would want no money."

She looked at me for a moment with an amused look on her face.

"Me, get back together with those fuckin' meatballs?"

Broke my heart.

Marshall Tucker Band

About a year before Lynyrd Skynyrd's plane crash, I had a "Colorado Sunday" at Mile High Stadium. It was a great lineup: Skynyrd, Marshall Tucker Band, Heart and the first Colorado appearance of Foreigner. But, those rat bastards in Marshall Tucker refused to go on in a way that made it seem they were a support act to Skynyrd, which they were; Skynyrd was the biggest draw of all of them. But, Marshall Tucker refused to go on unless I divided the show with a long enough intermission to make it clear that they weren't a throw in. By the way, there was no Marshall Tucker in the band. He was a blind piano tuner in South Carolina who had been in the space the band rented to rehearse and his name was still on the door. I would have been better off with him on stage.

It was such a debacle. Foreigner and Skynyrd played the first half and they were great. They killed. But, before Marshall Tucker would take the stage, they insisted on using their own monitors and the roadies took their sweet time changing out the gear. I was on stage, trying to hurry things along and making sure people who didn't need to be there weren't. One guy got in my way.

"Who are you?" I demanded.

"I'm Doug Graves." He was the lead singer for Tucker, but you wouldn't know him if you were standing next to him.

I told him to get off the stage. He said, "You throw me off, we're not going to play."

I said, "I don't give a fuck at this point. Go ahead, leave, all of you." They played, but it was such a long break between bands. The tear down and set up lasted an hour and 15 minutes. Remember, this was an all-day, outdoor show. I felt terrible for the fans.

Heart went on just before Marshall Tucker and ripped it up; the crowd was really into it until some asshole with Marshall Tucker turned off the power. It was ridiculous. People started booing and Heart, who didn't know what the fuck was going on, left the stage.

Marshall Tucker finally did their show, but it wasn't over until about 12:30 in the morning. There were still about 50,000 people there who'd been baking in the sun all day and had put up with Marshall Tucker's bullshit. I walked to the lip of the stage, sat down and took a mic in my hand and said, "I really want to apologize to all of you who've had to stand out there today and witness this shit. This is the worst show I've ever done. I apologize and if I could afford it, I'd give everyone of you your money back." That's how bad it was. Such a terrible day and after that the Marshall Tucker Band hated me, but I hated them more. I called their agent, Alex Hodges, and said, "Don't you ever try to sell me this piece of shit group again." They couldn't play for me for free.

But, pieces of shit or not, that was one great song, wasn't it? "Can't You See". Great song. Terrible people.

Michael Jackson and The New England Patriots

I know this isn't a news flash, but Michael Jackson was really strange. Unbelievably talented and his fans seemed to love him despite all of the weird stuff, but wow, what an unusual guy.

The 1984 "Victory" tour was a disaster. Not from what the audience saw—Jackson and his siblings sold out stadiums all over the country and it grossed $75 million, a record at the time for tours—but in how it was put together and financed. Chuck Sullivan, whose dad, Billy, owned the Boston Patriots which became the New England Patriots, bid a fortune for the Victory Tour. He way overbid for it and didn't know what he was doing. He guaranteed the Jacksons $41 million. That amount was unheard of in 1984. He got so far in the hole at one point that he reportedly stopped payment on a check for a couple of million to the Jacksons.

Their ticketing was a nightmare. Tickets were $30 each, which was a lot at that time and had to be bought four at a time AND had to be bought by mail with a newspaper coupon AND the only form of payment allowed was a U.S. Postal Service Money Order.

Sullivan lost his shirt and his dad's shirt on the Jackson tour and went bankrupt. That led to the Sullivans having to give up their NFL franchise, which allowed Robert Kraft to become the Patriots owner. The rest is history: Three Super Bowl championships since the Michael Jackson Victory Tour bled the Sullivan family dry. If you're a Patriots fan, you can thank the Jacksons for the Super Bowl trophies.

Don King was the co-promoter of the Victory Tour and would go to each city before the shows, take 200 tickets from the promoters and scalp them. That's one thing I like about Don King. He's never pretended to be anything other than what he is.

Despite all of that, the Denver shows went pretty well. September 7 and 8 of 1984. Over 50,000 each night at Mile High Stadium. And that Saturday night was quite a night for Feyline. Jackson at Mile

High Stadium, Elton John at McNichols and James Taylor at Red Rocks. Talk about a trifecta. Over 80,000 tickets in one night.

In 1988, Michael wanted to play three shows at McNichols Arena in Denver as part of his "Bad" tour. Now, two shows, he would have sold out, but I told him that three wouldn't and it would cost him money because of another night of expenses. He didn't care, he wanted three shows. March 23, 24 and 25 of 1988 and I was right: 11,000, 11,000, 12,000. Good shows, but not sellouts.

Miles Davis

The guy was a musical genius and after he'd gone "electric", blending more of what he borrowed from Jimi and Sly into his horn playing, I had him in concert in Denver. It was in 1970. He was a half hour late going on. I walked into the dressing room and he was all alone, staring at himself in the mirror. He didn't flinch, didn't move a muscle to acknowledge my presence, just kept staring at himself. I didn't say a word, because I knew he'd pick up and walk out if I dared suggest that he go on stage and do his job. I was scared to death of him. Miles was crazy. He was a brilliant musician. But, you didn't fuck with Miles.

The Moody Blues: Kansas City Here I Come

The Moody Blues were a beautiful group. I'd played them in Denver and just loved putting them on stage.

In December of 1970, I decided to take a chance and expand my reach by taking the Moody Blues to Kansas City.

As in Denver with KIMN, there was a rock station in Kansas City that had a lock on the market. When I went to talk with them about running some commercials for the concert, the station manager said, "Well, we usually do our own shows, but we'll let you do yours...." but he said it would cost me an enormous amount for commercials.

"You know how much you're going to get from me?" I said.

"What?"

"You're going to get nothing."

He said, "You're an asshole. You're going to die, you won't make it in this market. We'll run you out of this fucking town."

"Good luck. You won't be the first to try."

There was another station in town where Jerry Mills, a folk music guy, had a show. He was a mandolin player with the Ozark Mountain Daredevils in 1976. He was on for three hours a night and was the only live show on that station. I guess the rest of the day's programming came from a network or whatever. I went to see him.

"Jerry, I'm not going to use the big station for the Moody Blues concert. I'm going to use only you, so I expect to own your station." Tickets started selling real well.

When the big station saw how successful the concert was going to be, someone called and said, "We'll give you some airtime if you give us some tickets to give away."

"No. You get nothing."

"We'll promote the concert anyway."

"Don't you dare, I don't want you announcing anything. I want nothing to do with you."

We sold out and that brought the big station to its knees. They were nicer to me after that and we did some business together.

A little later, I went to Kansas City because I'd made a deal to book the Starlight Amphitheater, an 8000 seat outdoor theater for a couple of years. After that, Feyline had a 15,000 seat outdoor amphitheater built in a suburb of Kansas City, Kansas called Sandstone. I was in my room at the Crowne Plaza.

"Is this Barry Fey?"

"Yeah."

"This is Butch Civella."

"Yeah?" I didn't know he was reportedly part of the Kansas City mob. Carmen "Butch" Civella's brother, "Tony Ripes" Civella was known as the Godfather of Kansas City.

"I'd like to talk to you."

"About what?"

"Well, I'd like to work out a way to get tickets to your shows and if you ever have any union problems in this city, I'll take care of them for you and we'll work together. Let me send a car for you."

I was intrigued. "Okay, sure."

So a car picks me up and takes me to a club he owns.

Butch says, "I'd like to have access to good tickets and I'll pay for them. Maybe once in a while you can comp me a ticket, but I'd like to have access to good tickets. And if you have any problems in Kansas City, I'll take care of it."

Being from Chicago, I knew what was going on. But, we had a nice evening. He fed me—which is always the way to get to me; just feed me, I'm yours—and I'm getting ready to go back to the hotel and he says again, not to hesitate to call him if I need anything.

Then he says, "Here, take these two girls with you, spend some time with them."

I said, "No, no thanks, I'm kinda tired" and his guy drove me back to the hotel alone.

Butch and I would talk from time to time over the years, but nothing big. I didn't have any trouble for him to fix. He apparently got into some trouble, though. Years later, I got a call from him and he said he was in Vegas, where mob guys were often sent when they got in trouble. He wanted me to book a club in Vegas, but that didn't work out.

When we were booking the Sandstone in the early '80s, there was a record shop called Tiger Records that was a great ticket outlet for us. It sold a phenomenal number of tickets at its stores in Kansas City and Lawrence. The stores were named after the owner, Tony "Tiger" Cardarella. Tiger got to be slow paying and was to a point where he owed us $70,000. Now, I never thought to call Butch because I didn't want to be involved in any of that kind of bullshit. And, I didn't know anything about Tiger. I didn't know who he was or whether he was connected. But, my longtime Denver bookie, Paul Villano, with whom I bet college football games and who I'll talk about later, was on the phone with me one day and asked how I was doing. I happened to mention that Tiger Records owed me all that money. Paulie said, "That motherfucking Tiger. Let me make you a couple of calls." I thought it was interesting that Paulie, who was connected to the Smaldone mob family in Denver, would be so familiar with this Tiger Records. Within two or three days, I got a cashier's check for $70,000 from Tiger Records.

Within a month, I heard that Tiger's body had been found in the trunk of his Cadillac! It had nothing to do with me. Tiger had apparently pissed off a lot of other people. After his murder, I read that he'd been involved in a big fencing operation and over the years, police suspected him in several gangland murders. But, what may have gotten him killed is that he was known to hire professional shoplifters to steal records from competing record stores and he apparently had them steal from a Mafia rival. In what I guess was a sign of what he'd done to deserve such an end, his hands had been cut off.

Back to the Moody Blues: In 1989 when I decided to try to save the Denver Symphony, I had the idea of pairing the Moody Blues with the symphony. I tried for two years to set it up and finally, through Tom Hulett at Concerts West, I was able to make it happen. We had two sold out, magical nights at Red Rocks and PBS filmed it for a pledge drive special. It became the biggest selling, and most pledge producing item that PBS offered.

The Moody Blues loved playing with a symphony and Hulett started promoting similar concerts with symphonies all over the country. In return for my showing them the way, Hulett promised that I'd get 25% of all future shows.

Unfortunately, Tom discovered that a mole on his head was melanoma and he died a short time later. Our deal wasn't on paper and I didn't get my 25%. I did get some credit, though. When John Lodge and Justin Hayward were on the "CBS Early Show", they said that it was Barry Fey's idea for them to reconstruct their careers with the symphony concerts.

Paul Revere and the Raiders

Over the summer of 1966, I'd gotten friendly with the Metzger brothers, who owned the Mt. Fuji Ski Hill just a few miles north of Lake Geneva, Wisconsin. We decided to make some quick, easy money. Lake Geneva is a great resort town about an hour southwest of Milwaukee and an hour and a half northwest of Chicago. It's packed every weekend during the summer, but on Labor Day Weekend, it's ridiculous. It's a party destination for college-aged kids.

I booked Paul Revere and the Raiders for $25,000 for the Sunday of Labor Day Weekend and we sold 20,000 tickets at $3.50 each— mostly to college kids—and there was still a line of cars waiting to get in. There was no stage, as such. The band was going to be on top of the ski area's main building that sat at the bottom of the hill. But, when the Raiders' bus pulled up, a couple of the band members got out to look over the set up. They saw the "stage", got back on the bus and after talking it over with the others, they said, "We ain't playing. It's not safe." And they left.

We started refunding money to anyone with a ticket, but many people had been drinking and fights broke out in the lines as people clamored to get their precious $3.50 back. It was a mini-riot. Luckily, the Wisconsin National Guard, which was regularly sent to Lake Geneva on major summer holiday weekends, was there to keep us from being overrun by the mob. I was glad to see them. I wasn't making any money and sure didn't want to get beat up.

We sued Paul Revere and the Raiders for damages. Our attorney, oh, this is great: he stalked the band, watching where they were going to be playing. When they had a date at the Arie Crown Theater in Chicago's McCormick Place, he took the subpoena and bluffed his way backstage. While they were playing, he walked up to Paul, an Idahoan whose full name is Paul Revere Dick, and said, "The British are coming" and served the papers!

They settled for $10,000.

Paul Simon

What a brilliant song writer! Come on: "Bridge Over Troubled Water", "Sounds of Silence", "Still Crazy After All These Years" and on and on. There aren't many in his class.

His vanity got in the way, though. It cost him, and me, money. Whenever I played him in the early years with Artie, he insisted that there be no one seated in a position where they could see the back of his head, where they could see his bald spot. So, we had to rope off seats on the sides of the stages and a stage in the round was out of the question.

In later years, he wore a ball cap.

Richard Pryor

What a hilarious night at Red Rocks and that was before Richard even took the stage. It was in 1979. We had the place sold out and my staff and I were waiting backstage for him to show up. I'd sent someone to the airport to pick him up. About 20 minutes after the show was supposed to start, Richard wasn't there yet. My guy who picked him up stopped and called from somewhere along I-70 and said the plane had been delayed or whatever, but they were on their way, they'd be there soon. To make sure they got there as soon as possible, I asked the Denver cops to send a couple of cars to give him an escort the mile or so from the freeway exit to Red Rocks. One car in front, one in back. Well, Richard saw the one in front, but hadn't seen the one behind him until they were driving up the steep, winding road leading to the amphitheater. As they rounded a curve, Richard saw the lights flashing behind him and he thought they were being pulled over. So, he started throwing his dope out the window.

Rod Stewart

Rod's Rod. What can I say? Nice guy who had a great, if unusual, voice and knew how to entertain his audiences. He had a string of monster hits, first with Faces and then on his own that filled up the halls for me over and over again. "Maggie May", "I Think I'm Losing You" and many more.

At one point later in his career, I called his manager, Arnold Stiefel, who I really liked and suggested that Rod needed to change his repertoire, going more toward the pop classics and away from rock because his crowds were dwindling.

To his credit, Rod knew how to re-invent himself. A guy who started as "Rod The Mod" with the spiked hair and the British mod look in the '60s, kept that bed-head hair look, and, thanks to a certain wise promoter in Denver, is now packing theaters singing pop standards. Say what you want about him, he's a great entertainer.

But, my favorite memory of Rod is still his birthday party in London that I attended with McCartney and, despite the naked women and whatever else was there for the taking, the thick hamburgers are what stand out most.

Sly and The Family Stone

Sly could have been the Muhammed Ali of rock 'n roll, but he couldn't lay off the cocaine. He was huge, especially after the year he had in 1969, beginning with the album "Stand!" and capped off by Woodstock, where the world got to see and hear him. But, a lot of promoters wouldn't book him because of his propensity to not show up. Or, he'd show up but would decide not to play. In Chicago's Grant Park, a riot broke out when he didn't show.

Here's a funny story about Sly as told to me by a promoter based in Seattle. He'd booked Sly for a show there. But, the promoter was out of town and was going to be late for a plane back to Seattle that would get him there in time for the show. He was speeding through traffic, running through the airport, but missed his plane. The next flight available would get him into Seattle nearly two hours after the concert was scheduled to begin, but he figured he'd be able to make it for the end. When he walked on the plane, guess who's sitting in First Class? Sly Stone.

Sly couldn't handle success. He chose cocaine instead.

Snoop Doggy Dogg

In the '60s and '70s, I didn't promote a lot of black music. There's a difference between acts that play "black" music and black acts that play music white people like. I mostly stayed away from R & B because I didn't understand it and I thought it should be left to black promoters, but it turned out that they didn't exist or that they were flakes. It wasn't until later on, in the '90s, that they got organized. The exception was the George Clinton-P Funk-Mothership tour, which I talk about in another chapter.

But in that genre of black acts that played music white people like, I promoted a lot of them: Diana Ross and The Supremes at Red Rocks (on the eve of Woodstock), The Temptations, The Four Tops, Stevie Wonder, Lionel Richie—with and without The Commodores—and Earth Wind and Fire (called a Chicago band even though Phillip Bailey was from East High School in Denver) whose audiences were mostly white when it had big radio hits like "Shining Star" and "September" and "After The Love Is Gone" but got more black as time went on.

In 1993, when rap and hip-hop blew up, I decided—even though I didn't understand or like either genre—to try to get in on some of the money people were willing to pay to see those acts. I called Dick Klotzman, a promoter in Baltimore and I booked seven cities with Dr. Dre and Snoop Dogg. Earlier in the year, Snoop had been arrested while recording *Doggystyle* for driving the car when his bodyguard killed a member of a rival gang. (He pretty much got off, thanks to the efforts of his attorney, Johnnie Cochran.) But, Snoop was well known because of some songs he'd done before that and his album was eagerly awaited by the street. So, I booked them for 1994 across the Southwest—Denver, Vegas, Albuquerque and Southern California. Seven shows, all sold out.

Suge Knight and I got pretty friendly. I didn't know him from an apple tree, but, of course, he was the boss. Not only was he managing Dre, Snoop and other guys, especially Tupac Shakur, he owned their record label, *Death Row Records*. I suppose that name should have tipped me off to what I was getting into. My most interesting encounter with Suge and the rest was in early November, 1993, the same time as the second Holyfield-Bowe fight—the "Fan Man Fight". That's one of the truly strange moments in sports history. Some guy tried to parachute into the outdoor boxing ring at Caesars Palace. It was during the seventh round and everyone started looking up, even the fighters, and here was this guy coming down, almost into the ring. I read later that his chute got caught in the lights and he landed on the ropes for a moment before he fell or was pulled down into the crowd. It was on Bowe's side of the ring and his entourage and security guys beat the shit out of the guy.

Anyway, the fight was on the night of the day the Breeders' Cup was being run at Santa Anita. My wife Lisa and I were at the race and our plan was to fly into Vegas that night. Suge said he and his entourage including Dre and Snoop would be flying in, too, and asked me to get them rooms. No problem.

Remember, I had no idea what rap was about, or what the musicians were about, I just figured there was money to be made promoting them. About three in the morning, I get a call in our hotel room.

"Hey Barry, it's Suge."

"Hi, Suge. What's up?"

"Would you call Caesars and make sure they hold our reservations because we changed our minds. Instead of flying in, we're driving in."

"Yeah, sure, I'll call them." I wasn't going to ask any questions at that time of night.

I called Caesars Palace and made sure their rooms would be held. By that time, I was awake enough to wonder why these people would drive all that way instead of just getting on an airplane. It's just a 45-minute flight. Lisa was sharper than I was.

"Dummy, it's because they want to bring their guns."

I asked, "Why would they need guns?

"Because they're gangsters!"

See, I thought they were musicians playing gangsters. I didn't realize they were gangsters playing musicians.

Suge, Dre and Snoop were going to be my guests at the fight. I got tickets—great tickets, Hollywood stars like Bruce Willis were sitting behind us—for all of them and thought that would be a great bonding moment. I'd be the big shot hosting these rap stars at this fight that the whole world was watching.

Security at the big fights was really tight, but when we walked in—and we were hard to miss because Suge is huge, like 6'5" and 400 pounds—it was like the Red Sea parting. All of these security thugs got out of the way and pretty much bowed to my guests.

"Hey, Suge, how ya doin'? Whattya doin' Dre? Wassup Snoop..." All the security guys knew them. I thought, "My, God, look at this, I'm with real celebrities!" I didn't realize that most of the security were probably Bloods or Crips or whatever, but I felt that I'd wasted my money on tickets because these guys could have sat in the ring if they'd wanted.

So, the shows were sold out and I thought I going to do pretty well. But, one morning in January, 1994, I'm reading the paper and I see the headline: "Rapper Arrested". The story was about Dre. He'd been arrested after a police chase in Los Angeles.

I called Suge.

"Barry, it looks like we've got to cancel. It'll be 60 or 90 days before we can take care of this shit."

Fuck!

I lost over $150,000 in expenses—the hotel rooms, fight tickets, advertising...all of that and more—plus, I'd given Klotzman over $100,000 as a deposit for the groups.

I called Klotzman, who I knew well. We'd worked on several shows and I'd even stayed a couple of times at his mansion in Baltimore. I think he lost it later when he was sentenced to prison for tax evasion.

"Dick, send me my hundred thousand back."

"I ain't got it."

"Whaddya mean you ain't got it?"

"I sent it to Suge."

"I'm going to sue your ass."

"If you sue anybody, you need to sue Suge, because I can prove he got the money."

Well, I was ready to sue Suge, but pretty much everyone I knew advised me that suing Suge Knight was not really what I wanted to do. And, after carefully considering the possible ramifications of going after him for the $100,000, I decided it wasn't worth it.

That was my first, and only, attempt at promoting rappers.

Al Haymon was a black promoter from Boston. There were a lot of stories about how and why the big black acts, who'd been mostly represented by white promoters, fired them and went with Haymon. However it happened, it did. Then, he sold out to Live Nation and went into the boxing business, where he became equally huge. (By the way, the boxing business makes rock 'n roll promoters look like Mother Teresa.) As the Snoop-Dre-Suge fiasco was still in play, he called me.

"Barry, why are you messing with these acts?"

"Al, it seemed like a great idea; I could sell a lot of tickets. Plus, I have an edge."

"What's that?"

"I have them cross-collateralized." That means when you're giving a group a percentage, a guarantee plus a percentage, when it comes to the last date of your tour with them, if you'd paid them more in percentage than they had coming, you just keep everything from the last date. So, it's kind of a protection.

"Barry, you don't understand. Stick to what you know. Play home games, not away games."

"What are you talking about?"

"Let's say you come to the last date and they're ahead of you by $50,000. They aren't going to do a show for free. They'll go the hall manager and say, 'Fey's not going to pay us and you're going to have the biggest riot on your hands you've ever seen.' Now, what do you think that hall manager's going to do?"

I said, "If he's smart, he'll turn the ticket money over to the group."

"That's exactly right, so you can take your cross-collateralization and shove it."

That was probably good, sound advice, but by that time it didn't matter because after Dre-Snoop-Suge, I didn't have any dates, anyway.

It wasn't my last encounter with Suge, though. In September of 1996, I'm at the Tyson-Seldon fight at the MGM Grand and he's there with his entourage, including, as it turned out, Tupac. On the way out of the fight, I see a little scuffle between Suge's guys and some other guys. None of my business, so I keep going on my way. I heard the next day that it was about 20 minutes after I saw Suge that some guys pulled up next to the passenger side of his car where Tupac was sitting and opened fire. Tupac died about a week later. Suge had a bullet fragment in his head, but nothing else. How he survived, as huge of a target as he was, was amazing.

The one other time I attended a fight with music royalty was March 12, 1997. Richard Sturm, who's now President of Entertainment and Sports at the MGM Grand, told me he had a ticket for me for the Oscar De La Hoya–Sweet Pea Whitaker fight.

"Listen, Barry, I've got this ticket if you don't mind going with Smokey Robinson."

"Are you kidding? THE Smokey Robinson?" Would I mind! I played him several times and he always sold a lot of tickets. What a writer and performer. "Ooo Baby, Baby", "Tracks of My Tears" on and on. Amazing talent. We had a good time at the fight. Smokey's a great guy.

Steve Martin

When he was just starting out, Steve lived in Aspen and would often be the opening act for bands like Brewer and Shipley and The Nitty Gritty Dirt Band and others before he got way bigger than any of them. Chuck Morris, my own "wild and crazy guy", had booked him at Tulagi's in the early '70s. In fact, the Dirt Band showed up with Steve on their bus and asked Chuck to put him on before them and pay him $50. Chuck's relationship with Steve grew and we had him several times at Ebbets Field. But, the Steve Martin Show on New Year's Eve 1974 was probably the most memorable. It was snowing hard, but people showed up and packed the place, which wasn't hard; Ebbets only held about 260. After his show, Steve invited everyone to follow him out the door and down the street a half block to an all night diner, the White Spot, for coffee and doughnuts. He had balloons on his head and was wearing those big, funny glasses he used in his act and was standing in the middle of a downtown Denver street directing traffic in the blizzard. He walked into the diner and ordered 260 coffees, half with cream and sugar.

Here's how quickly he got big: from playing at Ebbets Field in 1974/75, to 1978 when he sold out back to back nights at Red Rocks. Between Ebbets and Red Rocks, he'd recorded an album called *Let's Get Small*, which contained the bit where he said, "Well, excuuuuuuuse me!" which became a national catchphrase. He appeared several times on "Saturday Night Live", too. So, by the time we booked him at Red Rocks, it was an automatic sell out. Red Rocks is where he recorded the second half of his next album, *A Wild and Crazy Guy*. And, the back up band when he did "King Tut", were members of the Dirt Band.

In 1979, when his "The Jerk" came out, he was in Denver and took us to the premier at the old Colorado Theaters at Mexico and Colorado Boulevard. We went to dinner before, maybe after, at the Cork 'n Cleaver.

One quick thing about Brewer and Shipley. Their big hit when Steve was opening for them was "One Toke Over the Line". I was always singing one song or another to myself or to whomever happened to be within earshot. Someone finally broke the news that it wasn't "one TOE over the line. Sweet Jesus.

Here's another story about my naiveté. Steve Jensen, an agent (now for Katy Perry and other big names) and a good friend of mine with a big firm in Los Angeles was transferred to New York and I met him in Manhattan for lunch. We've ordered and the waiter brought us some bread. As I'm buttering mine, Steve said, "Barry, I think you should probably know that I came out of the closet."

"Oh, okay, great," and kept eating. The conversation moved on to other things.

About half an hour later, I said, "Steve, let me ask you one question."

"Sure, Barry…anything."

"Why were you in a fucking closet?"

No one cared less about sexual persuasion than me. Gay, straight, this or that, I just didn't care. There were only two kinds of people: those who bought tickets and those who didn't.

Steve Miller

Here's a guy who always sold a lot of tickets for me and always put on great shows, but I bet 90% of the fans couldn't pick him out of a lineup. Chuck Morris said that Steve could be standing next to you at the supermarket buying lettuce or whatever and you wouldn't know him. He's one of the most faceless of the superstars.

Miller says he first picked up a guitar around the age of five, when Les Paul was a frequent visitor to his parents' home.

My son Tyler was a year younger when Steve gave him his first guitar lesson. At a 1995 Red Rocks concert, he looked off-stage between songs where Tyler and I were standing. He pointed at Tyler and waved him out. "Come here, come out here, Tyler." Steve sat down, put Tyler on his knee and gave him a quick guitar lesson in front of nearly 10,000 people.

Sting and The Police

Before they got big, we had The Police at the Rainbow Music Hall in Denver and several times later, when it became just Sting, at bigger venues. We never talked much—I probably didn't say more than 100 words to him during that period.

As I brought him back for shows in the '90s, we got better acquainted and had something in common: The Amnesty International tours. He was on the "Conspiracy of Hope Tour" that I promoted and again on the "Human Rights Now!" tour, where I saved the life of the Amnesty International board member with the Heimlich maneuver.

Tina Turner

Tina was a no-show for her first concert with me. But, it wasn't her fault. Nobody told her. In October of 1969, I'd heard that the Rolling Stones were going on tour. I called their agent, Ronnie Sunshine and asked for a date. "Ronnie, I've got to have Denver. They're a great audience, they deserve the Stones, we'll sell out", blah, blah, blah. Ronnie said "no", the show's opening in Los Angeles and there isn't room on the tour for Denver. But, I can be such a nudge and kept calling every day, but every day got the same answer.

Later in October, Ronnie called and said that the boys are a little nervous about opening in L.A. It had been a few years since their last tour and they played small venues then. This tour was in big arenas. He asked if I had any place they could open the tour, but it couldn't be Denver. I booked them in Fort Collins on November 7th at Moby Gym on the campus of Colorado State University. The Stones wanted black groups to open each show on their tour as a tribute to the early R & B guys who influenced Jagger's and Richards' songwriting. They chose Ike and Tina Turner for the Fort Collins show.

Ronnie said it had to be as low key as possible in terms of publicity, almost a secret until the day of the show, because the Los Angeles show was supposed to get all of the national media exposure for having the formal opening of the tour.

We—Feyline and the Stones' people—did such a good job keeping the show a secret, nobody told Ike and Tina about the show.

Beginning in the late '70s after she got out of her abusive marriage to Ike, I played Tina several times. She puts on a great show. Nice legs.

Whitney Houston

I played Whitney a few times and she was such a good singer, such a talent, but she had no personality. Her shows were boring. And each time I put her on, the crowds got smaller. Her concerts were like listening to albums. She sang her songs, did a great job, but that was it.

I dodged a huge bullet in 1991. Remember when she sang the national anthem at the Super Bowl in Tampa? My God, it was beautiful! Everyone was crying by the end of the song. The song had barely ended when I called my people.

"First thing Monday morning, we book every date on Whitney anywhere we can get her."

We called, but her manager said Whitney didn't want to travel west. I upped the ante: whatever she wants, she gets. But, she wouldn't come west.

When she toured up and down the East Coast, she left such a trail of promoter's blood, it was unbelievable. I had been so sure that the national anthem was going to propel her bigger than ever, but nobody showed up. I was so lucky not to get her.

The next year, she married Bobby Brown and we know how that turned out. Even Oprah couldn't revive her career.

But, what a beautiful voice.

Willie, Waylon and Some Guy Named Jessie

There was a tour of Willie Nelson and Poco in 1976, a national tour set up by a promoter out of St. Louis, that wasn't doing well. Mark Rothbaum, Willie's agent at the time, asked me if I'd be interested in taking over the tour because Poco was going to quit, apparently because they weren't getting paid.

"Who are you going to get?" I asked.

"How about Waylon Jennings?"

That was before "Luckenbach, Texas", their mega-hit together, but I thought it would be an interesting tour, and it was. Waylon was the poster boy for Outlaw Country—which I didn't much care about. Country music wasn't my thing. But, I knew that Waylon and Willie would be a big hit; we'd sell a lot of tickets.

We picked up the tour at Red Rocks in the summer of 1976. About two weeks before the date, my good buddy and country maven Chuck Morris, came into my office.

"We've got a chance to put Jessi Colter on the tour."

"Really?"

"Yeah, but I don't think Waylon will like it." Another employee overheard Chuck and agreed, "No, Waylon won't like that."

I asked, "Who the fuck is this guy Jessie that Waylon doesn't like?"

That's how much I knew about country music. I didn't have a clue that Jessi was Waylon's wife.

We sold out Willie, Waylon and Jessi all the rest of 1976 and all of 1977. We even booked New York City where—and who would have figured this—Andy Warhol asked me to get him a meeting with Way-

lon. He couldn't wait. Andy Warhol and Waylon Jennings! Backstage, you would have thought that Andy was a 13-year-old girl waiting to see The Beatles. He was beside himself, so excited to see Waylon. I don't know what happened, whether Andy ever painted Waylon or whether they hit it off and became friends.

Waylon and I were friendly, got along fine. But, Willie and I became very, very fast friends. He was such an easy guy to be around. No drama, no hysterics like

I'd endured with The Who, Stones and other rock acts. Backstage at Willie's concerts were very serene in comparison. He was just so mellow, and, of course, there's a well-documented reason for part of that demeanor. Willie smoked *all* the time.

One of the wildest dates we booked for Willie was the Willie Nelson Third of July Picnic in Tulsa in 1977. Joel Brandes, who had been with me off and on for several years and was one of my lead guys on national tours, thought that if Willie's picnics worked in Texas, they'd work in Oklahoma. He was right, but it was crazy in a number of ways. It was 100 degrees, not a cloud in the sky and over 50,000 people showed up, many of them wearing very little in the heat and many wearing much less as the day wore on.

After a couple of hours of beer drinking the lines at the port-a-potties were so long that people, men mostly, started going wherever seemed like a good spot. The State Fairgrounds were in a residential area and there were so many complaints of traffic and parking problems, not to mention public drunkenness and people urinating and fornicating on residents' lawns that the city banned concerts for ten years.

We booked Lynyrd Skynyd on the show with Willie and Waylon and several others. Skynyrd was opening for Peter Frampton on the 2nd and 4th of July in Oakland, so we sent a 727 to pick them up and take them back. But, on the way to Tulsa, the plane stopped in Los Angeles, supposedly to pick up Waylon. But, he'd taken another flight and told his friends with the Hell's Angels, who were often part of his entourage that they could ride on our plane. And not just the Angels. Their motorcycle mamas and cases of beer were loaded onto the plane. They took over the back of the plane and partied all the way to Tulsa. The plane finally got in about three in the morning. Skynyrd played at noon, packed up and flew back for their Oakland show.

Willie was playing in Hawaii and we'd visit each other in our hotel rooms, just hanging out. Willie said, "Why are we paying this hotel so much money? Why don't we just buy a home?" We looked up a realtor in the phone book and we bought a home together on Maui. It was in Spreckelsville, right on the ocean next to the Maui Country Club, very close to the airport on the Hana Highway. I used to take a hundred foot phone cord, sit on the beach and make my business calls.

We were there together once when Willie woke me up about two in the morning.

"Barry, would you mind doing me a favor and driving over to Long's Drug and buy me some Tucks?"

I didn't know what Tucks were, but told him, sure, I'd go.

Hemorrhoids weren't his only physical ailment in Hawaii. In 1981, one of his lungs collapsed while he was swimming in our pool, which not only forced him to cancel some concerts, it seriously hampered his smoking.

Willie's a fine, fine guy. We got very close. He had a good group of people in his band; his "family". Paul English on drums, who wasn't the best drummer I'd ever heard, but he doubled as security. He kept a couple of guns with him. Mickey Raphael on harp. He was dating Ali McGraw at the time.

At one point in our relationship, I decided to offer some musical advice. He always started his set with "Whiskey River" and the Texas flag would come down.

"Willie, I think people might be getting tired of that."

"But, Barry, my Texan fans expect that."

"Yeah, but there are fewer and fewer of them", meaning he was getting so big nationwide, worldwide, that the Texas flag thing was increasingly irrelevant. To his credit, he didn't listen to me.

Willie became a staple at Red Rocks, and sold out wherever he went. When he was in Las Vegas—I don't remember the year, but one afternoon, Willie called me in my office.

"Barry, can you fly out here, or send someone out and bring me a hundred thousand in cash?"

I said, "Yeah, no problem Willie."

I didn't ask what it was for. It didn't matter. I didn't care. I knew he'd pay me back, and he did. We were doing so much business together during that time, loaning Willie $100,000 wasn't a concern. One of my guys who did a lot of out of town work for me, Jeff Krump, flew out with the cash.

Another time I needed Krump was when Willie was touring and was scheduled to play in New Orleans during Mardi Gras. He had played in Oklahoma the night before and was supposed to catch a plane for New Orleans to do a press conference promoting the concert. But, Willie didn't want to and got on the bus which was headed for the next date in Oklahoma. I told Jeff to find Willie and get him to New Orleans. Our partner in that concert was Al Copeland, the man who started the Popeye's Chicken chain and owned a bunch of other restaurants. He had a private plane, a big one that he'd bought from Hugh Hefner. Krump got on the plane and headed west. He knew some cops in the area who put out an A.P.B. on Willie's bus and before long, the Oklahoma State Patrol pulled him over. Well, there wasn't an airport nearby that was big enough to handle Copeland's plane, so they landed in Enid. Jeff hired a crop duster, whose plane had no doors on it, and landed on a dirt road next to Willie's bus.

Willie still wouldn't go. The troopers patched Krump through their radio and he called me.

"Willie refuses to get off the bus. He says he's not riding on a crop duster. What do I do now?"

I told him to quit bothering Willie and go back to New Orleans.

Willie is a golf nut. The three things in life he seemed to love the most were music, golf and grass. No particular order. But he loves golf so much he bought a course in 1979 in Spicewood, Texas. Willie Nelson's Pedernales Cut 'n Putt Golf Club. He turned the clubhouse into a recording studio and the condos and houses around the course are home to a lot of Willie's family, friends, staff and roadies. Willie invited me down to learn how to play golf. What a miserable time that was. My allergies blew up because of the cedar trees around the course. My eyes watered non-stop and I was all stuffed up; it was terrible. But, I spent a weekend taking lessons from Willie's pro. Willie called me "a natural". He gave me a bag of golf clubs, which I took back to Denver with me, put in my garage and left them there.

Farm Aid

Willie was instrumental in starting "Farm Aid", the concert to raise money for American farmers. The first one was in Champaign, Illinois in 1985. The next year, Willie moved it to Austin. July 4th, 1986. I got a call from Bono in Ireland.

"Barry, I'd kind of like to fly over for Farm Aid and meet Willie. Can you arrange it?"

"No question at all."

Bono and his wife, Ali, flew to Austin. I picked them up at the airport and took them to the hotel where I introduced them to Willie. They were getting along great and the next day was going to be great.

The concert with Willie and his gang and other big groups like Alabama, Stevie Ray Vaughan and The Beach Boys. And Bono was there.

About 2:30 in the morning, Bono knocks on my door.

"Barry, can you take us to the airport?"

"Yeah, but why?"

"One of my best friends was killed in a motorcycle crash. We need to catch a plane back to Dublin."

What a shame. They'd flown all the way to Texas and weren't there five hours before they had to leave.

One funny moment from Farm Aid involved my son, Jeremy. He was 14 years old and I'd taken him with me. When I asked him to go out and get me a Coca-Cola, he came back with it and said, "Dad, there's some asshole out in the hall pretending to be Don Johnson." I took a peek into the hall. It was Don Johnson, the star of "Miami Vice", one of the top-rated television shows at that time.

ZZ Top

I started booking ZZ Top in 1972 and had them open several shows. They'd released a couple of albums by then, but didn't have any big hits yet. Their manager from the beginning, who pretty much created the group, Bill Ham, was a really good guy. I called him one day.

"Bill, I'm doing the Stones early next year in Hawaii. I'd like to open with your guys, but I can only give you $5000. Can you afford to get them over there?" I knew what his answer would be.

In January of 1973, I walked on stage at the Blaisdell Arena in front of 8,000 people. I wanted to say something more than just, "please welcome ZZ Top", but they were relatively unknown and unaccomplished, so I didn't have much to add. So, I threw in a few extra words that have stayed with them to this day.

"Ladies and gentlemen, please welcome that little ol' band from Texas, ZZ Top!" The crowd was silent. 8,000 people were staring at these guys they'd never heard of who were wearing cowboy hats, boots and jeans and were probably thinking they were a country band. This was way before Dusty and Billy grew the long beards. The crowd wasn't quiet for long. That was ZZ Top's first big show in terms of exposure; the first of many.

Later that year, in the summer of 1973, I had them at a football stadium at the University of Houston, Jeppesen Stadium. ZZ Top,

Wishbone Ash and Savoy Brown. Savoy Brown was supposed to be the opener, but the manager came up to me backstage.

"Barry, we're not going on before Wishbone Ash. We're bigger than they are."

I glared at him for a moment and pointed toward the stands. "You see that? All the tickets are sold. I don't give a fuck if you go on or not" and I walked away. Of course, they played. Maybe he was right about Savoy Brown being bigger, but I didn't care.

Bill Ham came up with an idea for a big stadium show in Austin: The ZZ Top Barn Dance and Barbecue at Memorial Stadium on Labor Day Weekend in 1974.

"It's going to be so big that I don't know if you can handle it alone. I'd like you to have a piece, Don Fox to have a piece, Terry Bassett to have a piece and Alex Cooley, a promoter from Georgia, to have a piece."

That "promoter by committee" was a disaster. Everyone was arguing with each other about how to do things, advertising wasn't being done right, tickets weren't selling, so Bill called a meeting in Houston.

Well, I had an ear infection and couldn't fly.

Bill said, "Barry, I'm sorry, I can't change the date. We're all going to be here. You've got to get here somehow so we can get this thing fixed."

Chuck Morris and I hired a Rolls Royce limousine that would drive us from Denver to Houston. Before leaving, I went to a deli, loaded up on sandwiches and we took off. We stopped in Pueblo and picked up a 12 volt TV from a buddy, Tony Spicola. Well, Rolls Royce or not, it wasn't a very comfortable car and the TV didn't work very well. Neither of us could sleep and we were dog tired when we got to Houston. At the hotel, we met with the other promoters and Chuck and I laid out the advertising plan, how to promote it and get tickets sold. Things immediately started to pick up.

There were two major problems. Darrell Royal, the University of Texas football coach and the caterer, the stadium food service guy.

First, Royal, who was king in Texas, or at least that part of it, didn't want to let us use the stadium at all, but after the university said he had to, he demanded that every blade of plastic grass on the field be covered. They'd just installed new Astroturf and he wanted it covered. When we're setting up on Sunday morning, we ran out of plywood to cover the field. Royal saw the amount we had covered,

With Billy, Dusty and Frank at the final concert before McNichols Arena was torn down.

which was most of the field, but that wasn't good enough. He said the gates weren't opening until the whole field was covered.

We sent a guy out with a truck and $10,000 in cash to get more plywood. Good plan, but, where are you going to find a lumber yard that's open on the Sunday morning of Labor Day Weekend in Texas? I told him, "Go to the biggest lumber yard you can find and drive through the gates, through the fence. Don't get out of your truck because they probably have guard dogs. The alarms are going to go off, but just wait in the truck until the police show up, who are going to notify the owner. When the owner comes, tell him you've got $10,000 and you need plywood. He won't turn you down." And it went just like that, just like we drew it up.

Still, we came about ten yards short of covering the field. Royal said, "The gates aren't opening, we don't have a deal."

I said, "Coach Royal, has anybody ever told you to go fuck yourself? There are 60,000 people waiting to get in and you're going to go tell them you aren't letting them in, right? Fuck you. We're opening the gates." He was furious.

Then there was the catering genius. He decided that we'd be lucky to sell 20,000 tickets and that's all he prepped for. On the day of the show, it was sunny and hot and the moron had run out of food and drinks before the show started! As we were still selling walk up tickets on one end of the stadium, there was a line of people leaving to buy food and drinks and bring it back in. On top of that, the water pressure in the stadium was low and the fountains weren't working. A few of them were ripped off the walls by unhappy fans.

We should have made a fortune on that show, but there was a class action lawsuit by people who said that we were guilty of false advertising because the ticket said, "ZZ Top's Barn Dance and Barbecue" and that implied that there'd be free barbecue. We had no chance in the Texas courts. We were chased out of there and after attorneys' fees and everything, were lucky to have made $5000.

To make it worse, I had Joni Mitchell at Red Rocks that weekend, and we were snowed out! I came home the next day and we did the show at the Auditorium Arena. What a disastrous weekend.

During another ZZ Top show at the Denver Coliseum, Billy Gibbons cut his hand on something backstage. I walked onto the stage, grabbed a microphone and said:

"Ladies and gentlemen, we've got a problem backstage...a bit of a medical emergency. Billy Gibbons cut his hand. Does anyone out there have something that will relieve his pain?"

People started walking up to the stage offering a variety of medications. We took some of them backstage and Billy was fixed up. It was a deep cut, but he played the whole show, with a little pharmaceutical help from the crowd.

ZZ Top was the first, and last, rock show to play at McNichols Arena in Denver.

In 2009, ZZ Top was playing Fiddler's Green in Denver. They invited me to the show and asked me to introduce them, just like the old days. I walked out on the stage, stood there for a moment as the crowd recognized me and applauded, put on those signature big sunglasses the boys wear and said, "Ladies and gentlemen, please welcome that little ol' band from Texas...ZZ Top!"

Part Ten

ENCORE

- ○ **The Fey Lists**

- ○ **A Few Final Words**

THE FEY LISTS

I searched "Lists" and came up with 1,510,000,000 hits in .08 seconds. I guess lists allow us to at least have the illusion of creating order from chaos and make short work of an overwhelming amount of information. If you've gotten this far in this book, you know that my business was chaotic. It feels rather satisfying to look back on it all, making categories and fill them up as I see fit.

With the exception of the Beatles, I've seen, heard and worked with all the greats many times. Putting them in order of preference was difficult. If you don't agree, send me a message on Facebook.

Best Rock Band

1. The Beatles
2. The Rolling Stones
3. The Who
4. Led Zeppelin
5. Pink Floyd
6. U2
7. Queen
8. The Doors
9. Jimi Hendrix Experience
10. The Grateful Dead
11. Eagles
12. Springsteen E/Street Band
13. AC/DC
14. Metallica
15. Black Sabbath
16. Aerosmith
17. Beach Boys

Best Rock Band Performance

1. The Who
2. The Rolling Stones
3. Led Zeppelin
4. Springsteen/E Street Band
5. Jimi Hendrix Experience
6. All the rest

Best Rock Showman

1. Mick Jagger
2. Jimi Hendrix
3. Elvis Presley
4. Jim Morrison
5. Bruce Springsteen
6. David Lee Roth
7. Bono
8. Roger Daltrey
9. Freddie Mercury
10. Ozzy Osbourne
11. Angus Young
12. Steven Tyler
13. Sly Stone
14. Robert Plant
15. Elton John
16. Otis Redding

Best Female Rock Singer

1. Janis Joplin
2. Aretha
3. Annie Lennox
4. Tina Turner
5. Stevie Nicks
6. Chrissie Hynde
7. Mama Cass
8. Grace Slick
9. Joni Mitchell
10. Bonnie Raitt

Best Male Rock Singer

1. Robert Plant
2. Jim Morrison
3. Freddie Mercury
4. Roger Daltrey
5. Mick Jagger
6. Axl Rose
7. John Lennon
8. Steven Tyler
9. Bruce Springsteen
10. David Bowie
11. Paul McCartney
12. Bono
13. Elton John
14. Bon Scott
15. Meat Loaf
16. Phil Collins
17. Van Morrison

Best Rock Drummer

1. Keith Moon
2. Neil Pert
3. Clive Bunker
4. Bill Bruford
5. John Bonham
6. Ginger Baker
7. Carl Palmer
8. Carmen Appice
9. Mitch Mitchell
10. Lars Ulrich

Best Rock Bass Guitarist

1. John Entwistle
2. Everyone else

Best Rock Lead Guitar

1. Eric Clapton
2. Jimi Hendrix
3. Jeff Beck
4. Jimmy Page
5. Stevie Ray Vaughn
6. Pete Townshend
7. Eddie Van Halen
8. Stevie Vai
9. Peter Green
10. Tommy Bolin
11. Carlos Santana
12. Tony Iommi
13. Duane Allman
14. Slash

Best Songwriters

1. Lennon/McCartney
2. Bob Dylan
3. Jagger/Richards
4. Bruce Springsteen
5. Brian Wilson
6. Plant/Page
7. Neil Diamond
8. Paul Simon
9. Pete Townshend
10. Bono
11. Queen
12. Neil Young
13. Jim Morrison

Best Songs

1. *Stairway to Heaven*
2. *Free Bird*
3. *Hey Jude*
4. *Satisfaction*
5. *Born to Run*
6. *Light My Fire*
7. *Baba O'Reilly*
8. *Bohemian Rhapsody*
9. *Sweet Child of Mine*
10. *Hotel California*
11. *Suite: Judy Blue Eyes*
12. *Bridge Over Troubled Water*
13. *Dream On*
14. *Sounds of Silence*
15. *You Can't Always Get What You Want*
16. *Won't Get Fooled Again*
17. *With or Without You*
18. *Layla*
19. *Piano Man*
20. *Jump*
21. *Holly Holy*

Best Albums

1. Sgt. Pepper
2. Dark Side of the Moon
3. Led Zeppelin IV
4. Revolver
5. Abbey Road
6. A Night at the Opera
7. Joshua Tree
8. Led Zeppelin II
9. Stranger In Town
10. Back in Black
11. Hotel California
12. The Doors
13. Mamas and Papas 30 Golden Hits
14. Who's Next
15. Appetite for Destruction
16. The Wall
17. The White Album
18. Tommy
19. Tea for the Tillerman
20. Endless Summer

A FEW FINAL WORDS...FOR NOW

I wish that I would have been nicer.

ACKNOWLEDGMENTS

There are many, many people who contributed to the compilation and completion of this book. Most significantly: Steve Alexander, who spent dozens of hours listening to me tell my stories, reworked and researched them and turned them into what you see here; his co-researcher and proofreader, Diane Montiel of Bantry Bay Media, whose sharp eye, love of books and thoughtful editing added immeasurably to the finished product; Rich Wolfe, whose publishing expertise is legendary and who created a business model that has left the big New York publishing houses wondering how they missed the boat; Dan Fong of The Creative Eye (thecreativeeyellc.com) and Michael Goldman for their historic rock 'n roll photos; Lisa Liddy of The Printed Page (www.ThePrintedPage.com), for her book design; and to Daniela Stolfi (www.bosshi.com) for her digital assistance.

Also, thanks to the following for their gracious and invaluable assistance:

- Joel Brandes
- J. Wendel Cox, Ph.D.,
  Denver Public Library Western History and Genealogy
- Alan Fey
- Geoffrey Fey
- Jeremy Fey (who came up with the name, *Backstage Past*)
- Tyler Fey
- Tony Funches
- Celia Gause
- Leslie Haseman
- Jack Healey
- Jeff Krump
- Cathy Millward Kreutz
- Phil Lobel
- Pam Moore
- Chuck Morris
- James Pagliasotti
- *The Denver Post*
- *The Rocky Mountain News*
- Todd Schiffman
- Larry Sessler
- Lisa Wheeler
- Steve Wozniak